My Neighbor
TOTORO

4

WRITTEN AND DIRECTED BY
HAYAO MIYAZAKI

Father
Satsuki and Mei's father. He's a researcher at the university's archaeology department.

Mei
Satsuki's four-year-old sister. She's worried about her mother's condition.

Satsuki
A sprightly young girl who looks after her younger sister.

Big Totoro
A forest creature who calls on the Cat Bus to help Mei and Satsuki.

Kanta
A local farm boy who's also Satsuki's classmate. He's kind.

Granny
Kanta's grandmother. She looks after Satsuki and Mei.

Cat Bus
This cat shaped bus runs on 12 legs and flies across the sky.

The Villagers
Inhabitants of Matsugô village.

Matriarch of Kanta's Family
A member of Kanta's extended family. She is the only villager who owns a phone.

My Neighbor TOTORO
CHARACTER INTRODUCTION

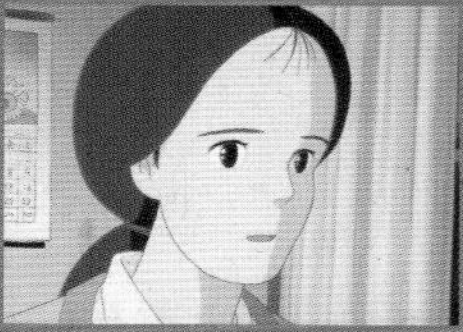

Mother
Satsuki and Mei's mother is resting at the hospital. Her children become worried when her condition worsens.

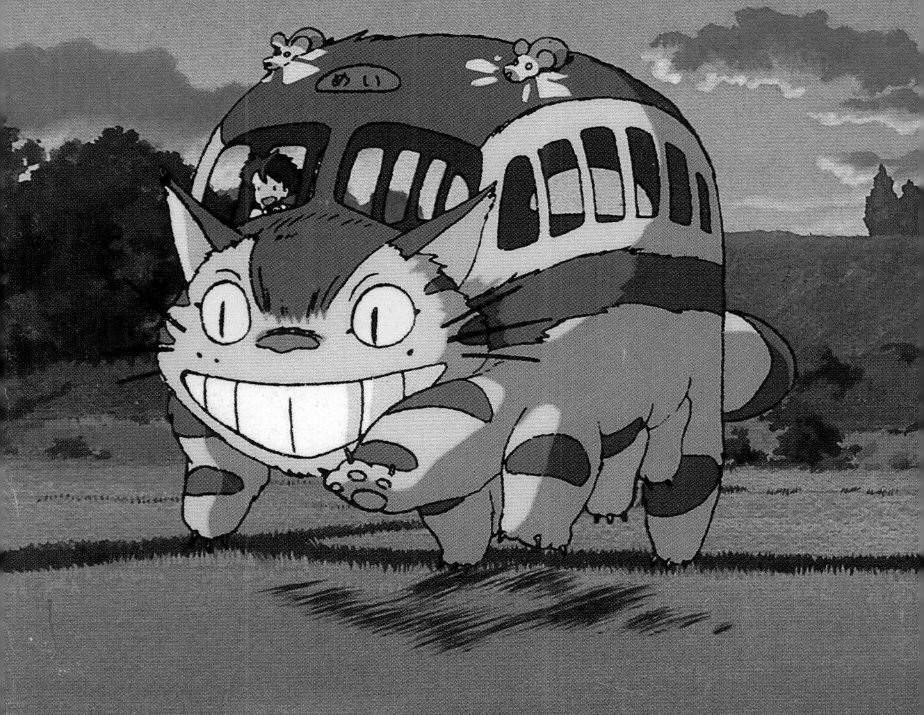
めい

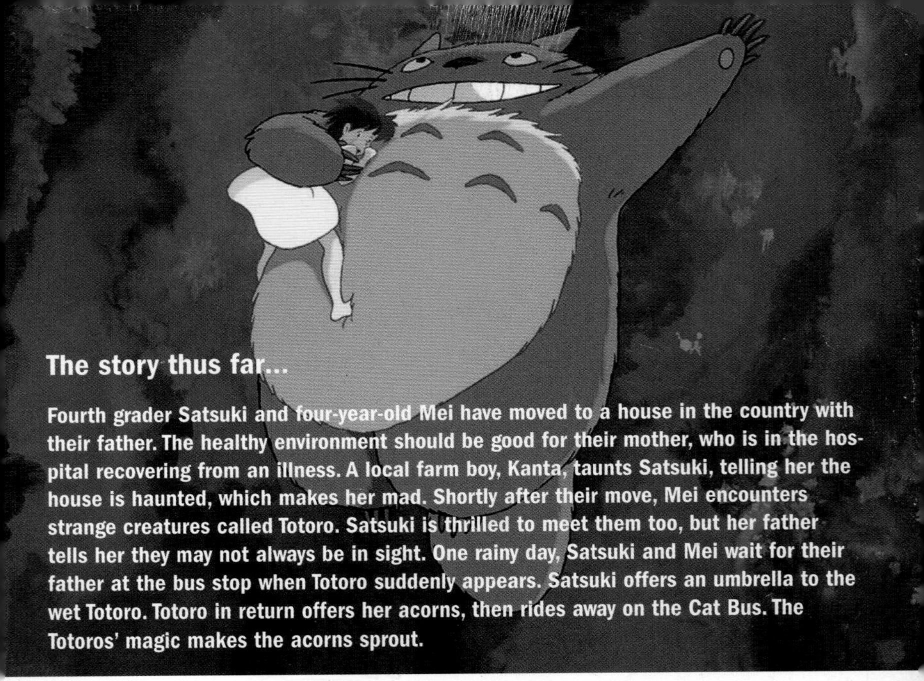

The story thus far...

Fourth grader Satsuki and four-year-old Mei have moved to a house in the country with their father. The healthy environment should be good for their mother, who is in the hospital recovering from an illness. A local farm boy, Kanta, taunts Satsuki, telling her the house is haunted, which makes her mad. Shortly after their move, Mei encounters strange creatures called Totoro. Satsuki is thrilled to meet them too, but her father tells her they may not always be in sight. One rainy day, Satsuki and Mei wait for their father at the bus stop when Totoro suddenly appears. Satsuki offers an umbrella to the wet Totoro. Totoro in return offers her acorns, then rides away on the Cat Bus. The Totoros' magic makes the acorns sprout.

Japanese Production Credits

Publicity Coordination
Hakuhodo Inc.
Tokuma Shoten
Animage Editorial Dept.

Distribution
Toho

Production
Studio Ghibli

Producer
Toru Hara

Main Cast

Satsuki	Noriko Hidaka
Mei	Chika Sakamoto
Father	Shigesato Itoi
Mother	Sumi Shimamoto
Kanta	Toshiyuki Amagasa
Granny	Tanie Kitabayashi
Big Totoro	Hitoshi Takagi
Mitchan	Chie Kojiro
Teacher	Machiko Washio

Editing
Takeshi Seyama

Titles
Takagu Atelier

Color Design
Michiyo Yasuda

Audio Director
Shigeharu Shiba

Recording and Sound Mixing
Shuji Inoue

Sound Effects
Kazutoshi Sato

Audio Recording
Omnibus Promotion

Production Manager
Eiko Tanaka

Production Desk
Hirokatsu Kihara
Toshiyuki Kawabata

Music Production
Mitsunori Miura
Takashi Watanabe
Tokuma Japan Co., Ltd.

Executive Producer
Yasuyoshi Tokuma

Associate Executive Producers
Tatsumi Yamashita
Hideo Ogata

Original Story and Screenplay Written and Directed by
Hayao Miyazaki

Supervising Animator
Yoshiharu Sato

Art Direction
Kazuo Oga

Music
Joe Hisaishi

Animation Check
Yasuko Tachiki
Hitomi Tateno

Color Design Assistant
Nobuko Mizuta

Camera Supervisor
Hisao Shirai

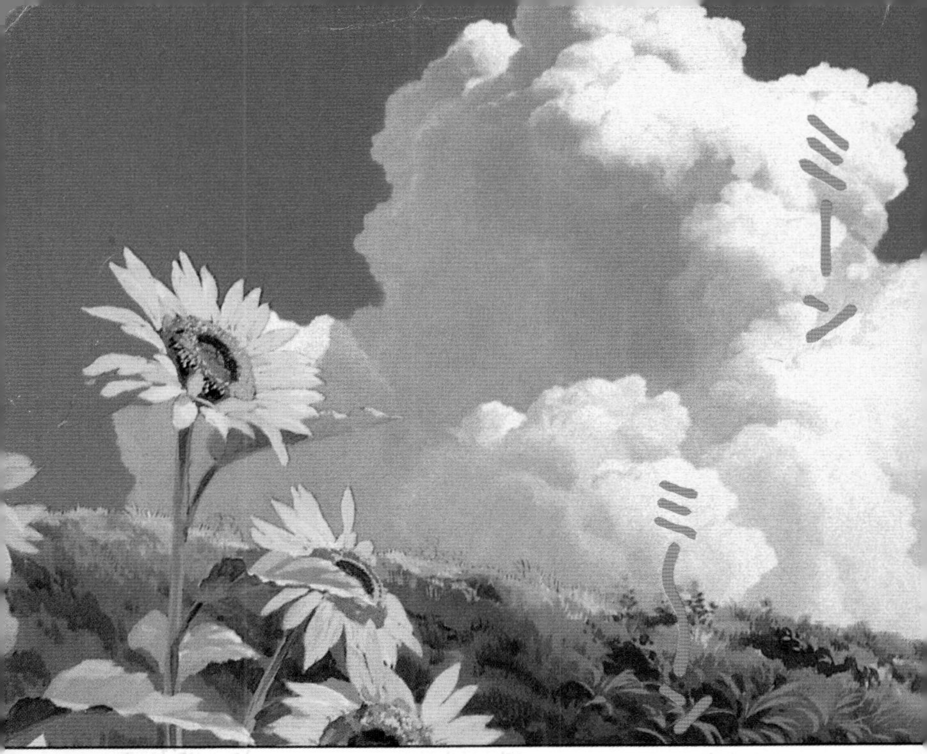
ミーン
ミー
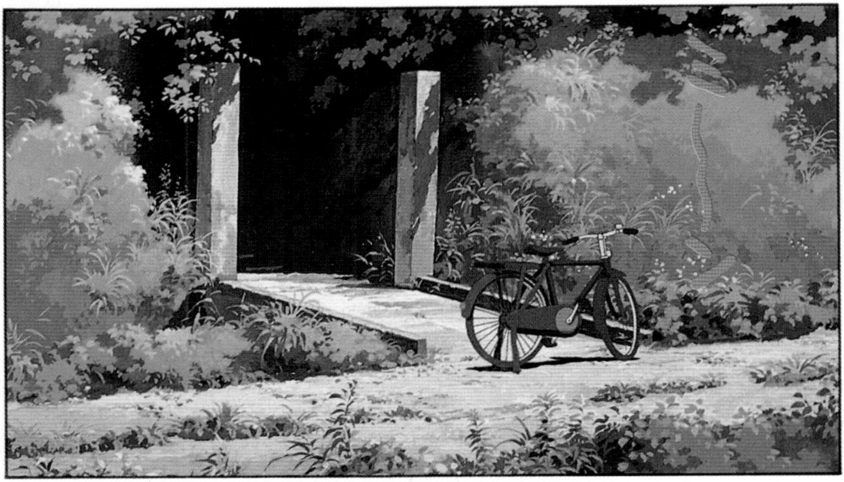

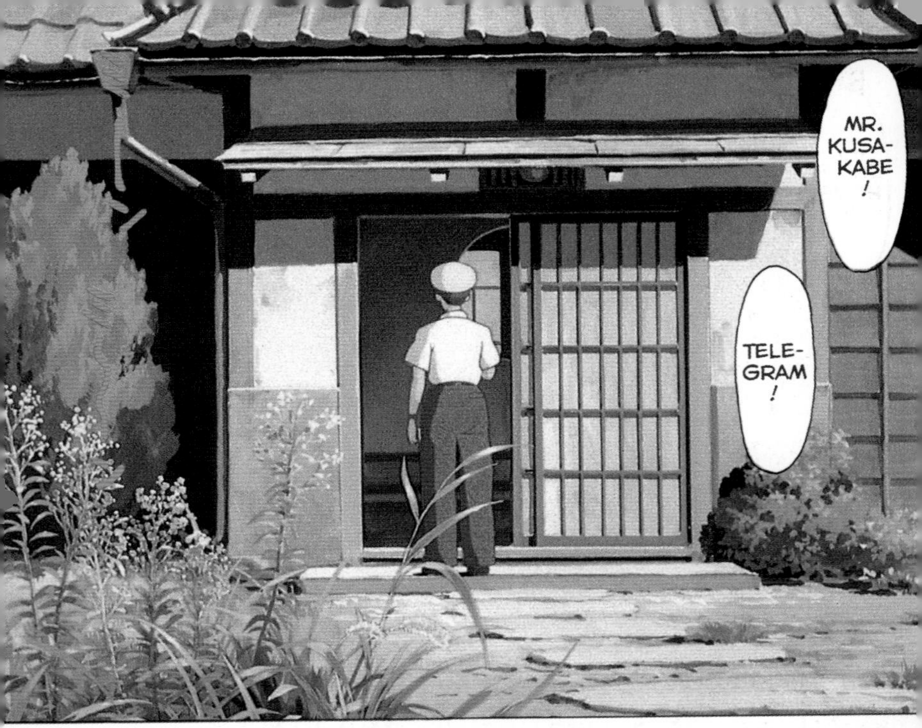
MR. KUSA-KABE!
TELE-GRAM!
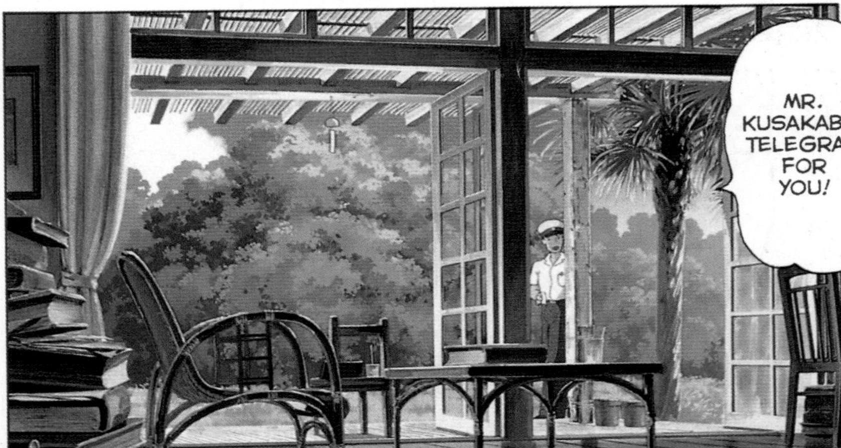
MR. KUSAKABE! TELEGRAM FOR YOU!

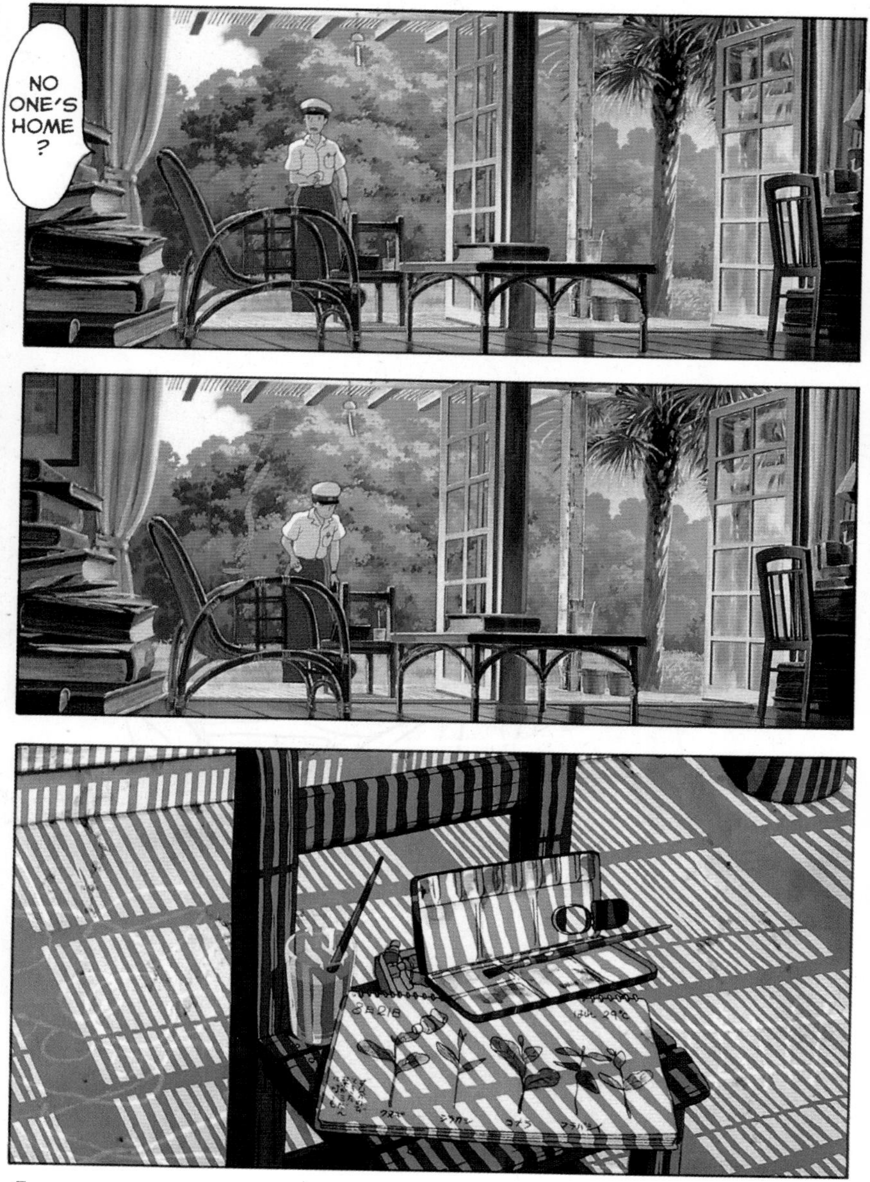
NO ONE'S HOME ?

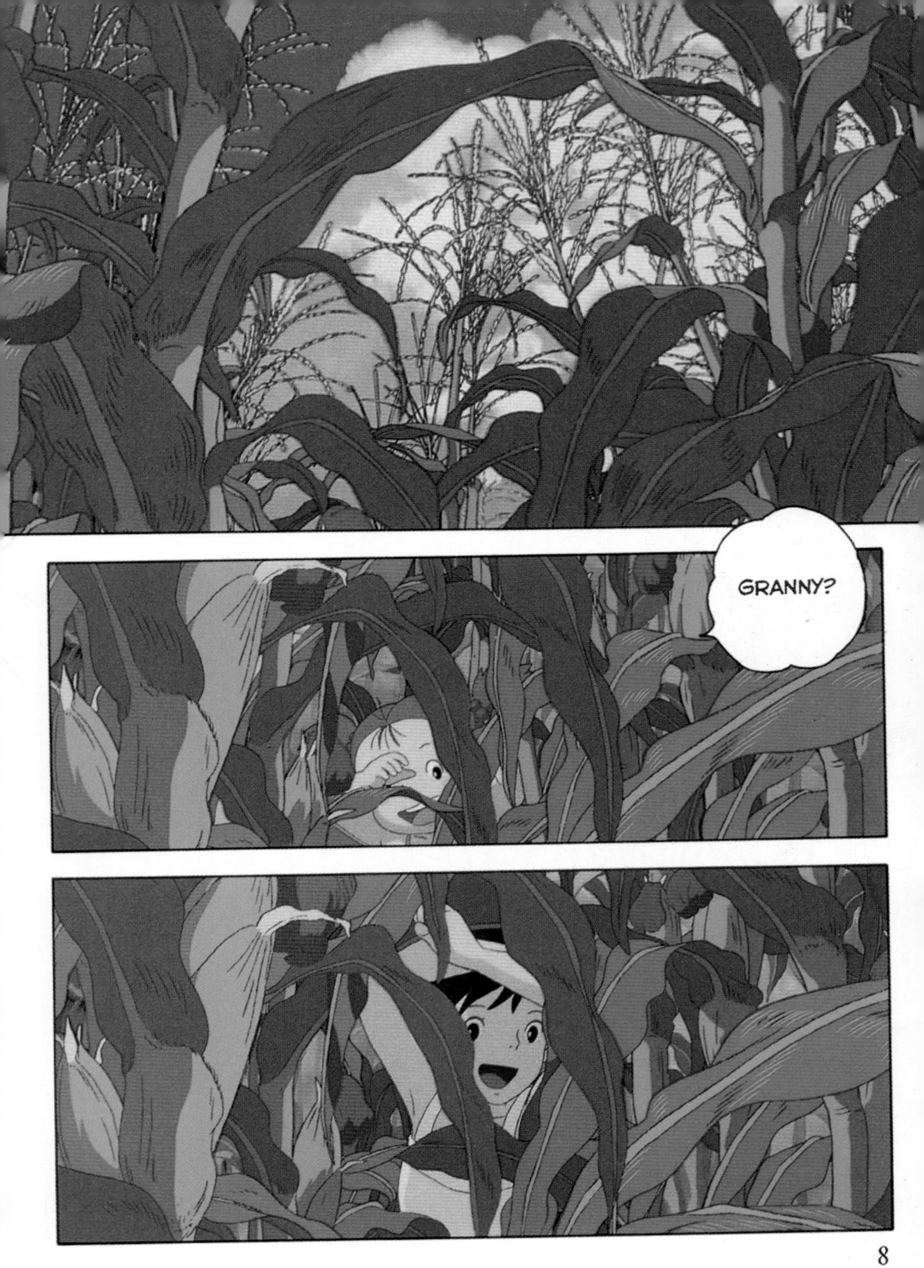
GRANNY?

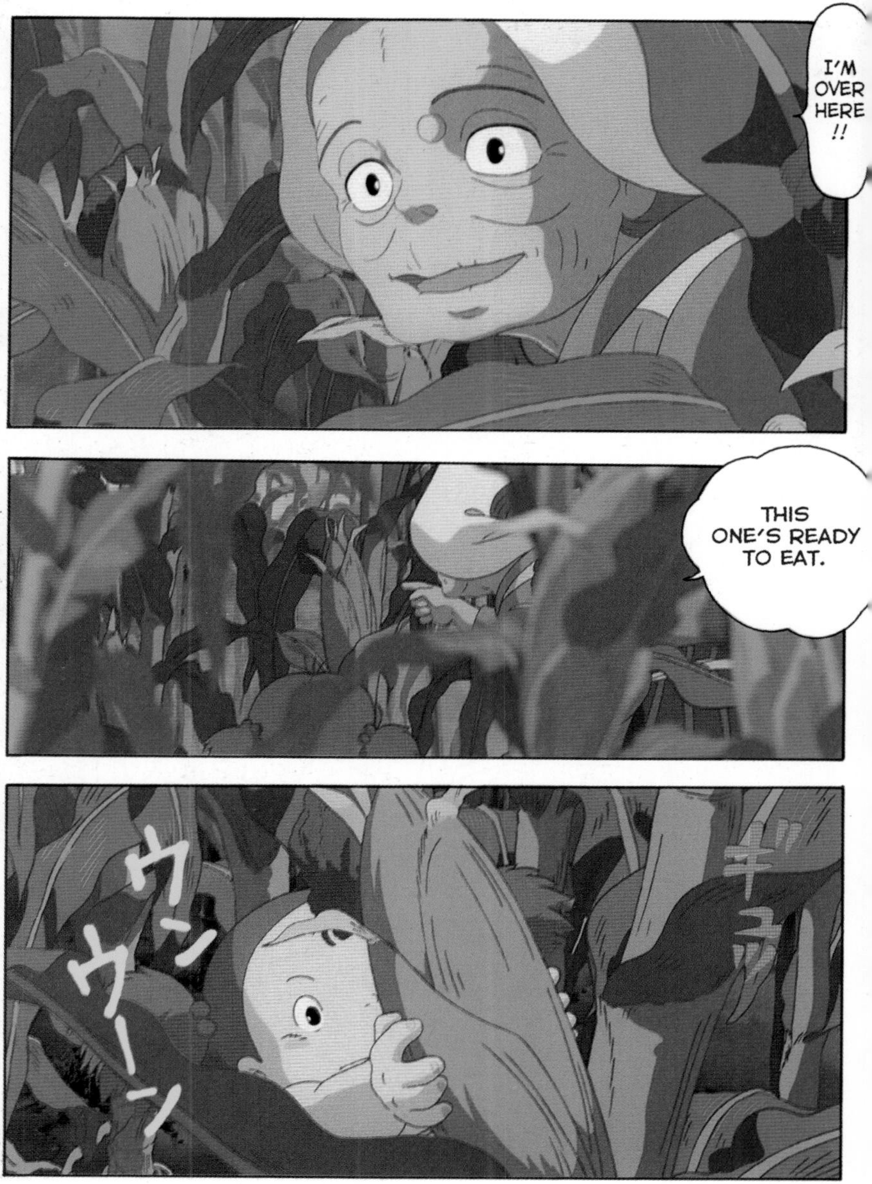
I'M OVER HERE !!
THIS ONE'S READY TO EAT.
ギュ
ウンウーン

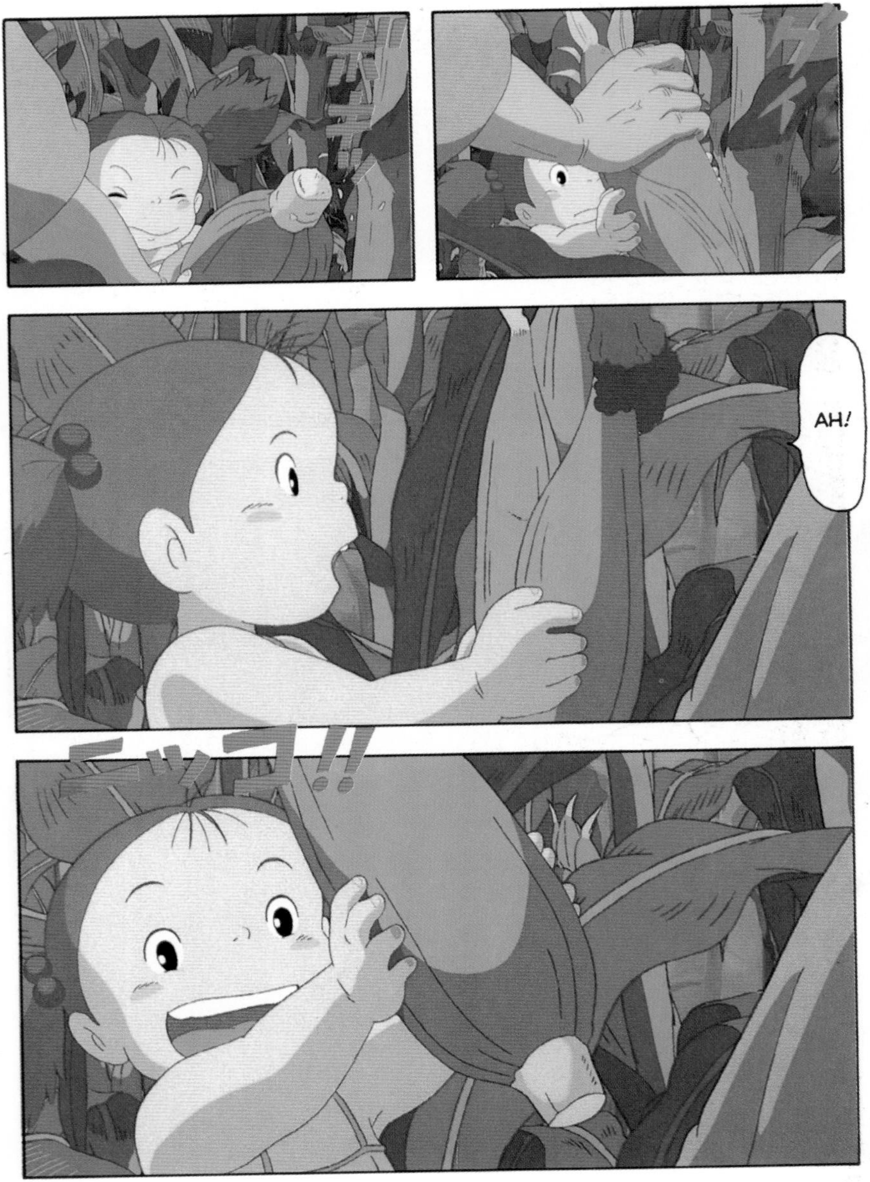
AH!

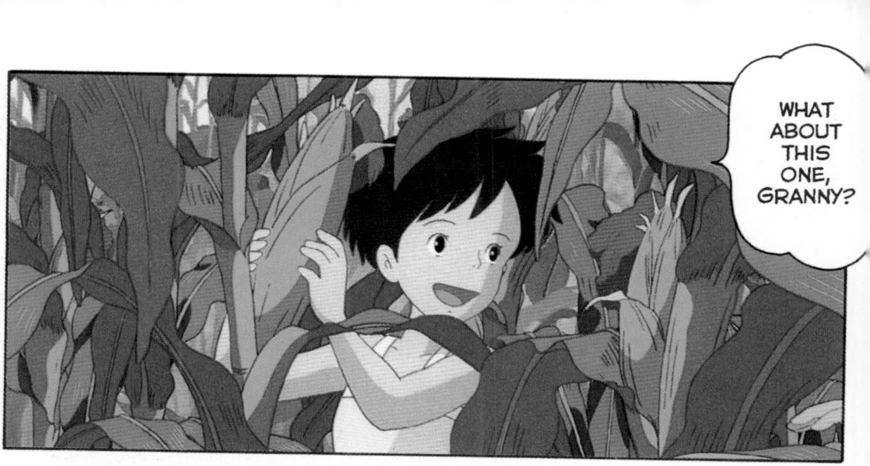
WHAT ABOUT THIS ONE, GRANNY?

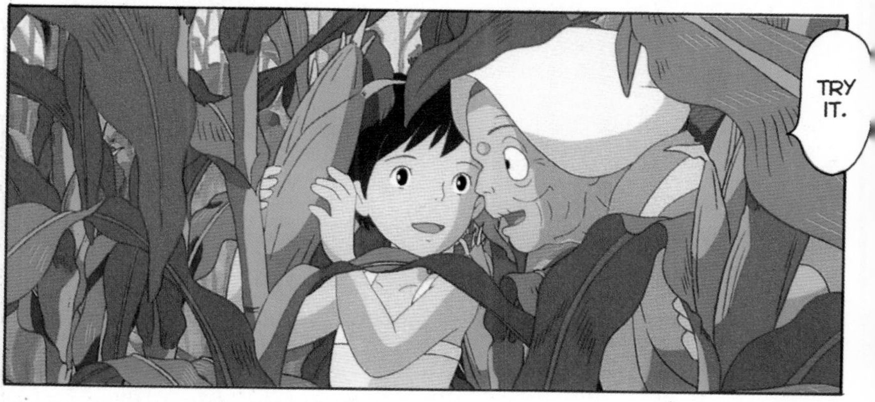
TRY IT.

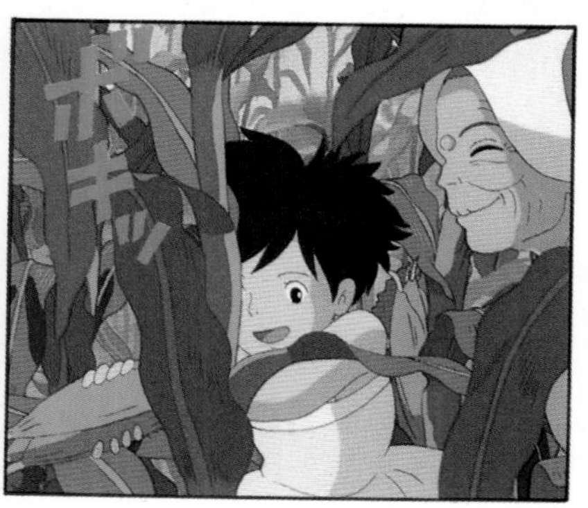
ボキッ

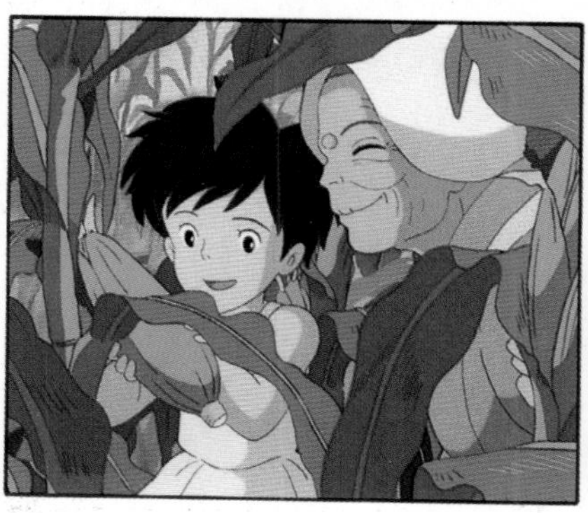

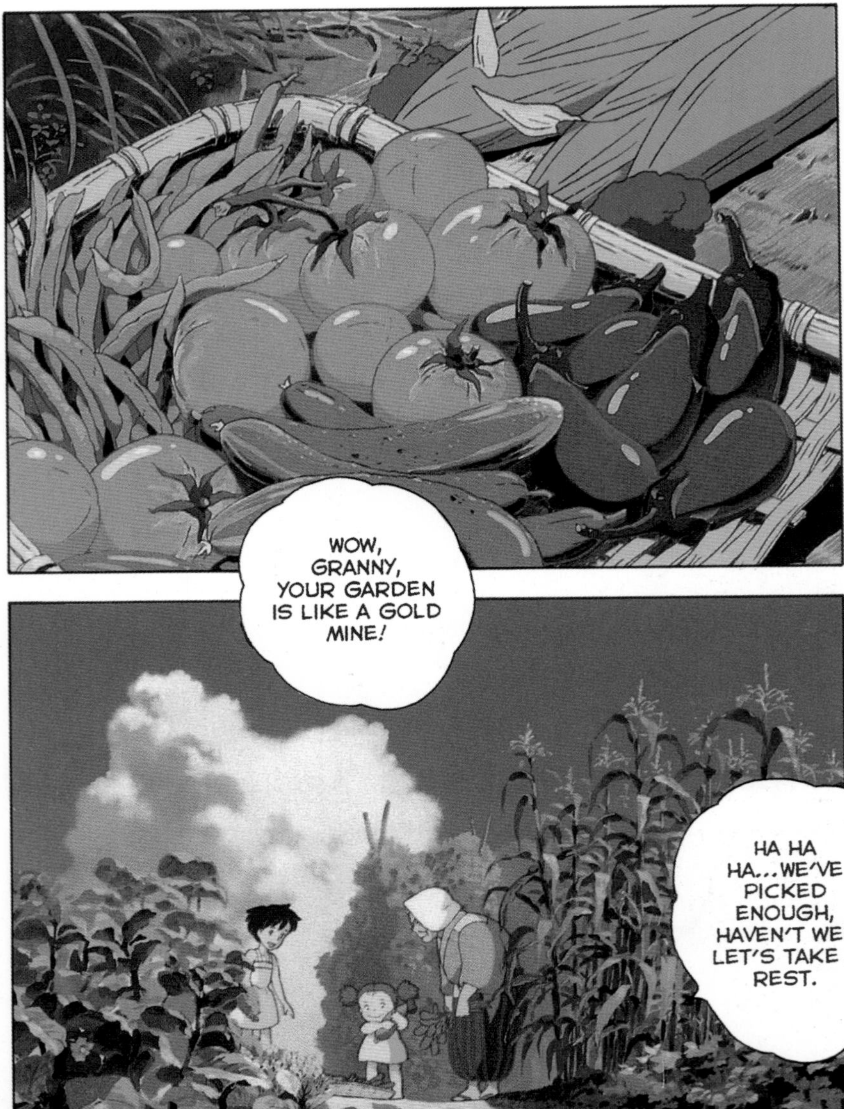
WOW, GRANNY, YOUR GARDEN IS LIKE A GOLD MINE!
HA HA HA...WE'VE PICKED ENOUGH, HAVEN'T WE? LET'S TAKE A REST.

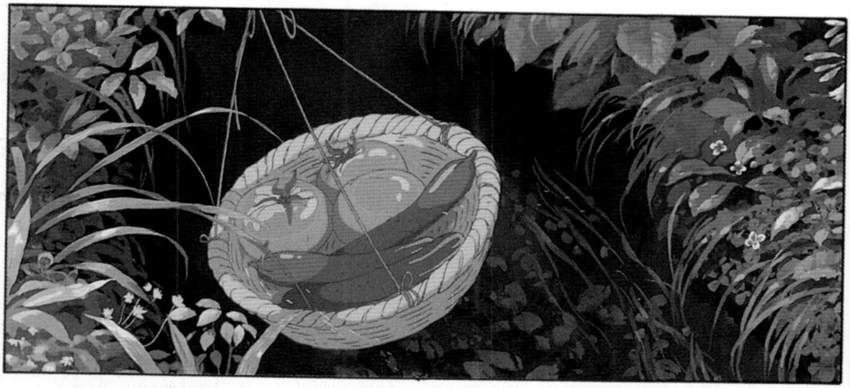

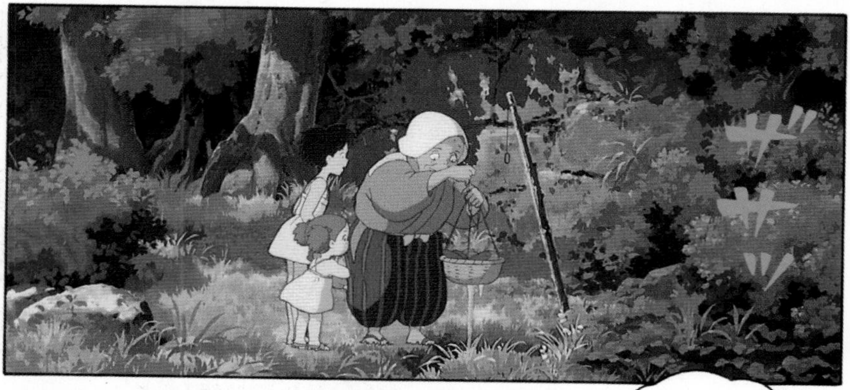
ザッ
ザッ

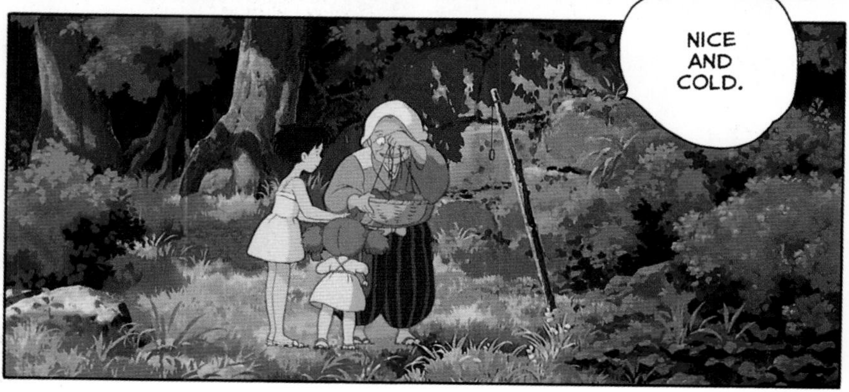
NICE AND COLD.

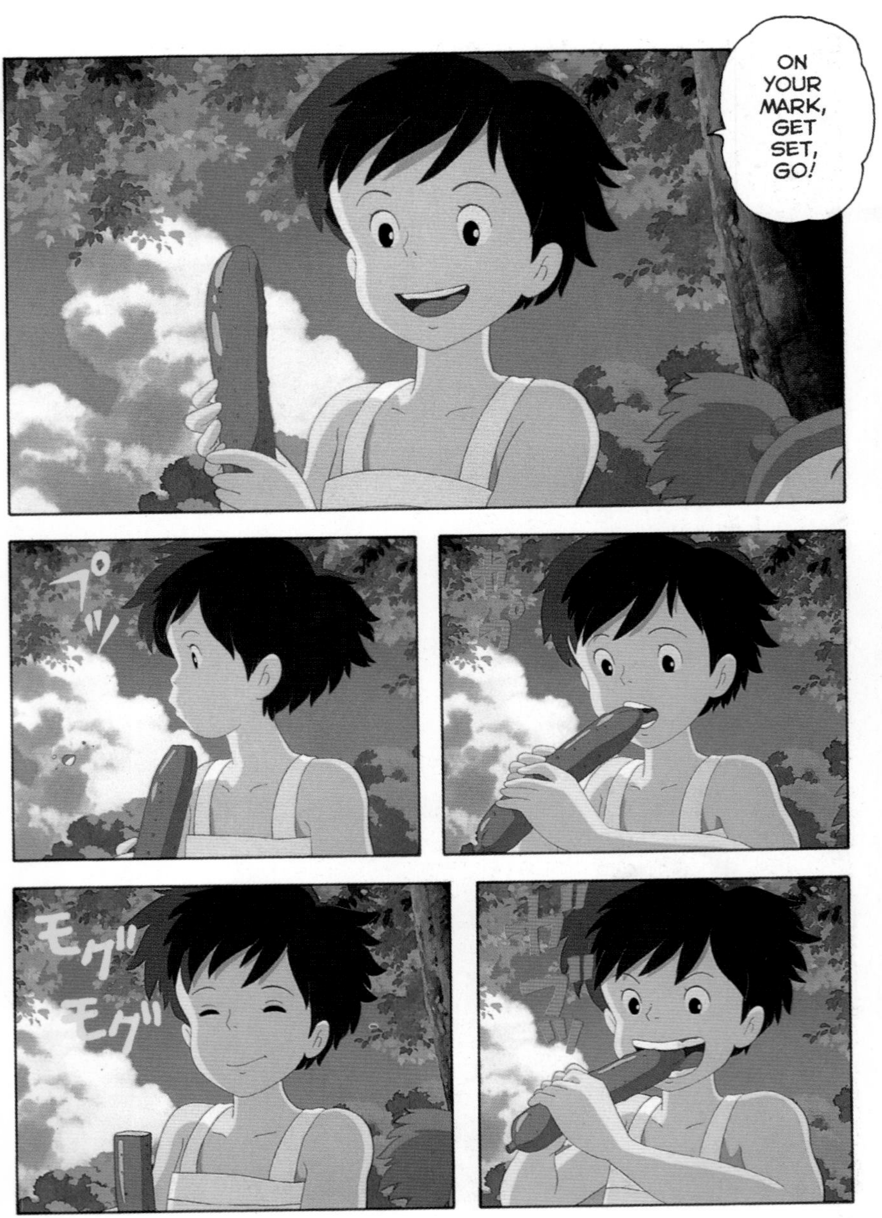
ON YOUR MARK, GET SET, GO!
プッ
モグ モグ

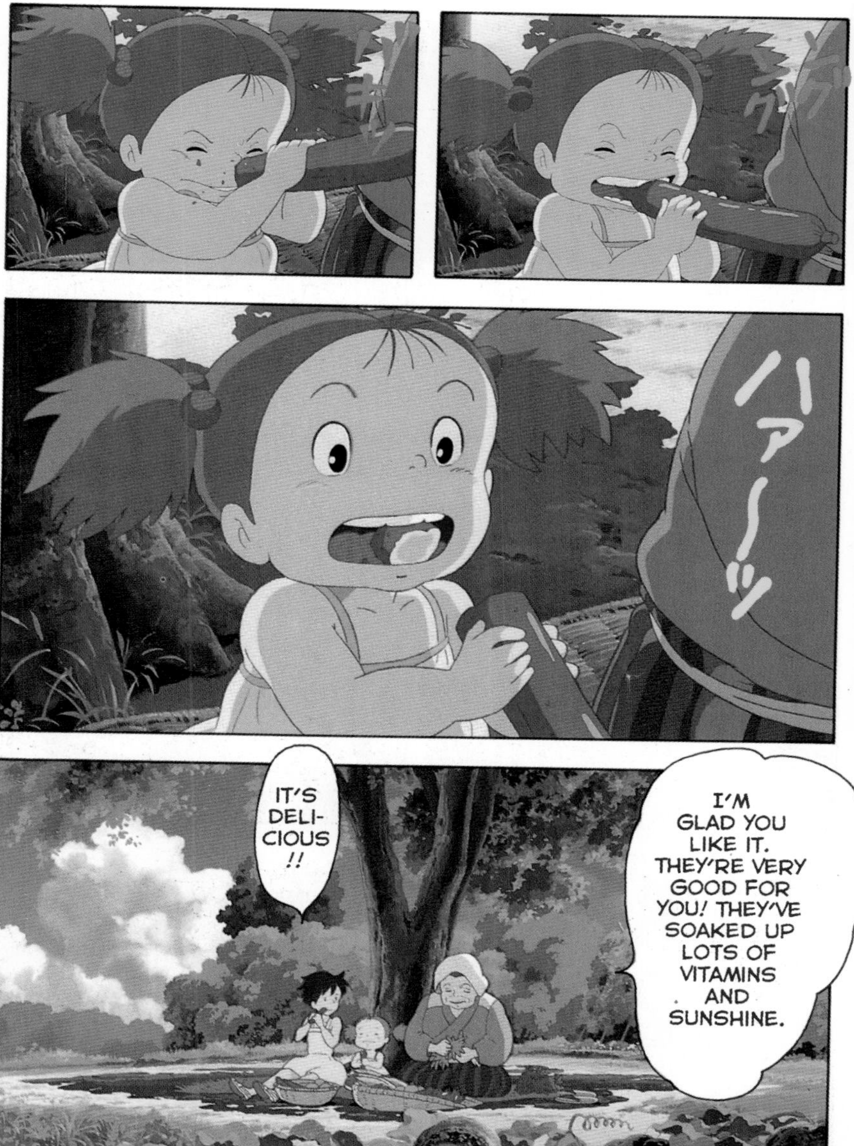
ハア～～ッ
I'M GLAD YOU LIKE IT. THEY'RE VERY GOOD FOR YOU! THEY'VE SOAKED UP LOTS OF VITAMINS AND SUNSHINE.
IT'S DELI-CIOUS !!

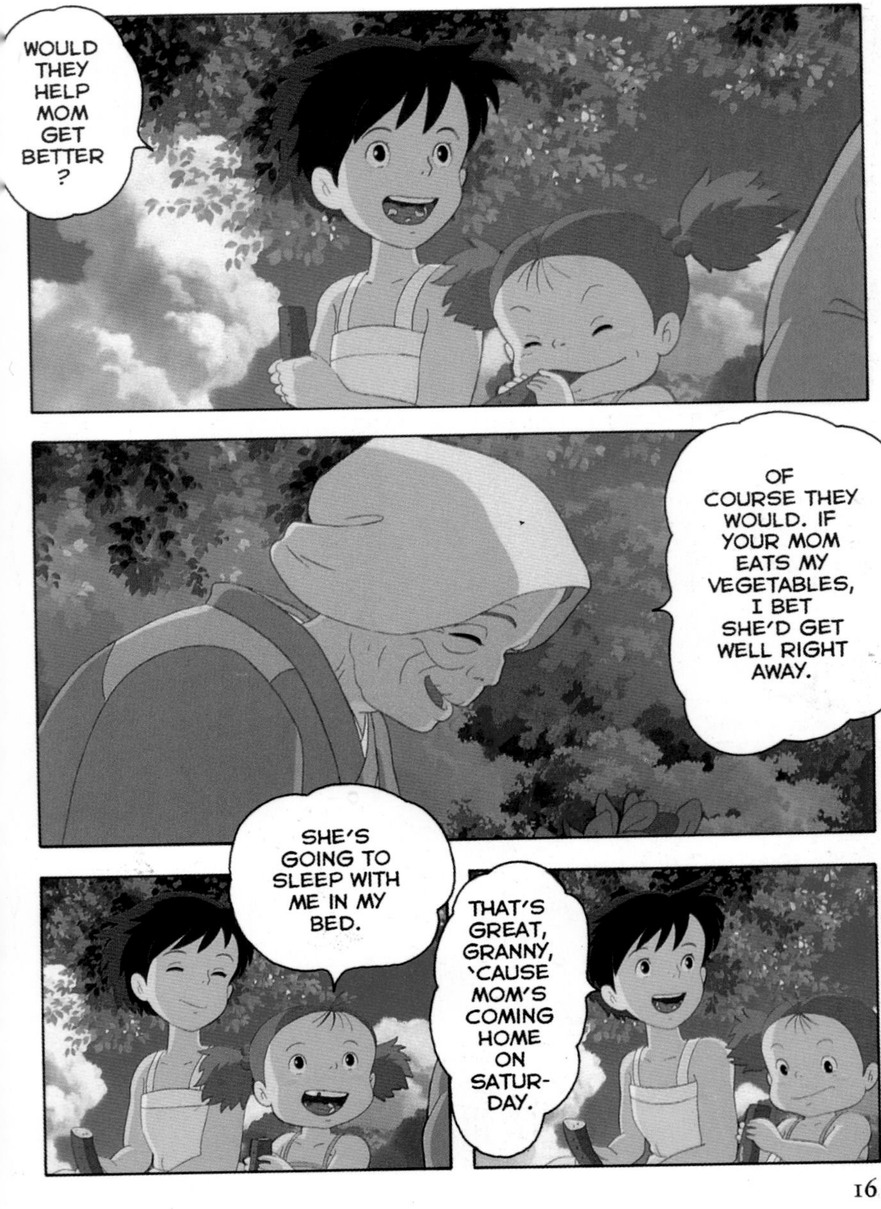
WOULD THEY HELP MOM GET BETTER ?
OF COURSE THEY WOULD. IF YOUR MOM EATS MY VEGETABLES, I BET SHE'D GET WELL RIGHT AWAY.
THAT'S GREAT, GRANNY, 'CAUSE MOM'S COMING HOME ON SATUR-DAY.
SHE'S GOING TO SLEEP WITH ME IN MY BED.

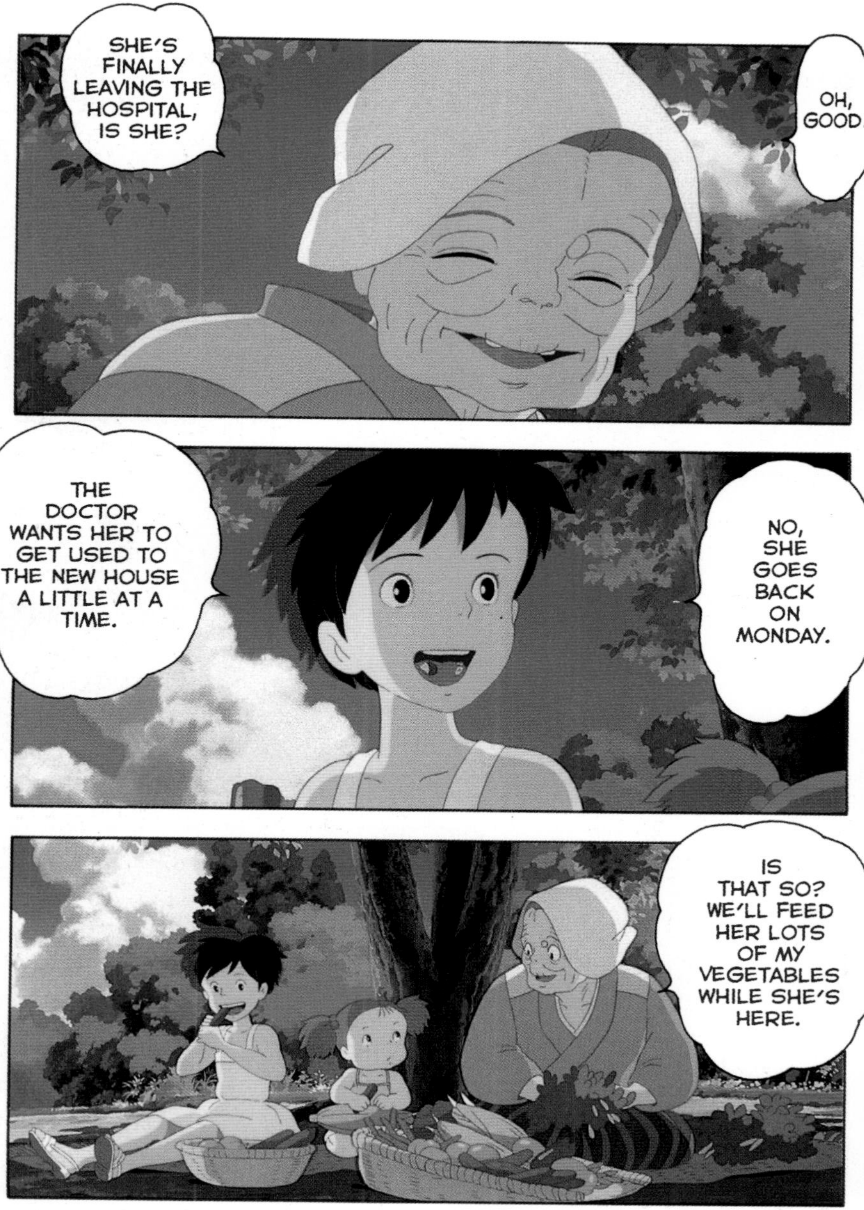
OH, GOOD.
SHE'S FINALLY LEAVING THE HOSPITAL, IS SHE?
NO, SHE GOES BACK ON MONDAY.
THE DOCTOR WANTS HER TO GET USED TO THE NEW HOUSE A LITTLE AT A TIME.
IS THAT SO? WE'LL FEED HER LOTS OF MY VEGETABLES WHILE SHE'S HERE.

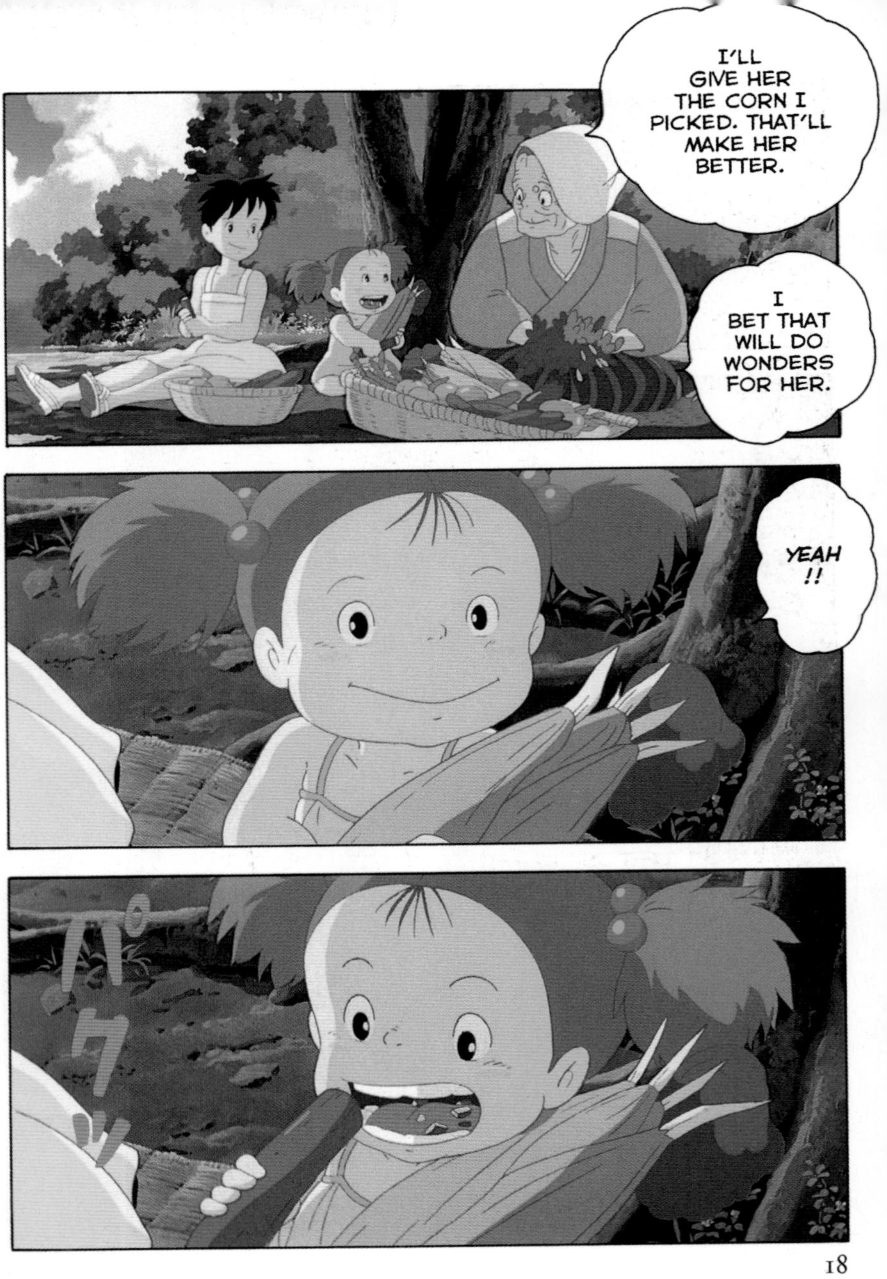
I'LL GIVE HER THE CORN I PICKED. THAT'LL MAKE HER BETTER.
I BET THAT WILL DO WONDERS FOR HER.
YEAH !!
パクッ

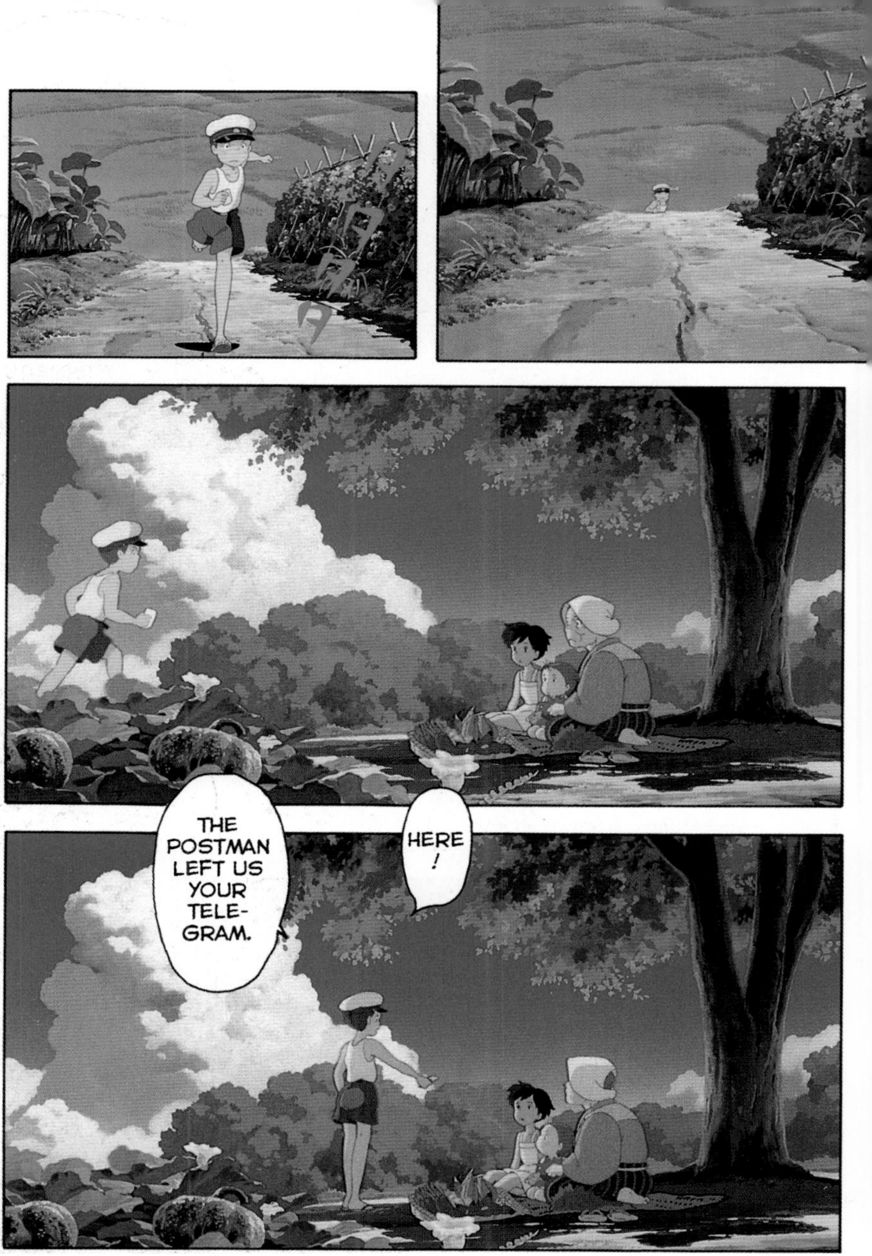
HERE!
THE POSTMAN LEFT US YOUR TELEGRAM.

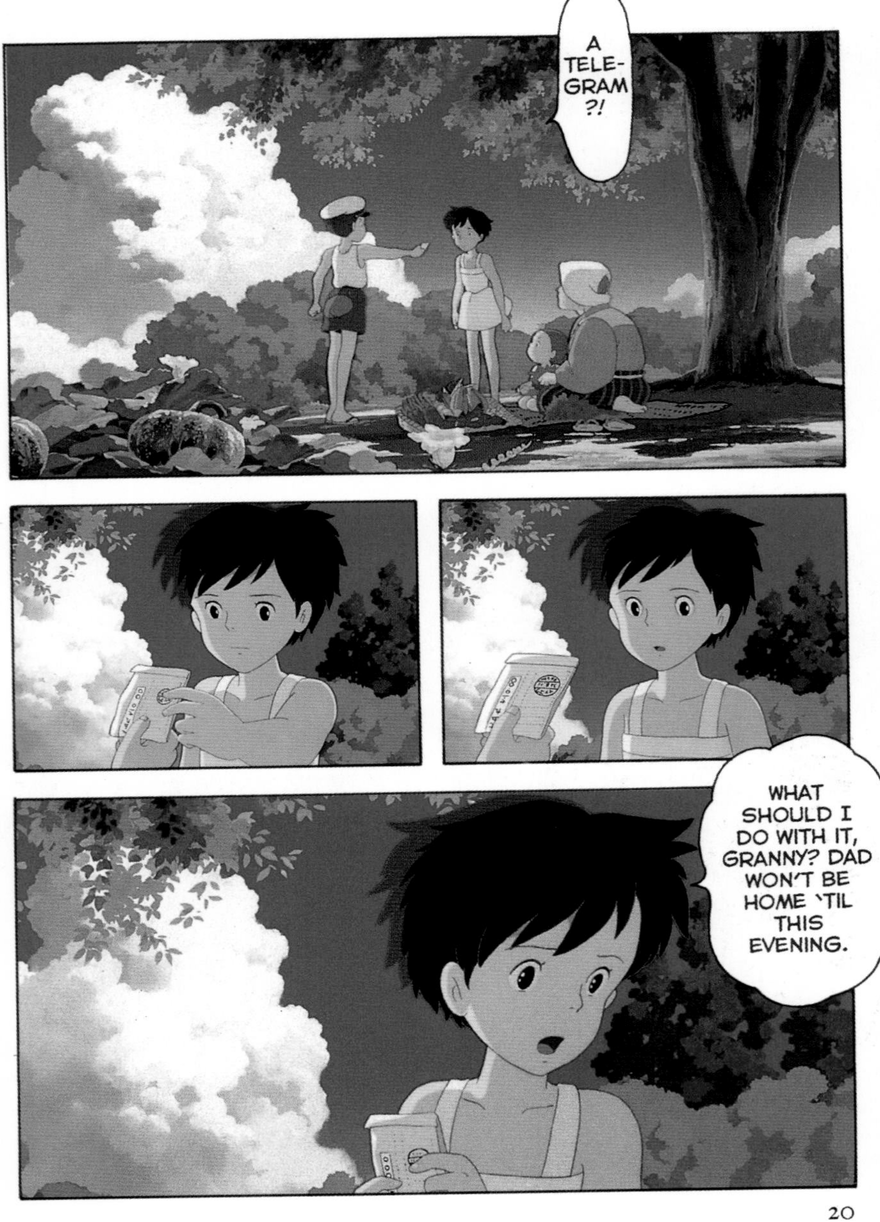
A TELE-GRAM?!
WHAT SHOULD I DO WITH IT, GRANNY? DAD WON'T BE HOME 'TIL THIS EVENING.

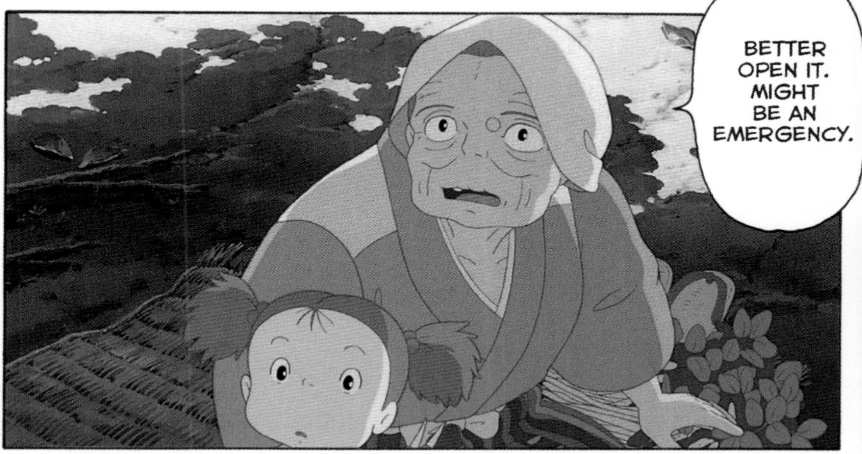
BETTER OPEN IT. MIGHT BE AN EMERGENCY.

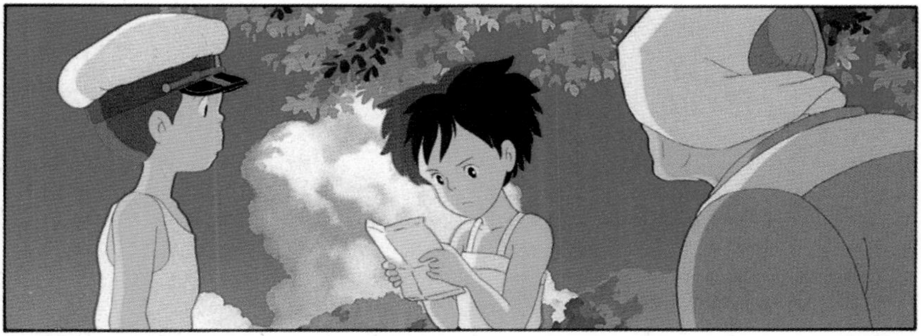

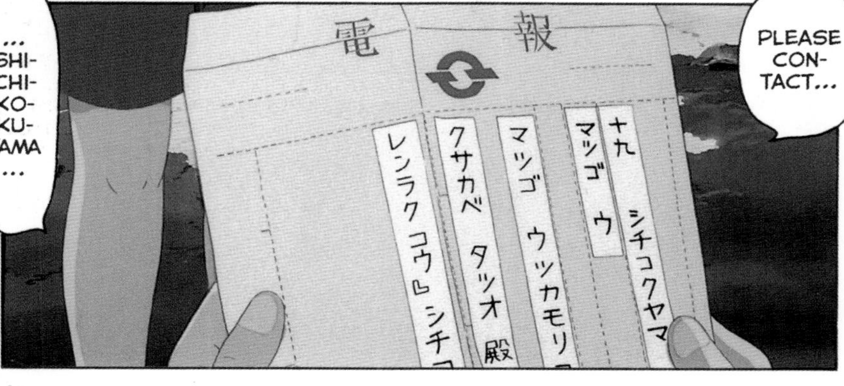
PLEASE CON-TACT...
電報
十九 シチコクヤマ
マツゴ ウ
マツゴ ウツカモリ
クサカベ タツオ 殿
レンラク コウ』 シチ
... SHI-CHI-KO-KU-YAMA ...

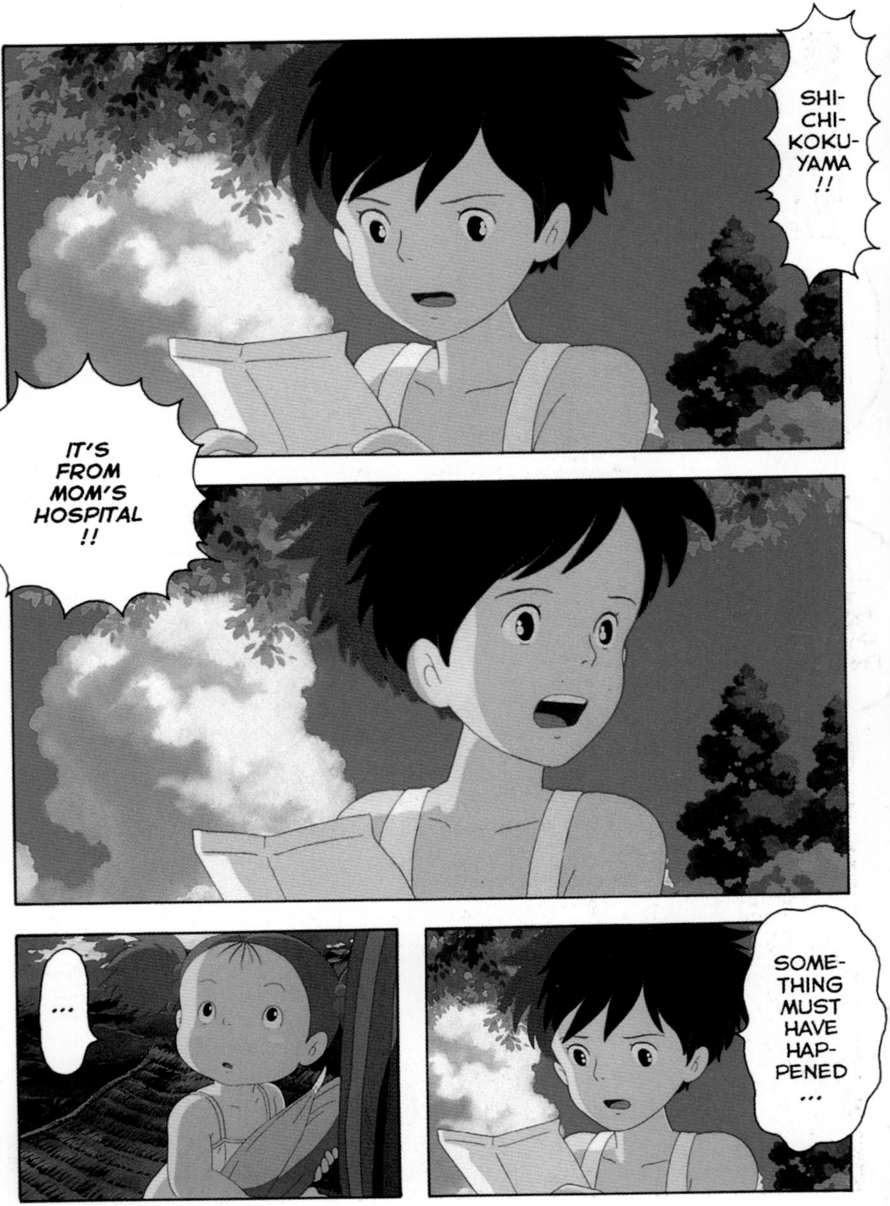
SHI-CHI-KOKU-YAMA !!
IT'S FROM MOM'S HOSPITAL !!
SOME-THING MUST HAVE HAP-PENED ...
...

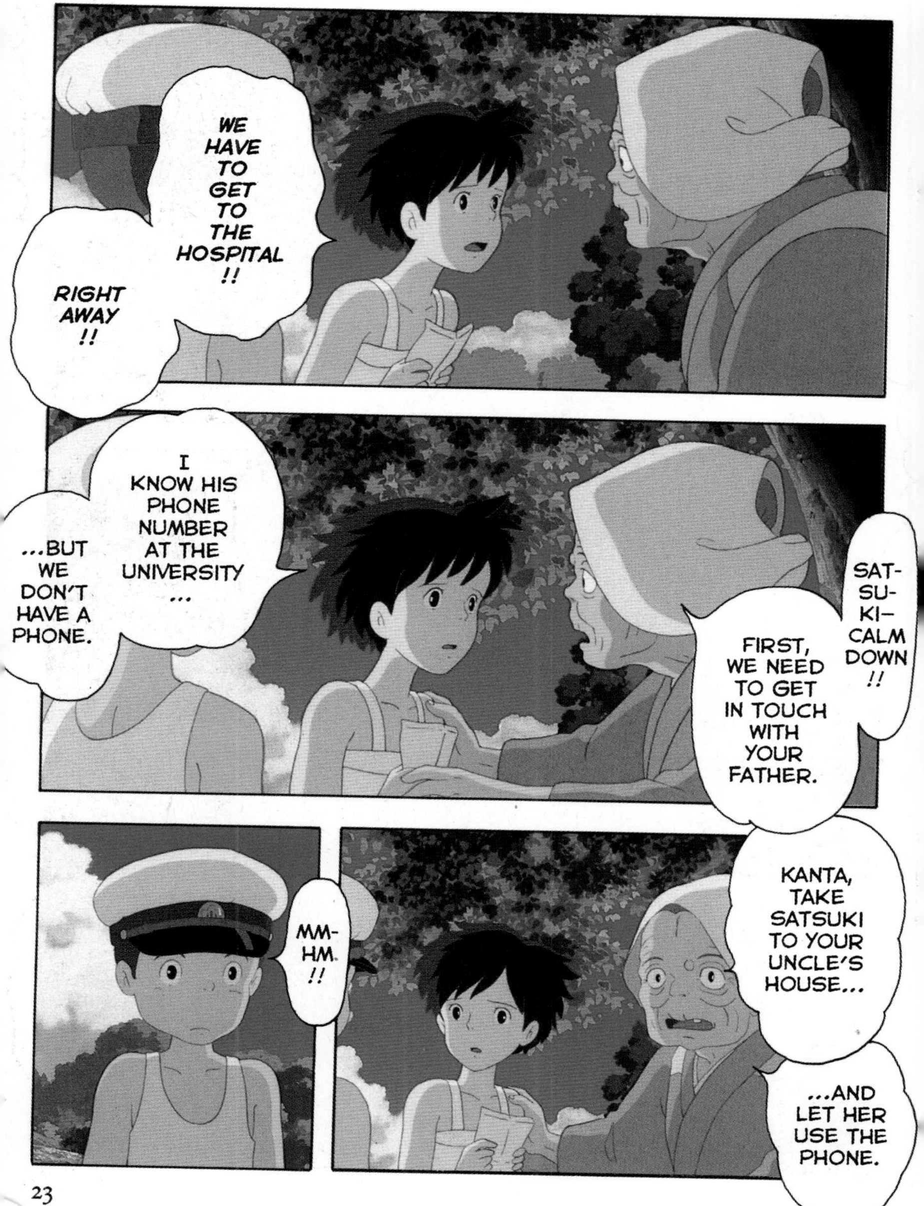
WE HAVE TO GET TO THE HOSPITAL!!
RIGHT AWAY!!
SAT-SU-KI—CALM DOWN!!
FIRST, WE NEED TO GET IN TOUCH WITH YOUR FATHER.
I KNOW HIS PHONE NUMBER AT THE UNIVERSITY...
...BUT WE DON'T HAVE A PHONE.
KANTA, TAKE SATSUKI TO YOUR UNCLE'S HOUSE...
...AND LET HER USE THE PHONE.
MM-HM!!

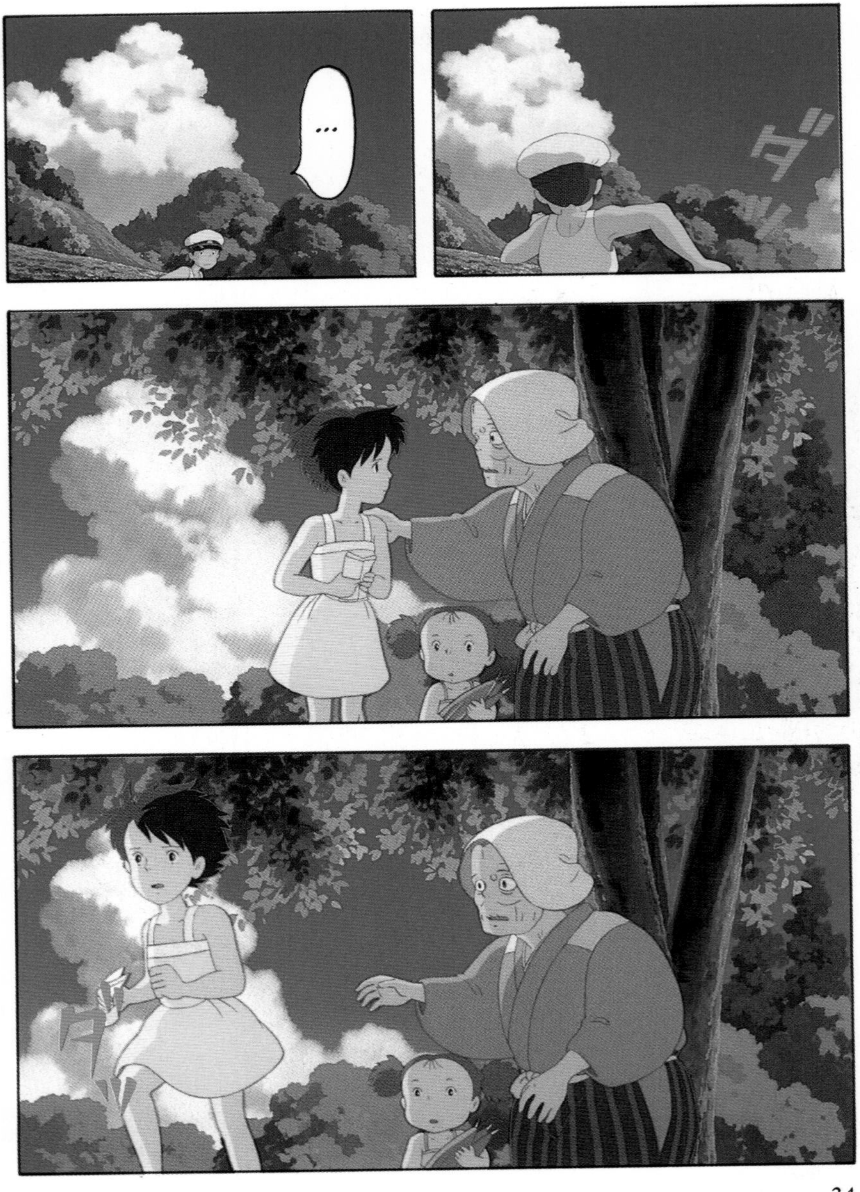
ダッ
...

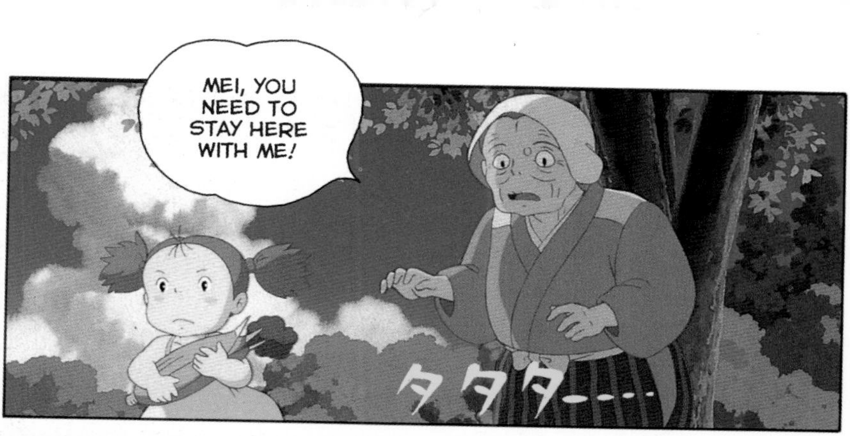
MEI, YOU NEED TO STAY HERE WITH ME!
タタタ....

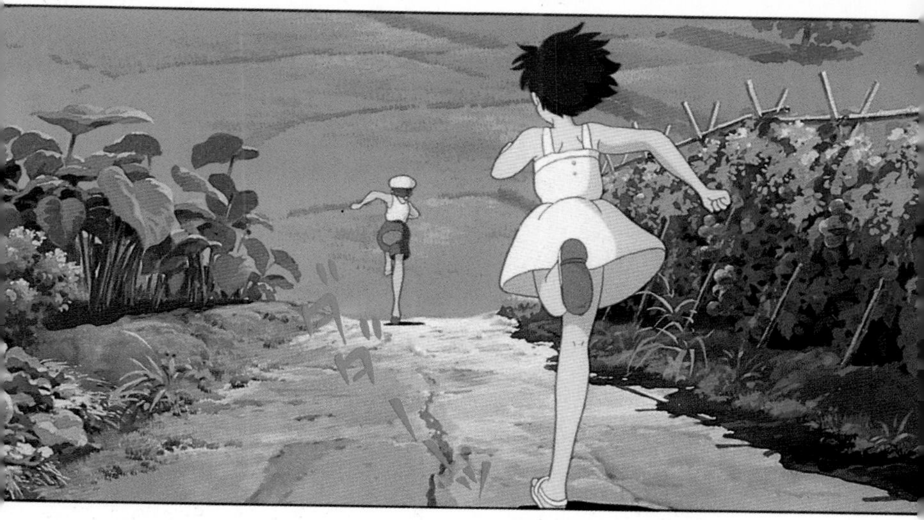

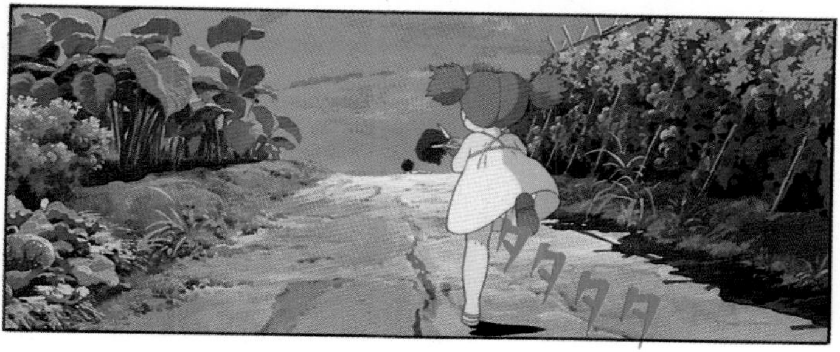
タタタタタ

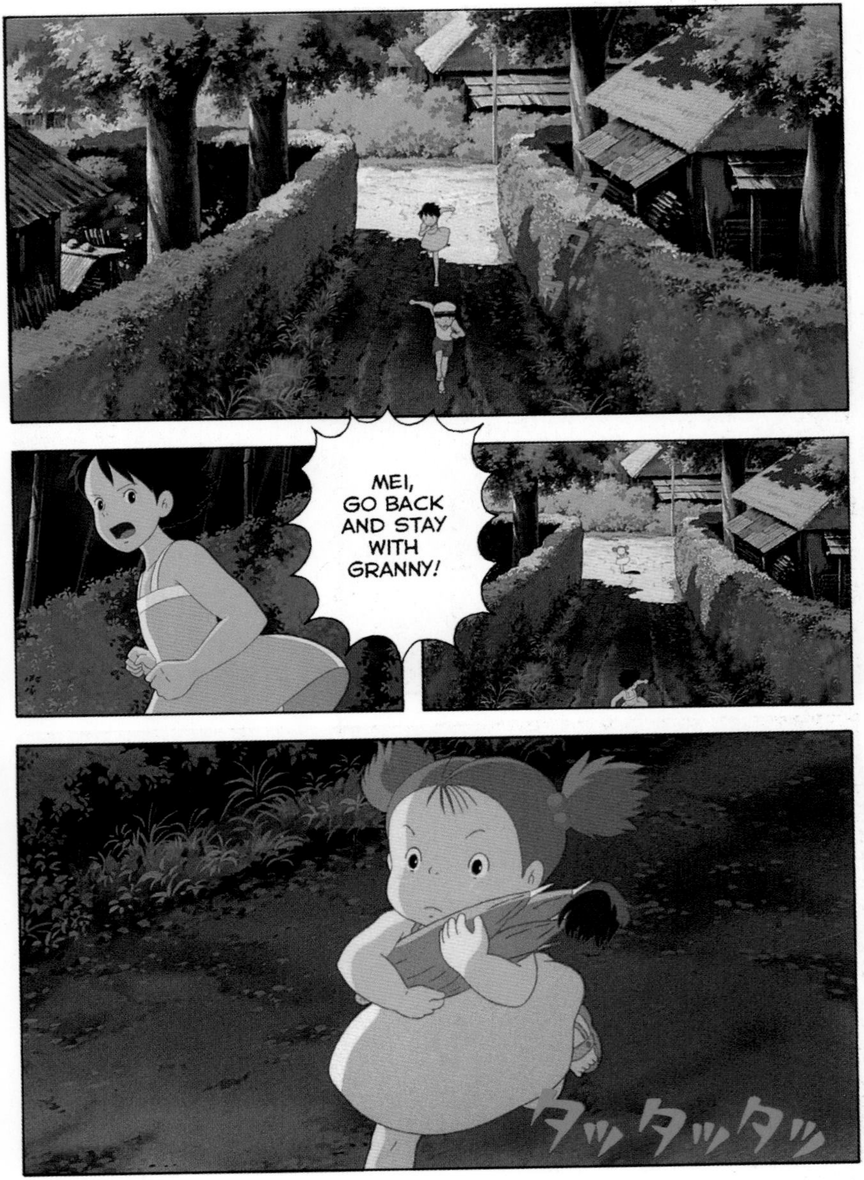
MEI, GO BACK AND STAY WITH GRANNY!
タッタッタッ

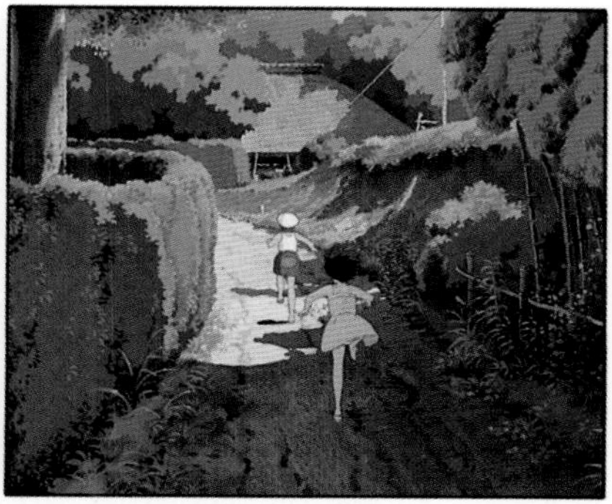

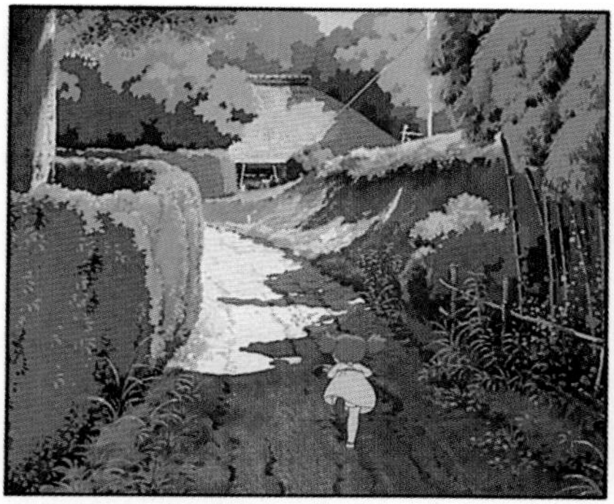

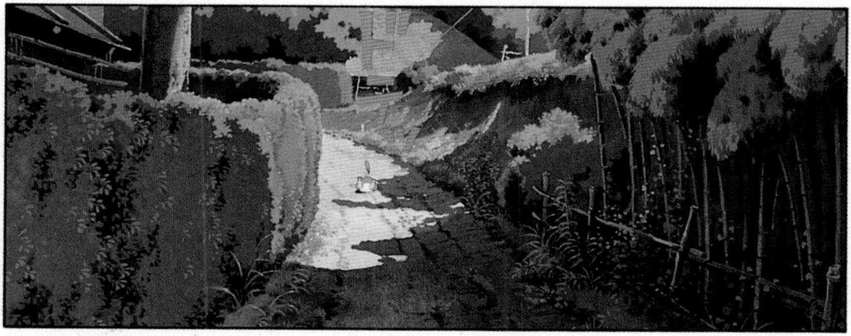

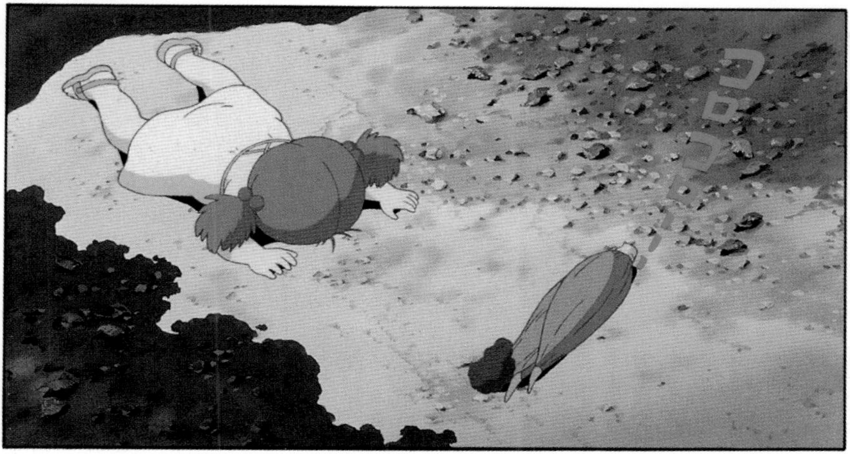
コロコロ…

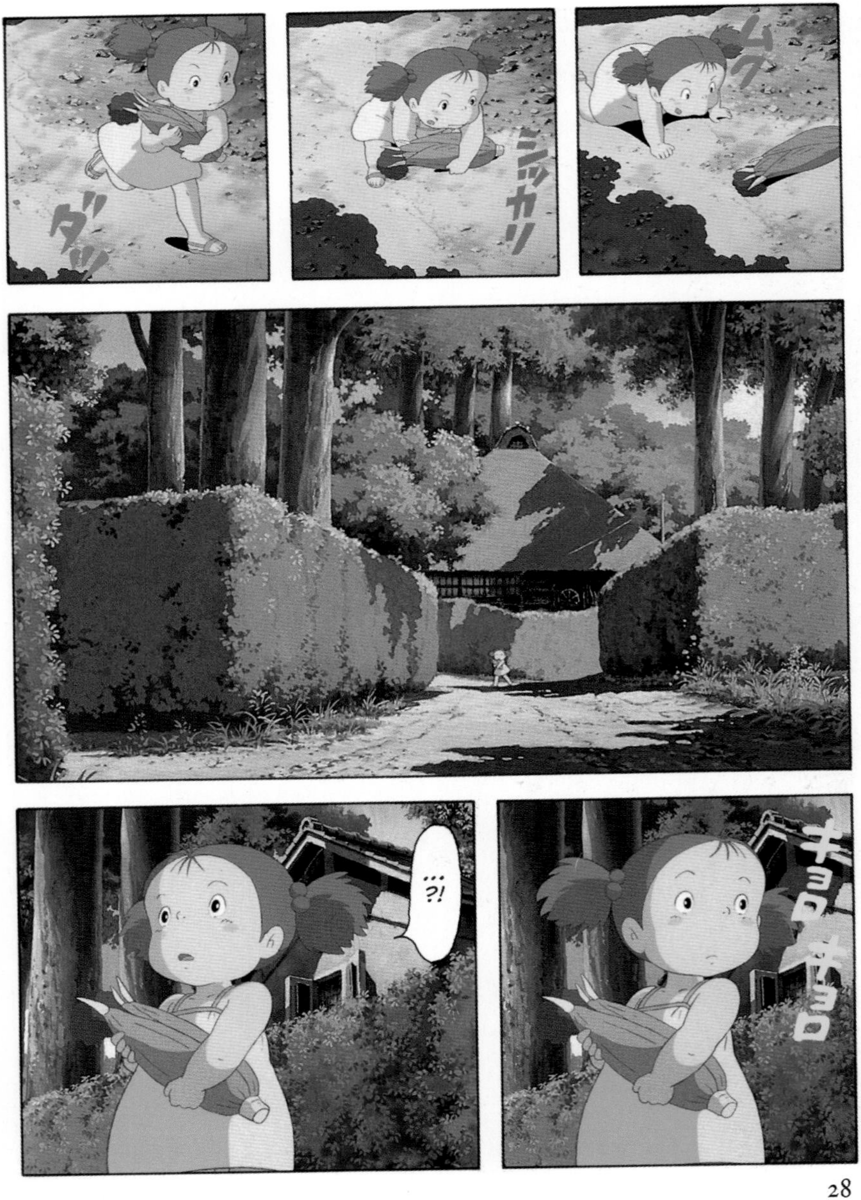
ムク
シッカリ
ダッ
キョロキョロ
...?!

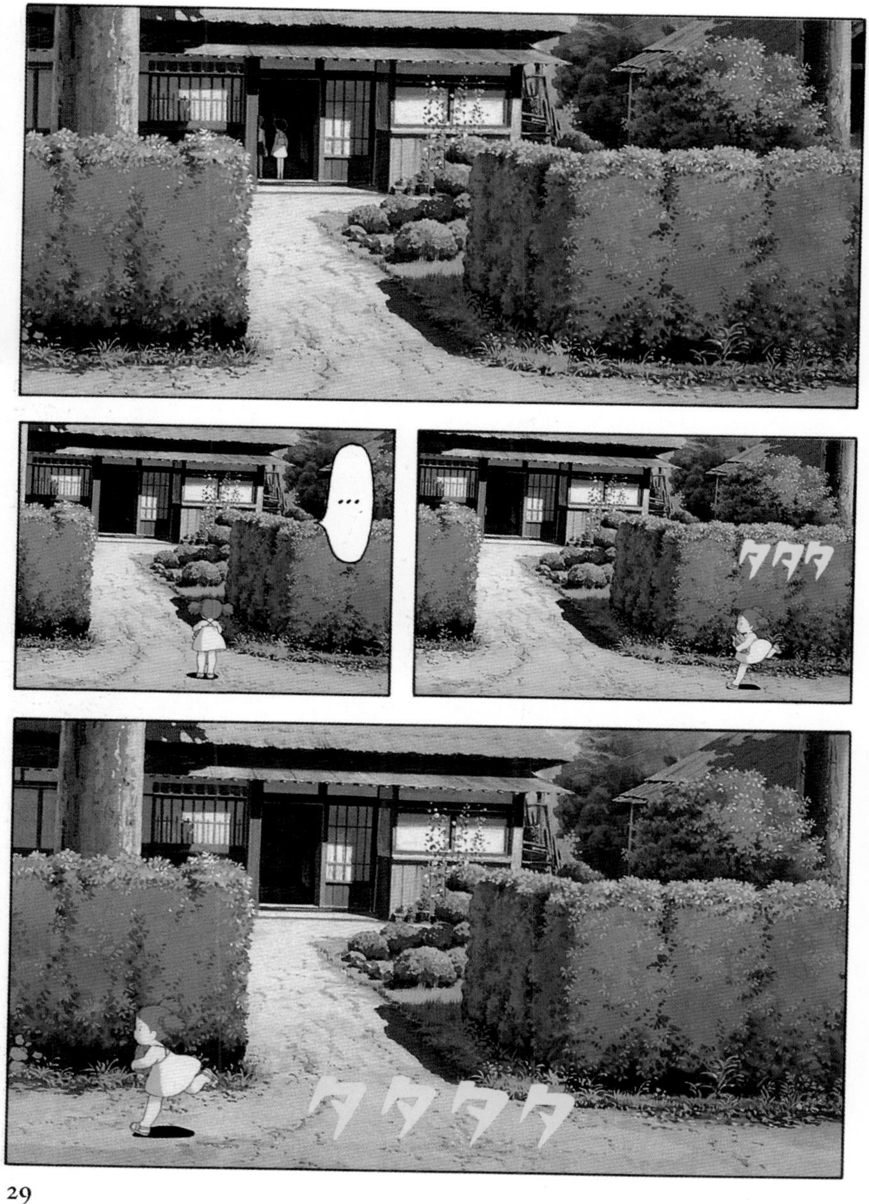
タタタ
...
タタタタ

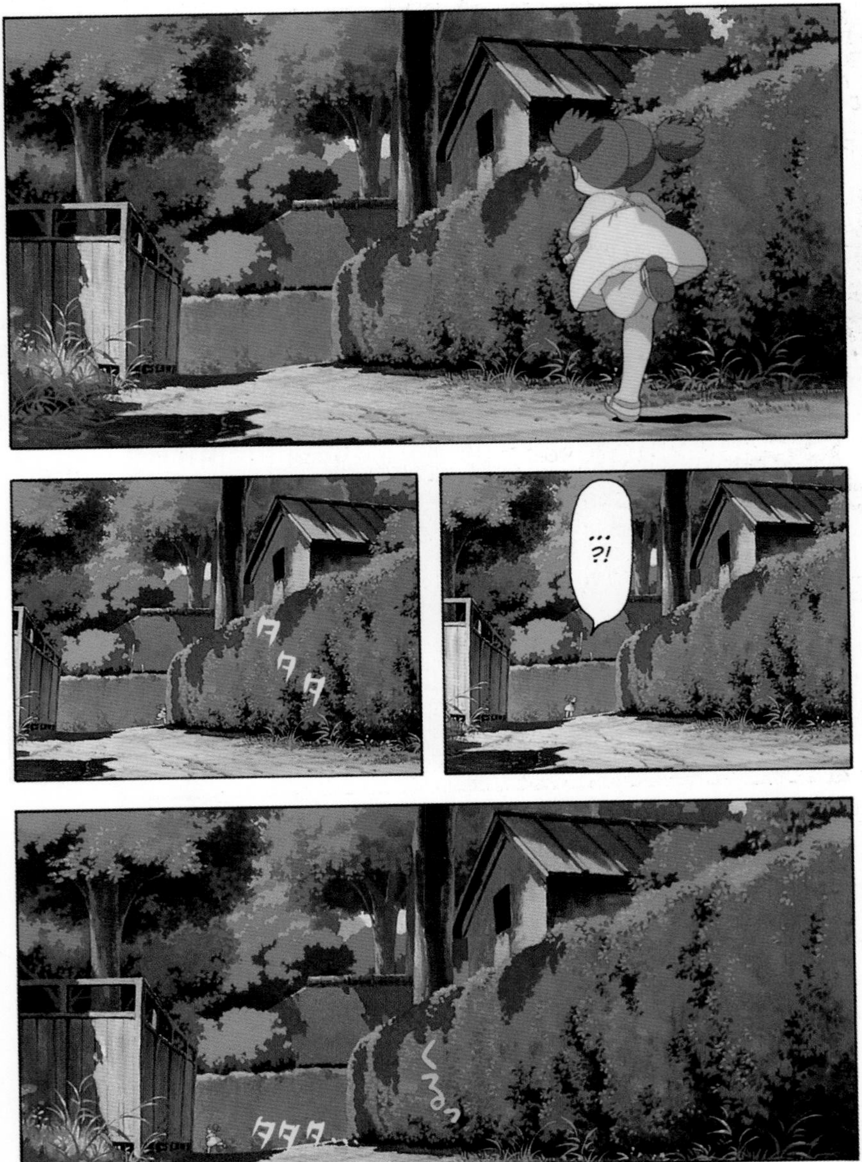
...?!
タタタ
くるっ
タタタ...

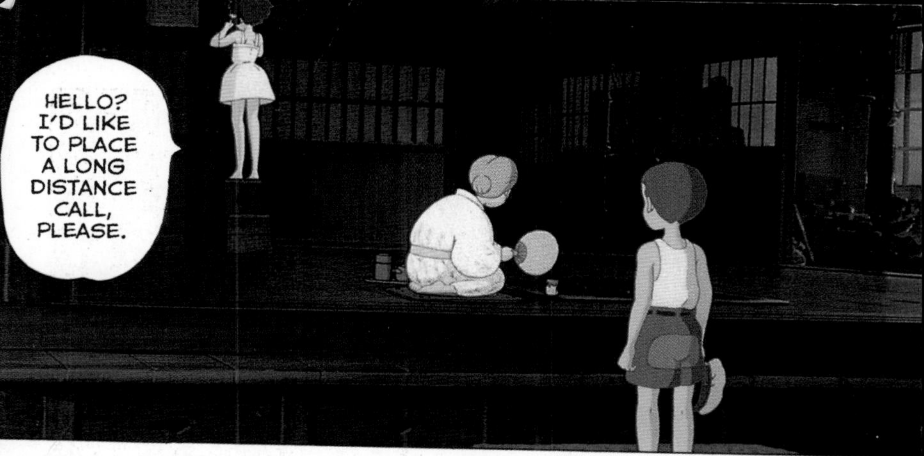
HELLO? I'D LIKE TO PLACE A LONG DISTANCE CALL, PLEASE.

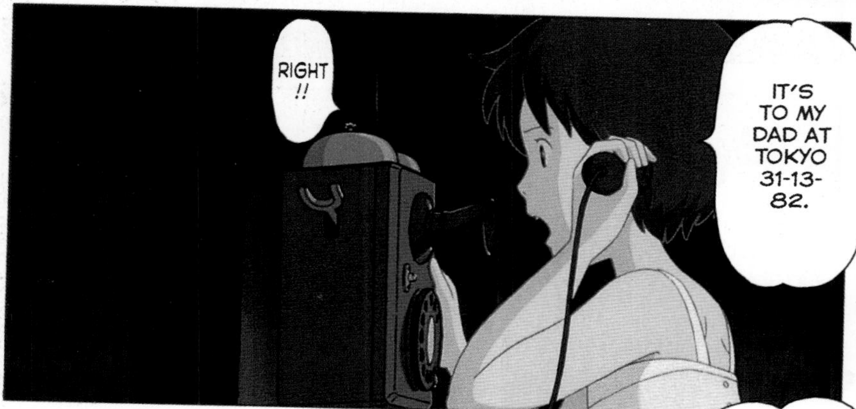
IT'S TO MY DAD AT TOKYO 31-13-82.
RIGHT !!

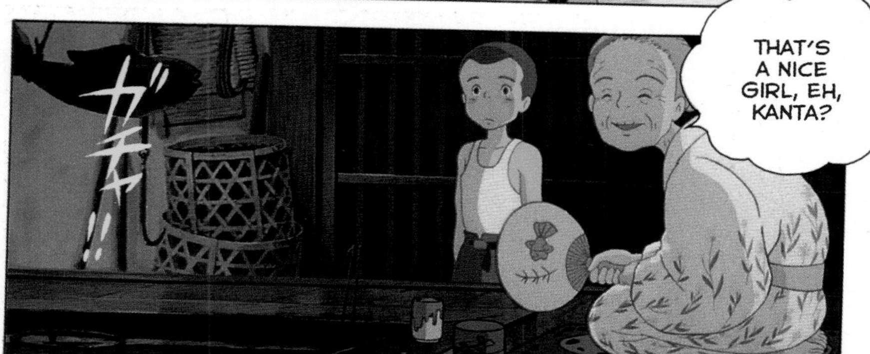
THAT'S A NICE GIRL, EH, KANTA?
ガチャ!!

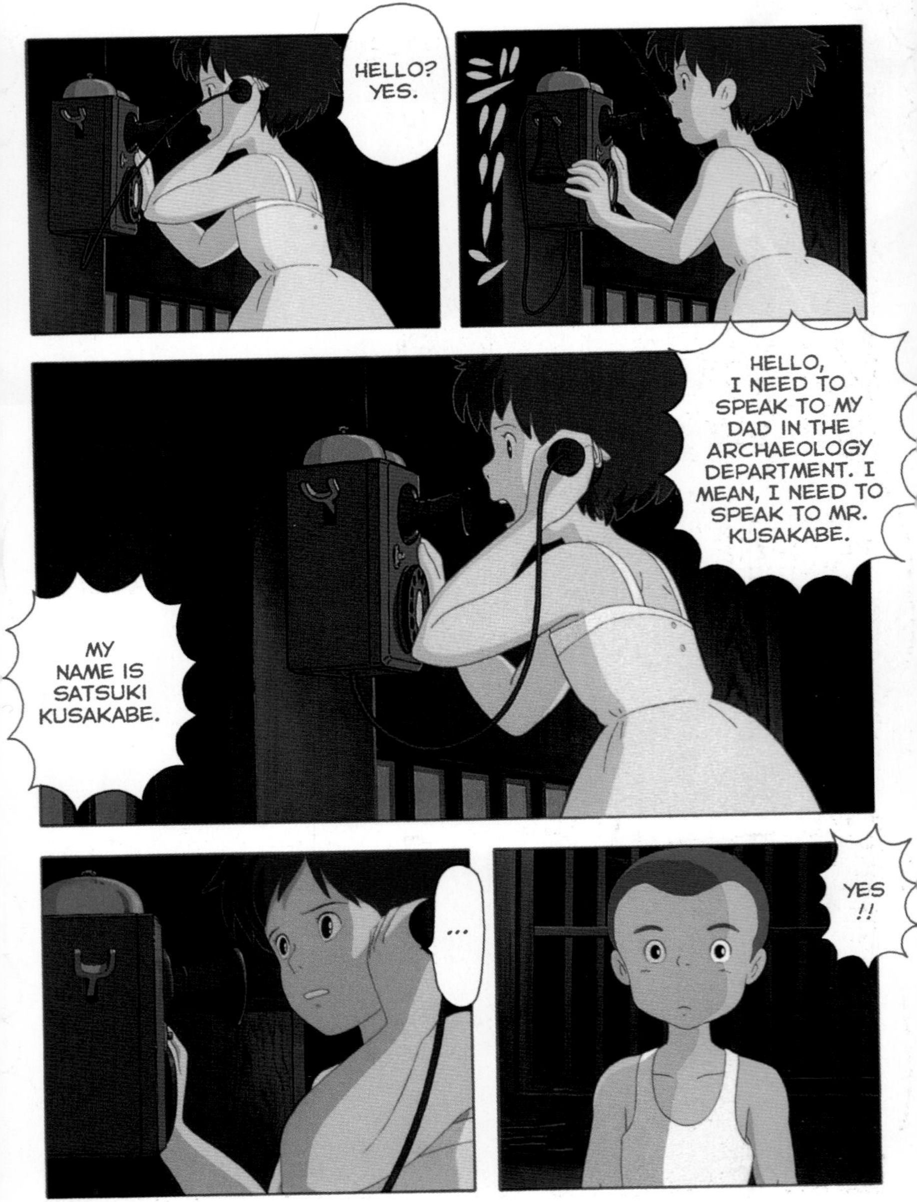
HELLO? YES.
HELLO, I NEED TO SPEAK TO MY DAD IN THE ARCHAEOLOGY DEPARTMENT. I MEAN, I NEED TO SPEAK TO MR. KUSAKABE.
MY NAME IS SATSUKI KUSAKABE.
YES !!
...

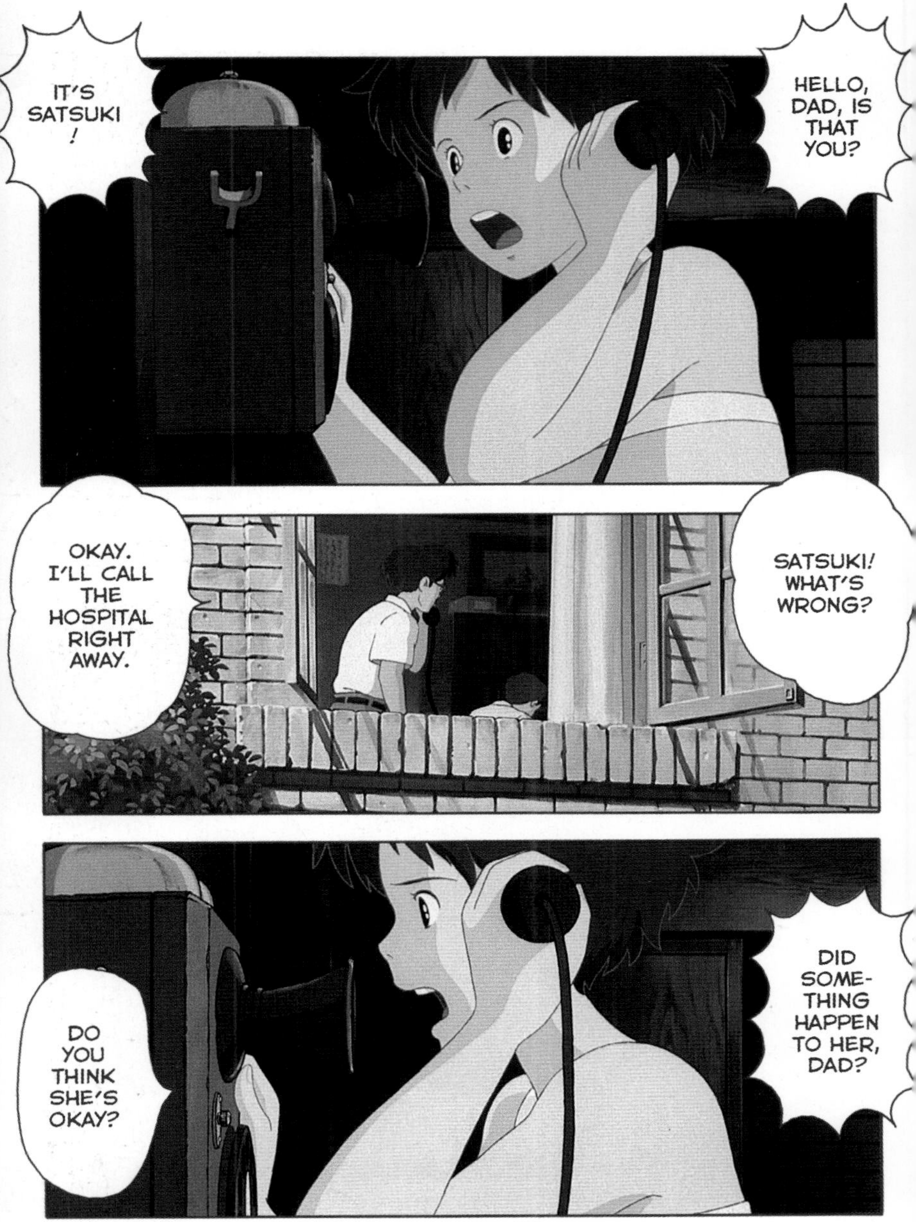
HELLO, DAD, IS THAT YOU?
IT'S SATSUKI!
SATSUKI! WHAT'S WRONG?
OKAY. I'LL CALL THE HOSPITAL RIGHT AWAY.
DID SOMETHING HAPPEN TO HER, DAD?
DO YOU THINK SHE'S OKAY?

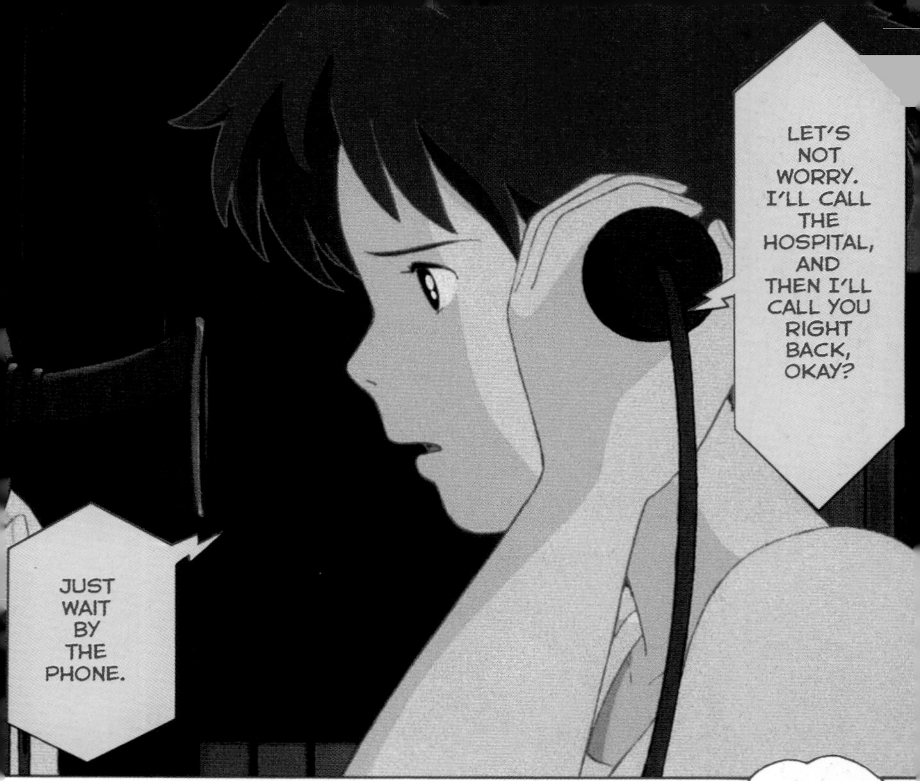
LET'S NOT WORRY. I'LL CALL THE HOSPITAL, AND THEN I'LL CALL YOU RIGHT BACK, OKAY?
JUST WAIT BY THE PHONE.

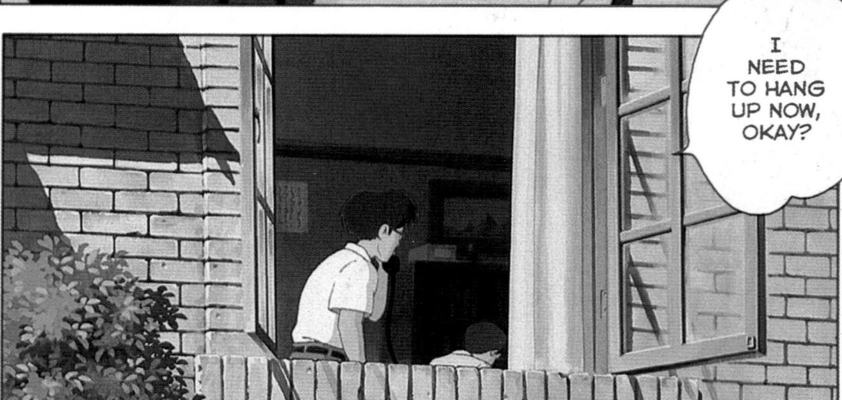
I NEED TO HANG UP NOW, OKAY?

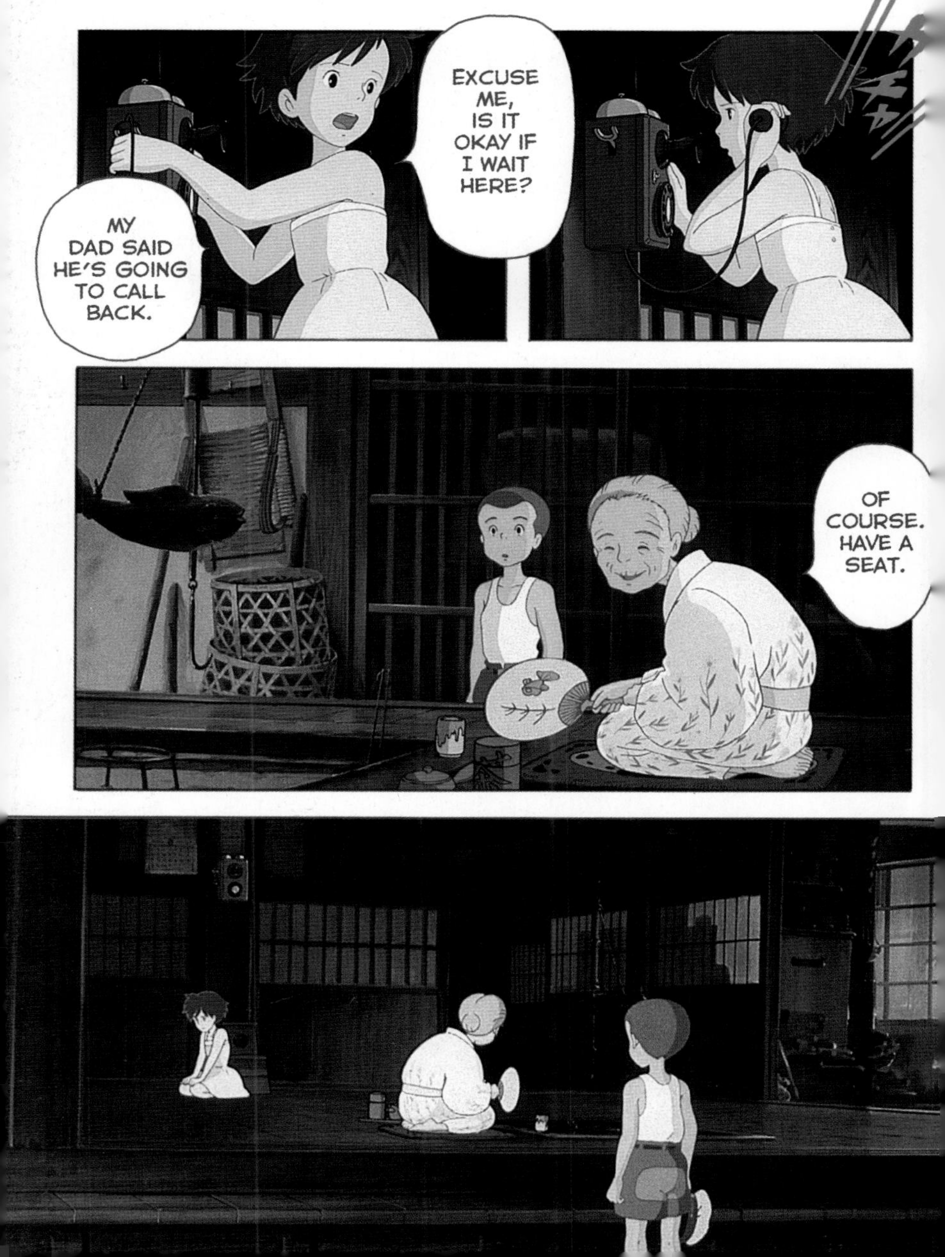
EXCUSE ME, IS IT OKAY IF I WAIT HERE?
MY DAD SAID HE'S GOING TO CALL BACK.
OF COURSE. HAVE A SEAT.

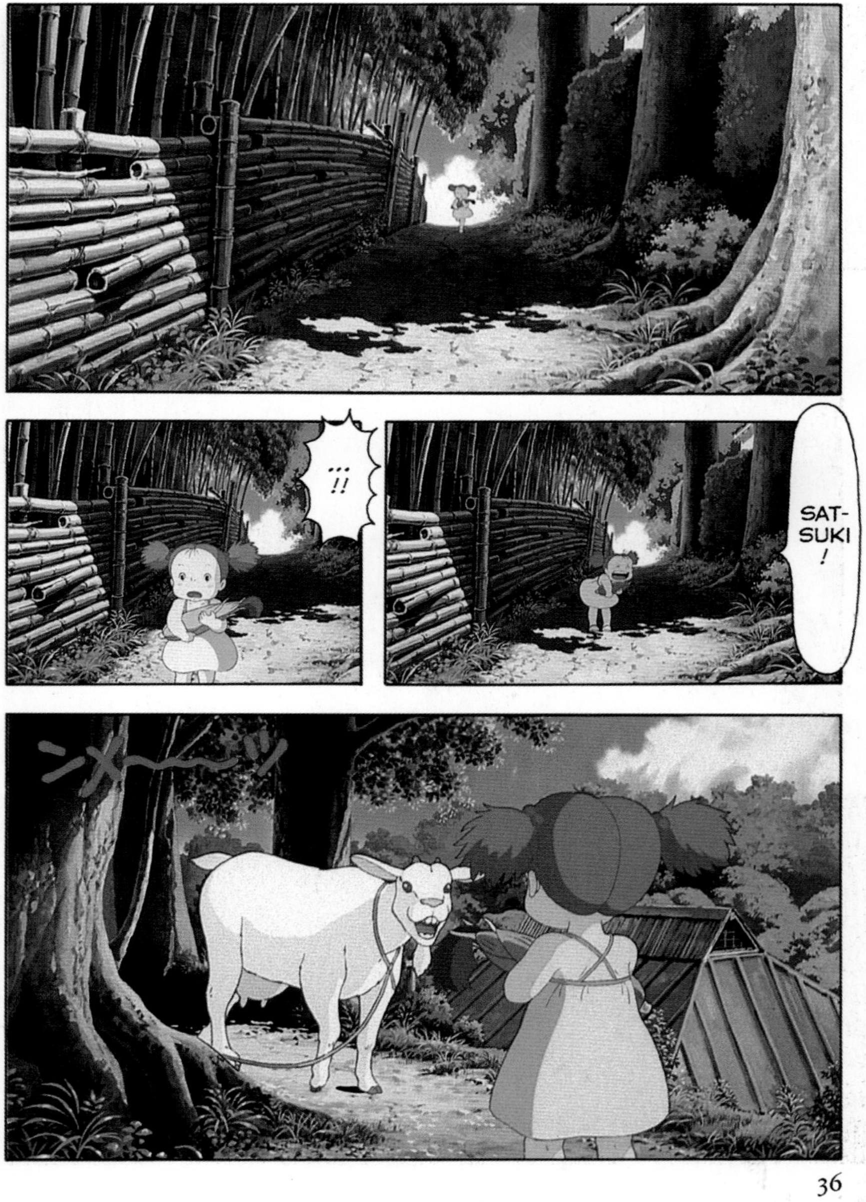
..!!
SAT-SUKI!
ンメーーッ

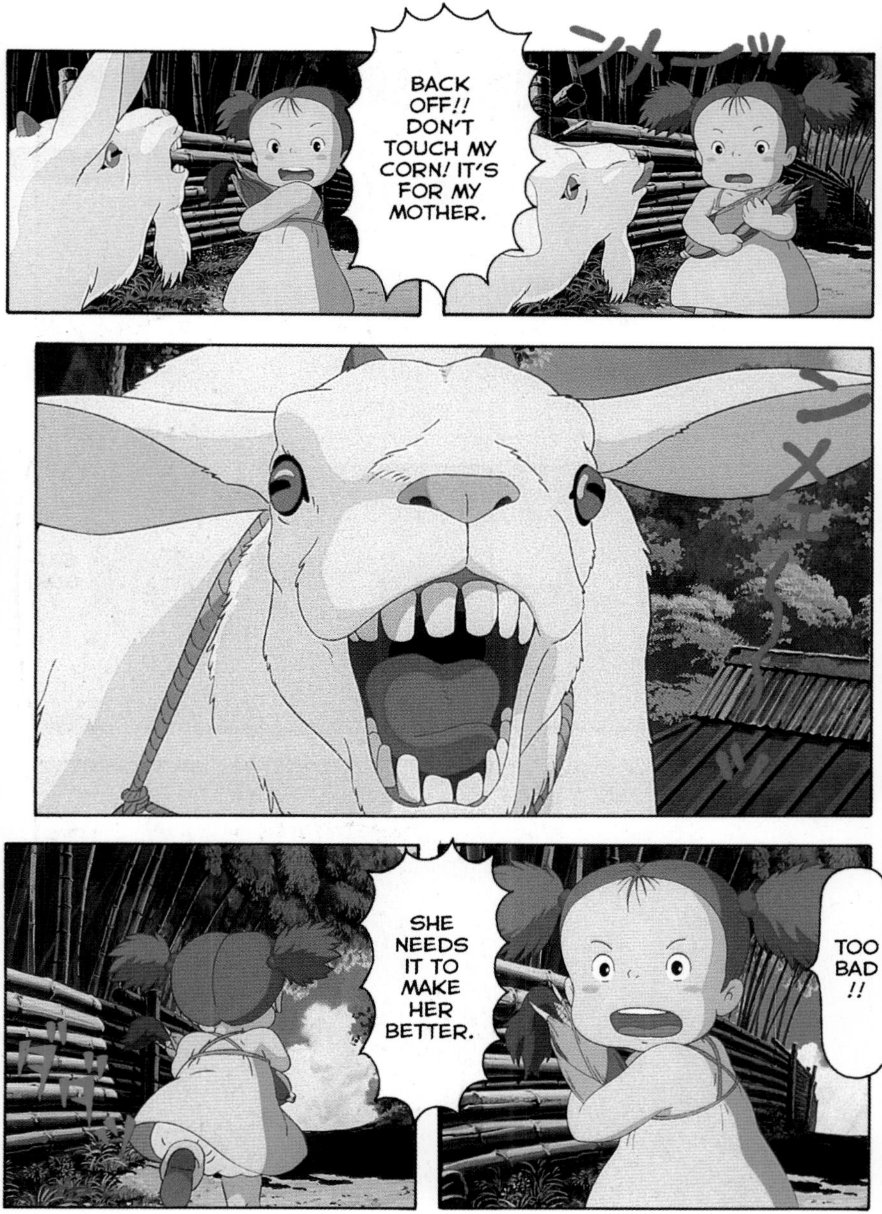
BACK OFF!! DON'T TOUCH MY CORN! IT'S FOR MY MOTHER.
TOO BAD!!
SHE NEEDS IT TO MAKE HER BETTER.

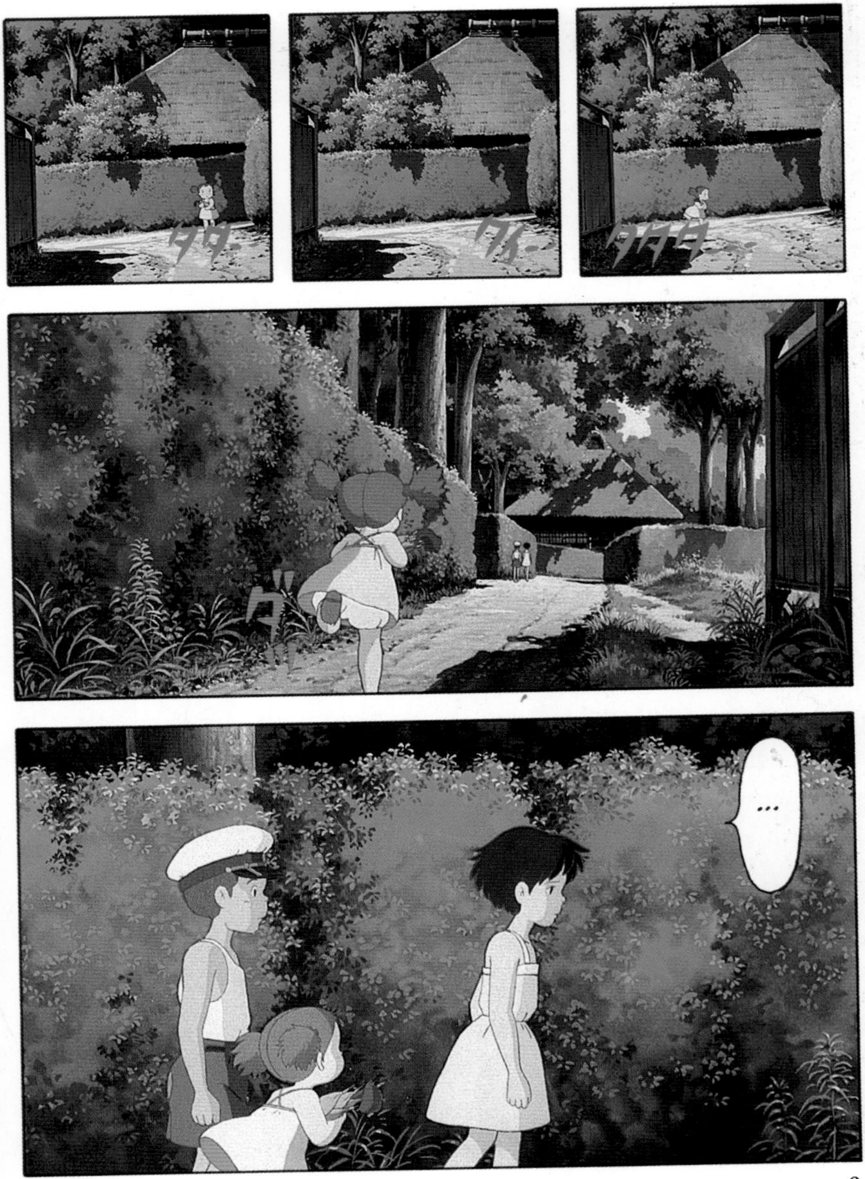
タタタ
クィー
タタ…
ダッ
...

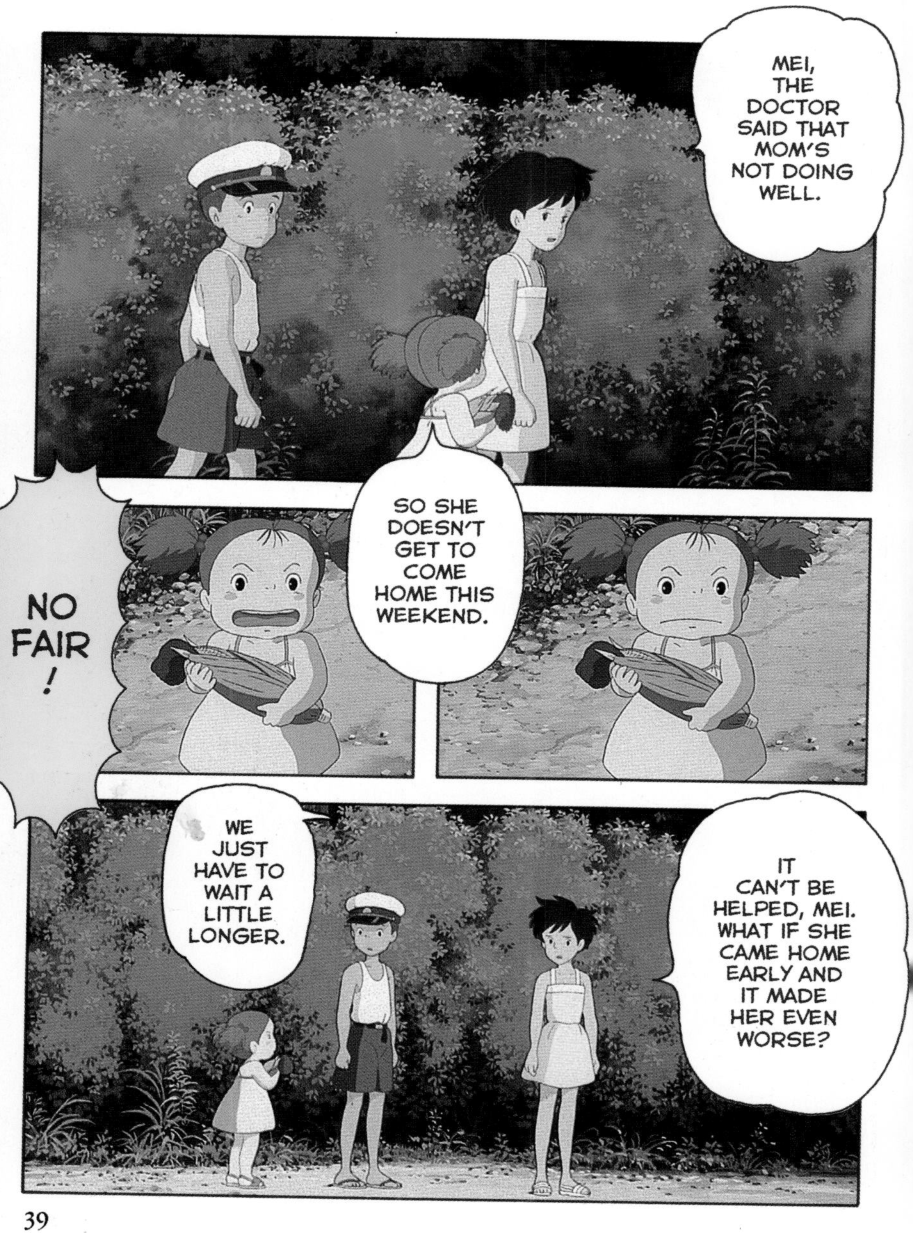
MEI, THE DOCTOR SAID THAT MOM'S NOT DOING WELL.
SO SHE DOESN'T GET TO COME HOME THIS WEEKEND.
NO FAIR!
IT CAN'T BE HELPED, MEI. WHAT IF SHE CAME HOME EARLY AND IT MADE HER EVEN WORSE?
WE JUST HAVE TO WAIT A LITTLE LONGER.

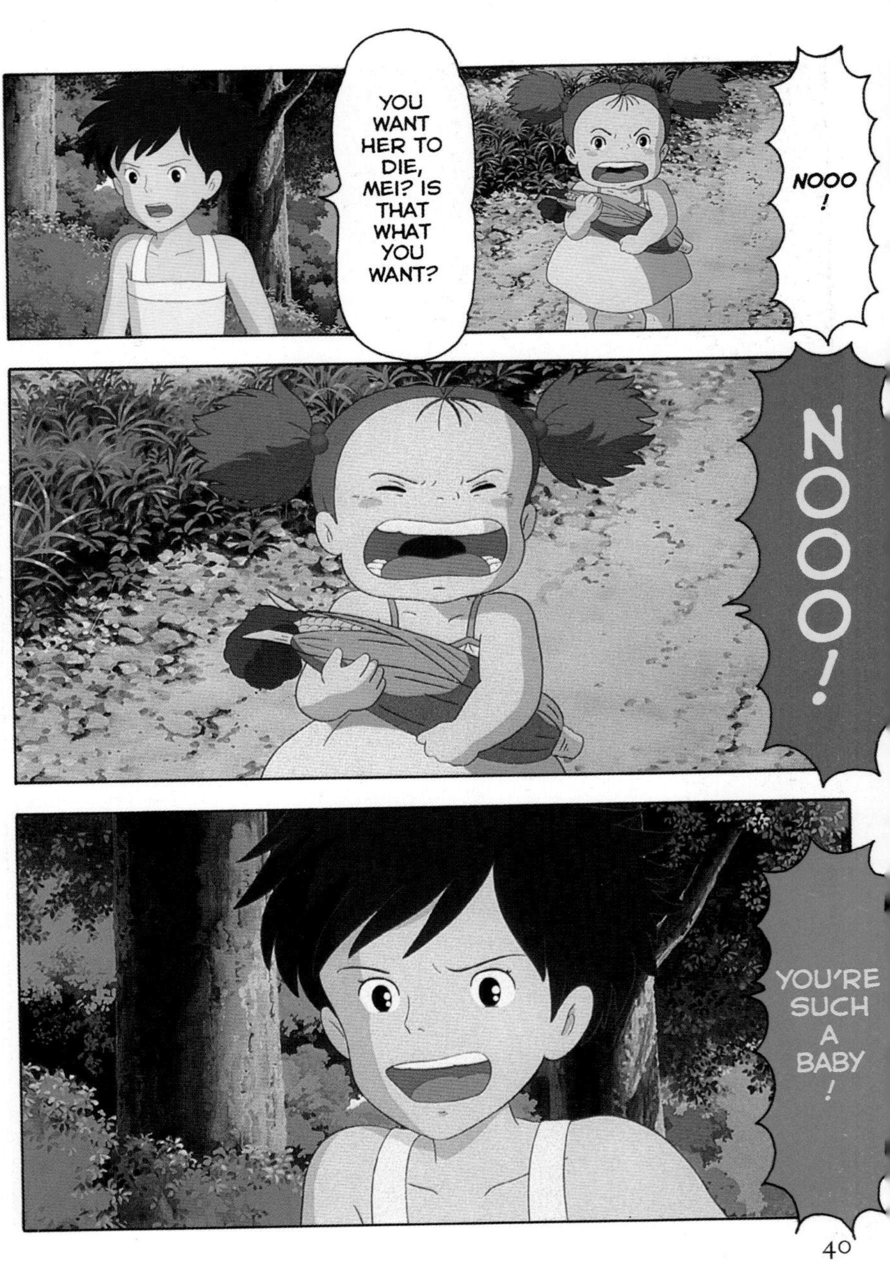
YOU WANT HER TO DIE, MEI? IS THAT WHAT YOU WANT?
NOOO!
NOOO!
YOU'RE SUCH A BABY!

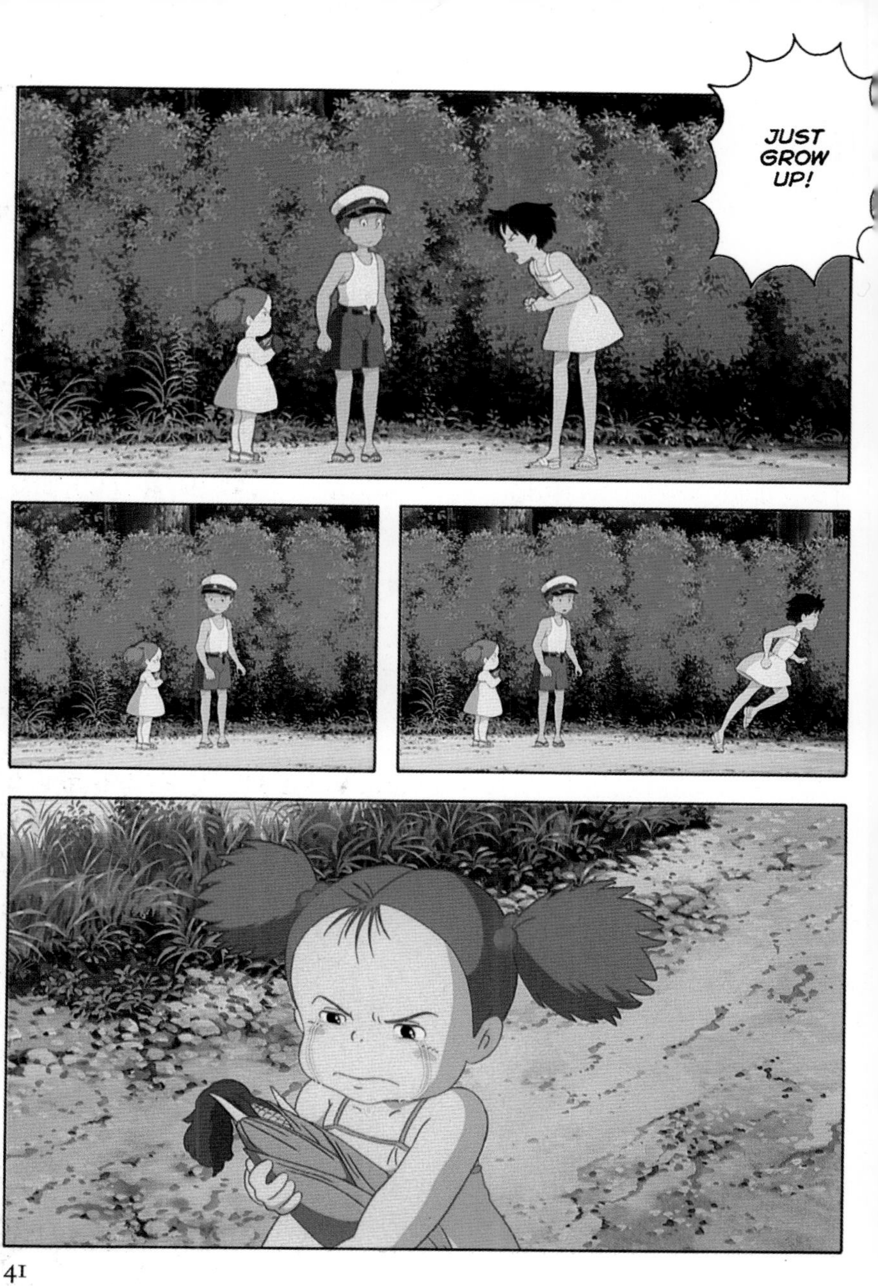
JUST GROW UP!

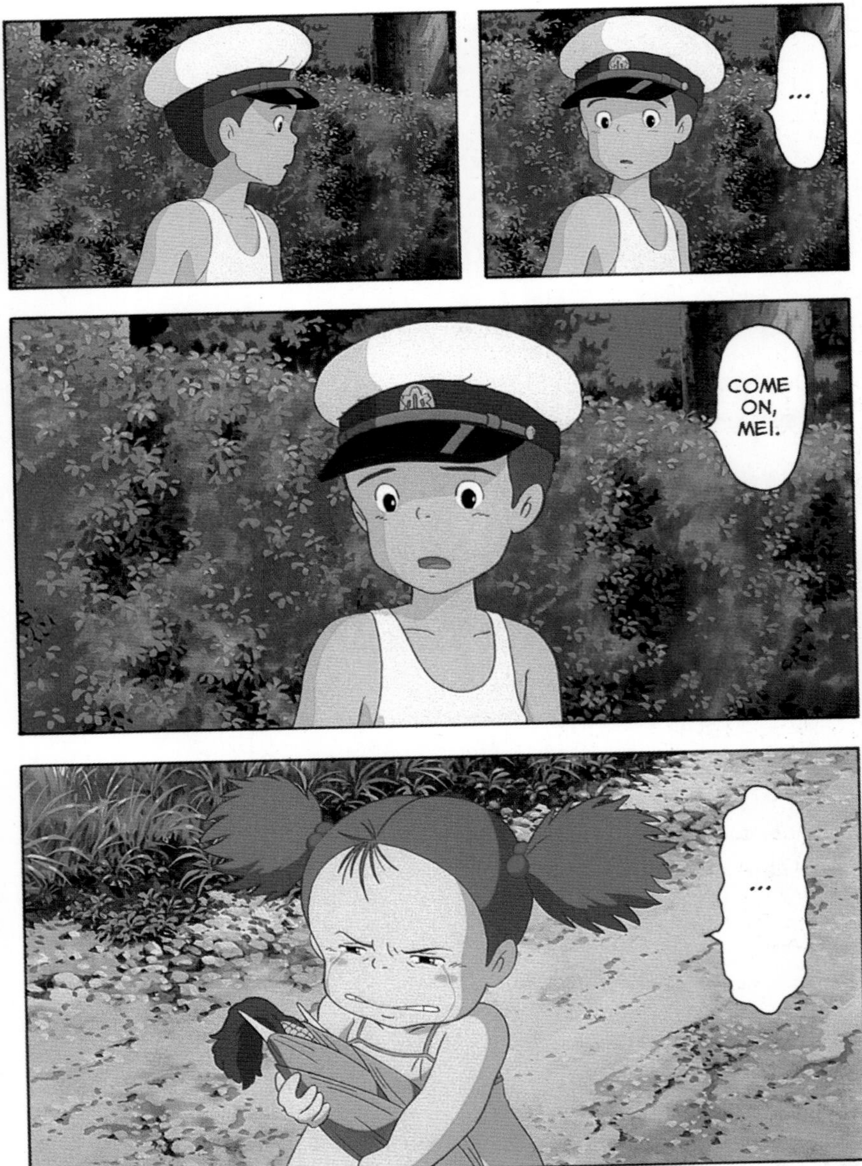
...
COME ON, MEI.
...

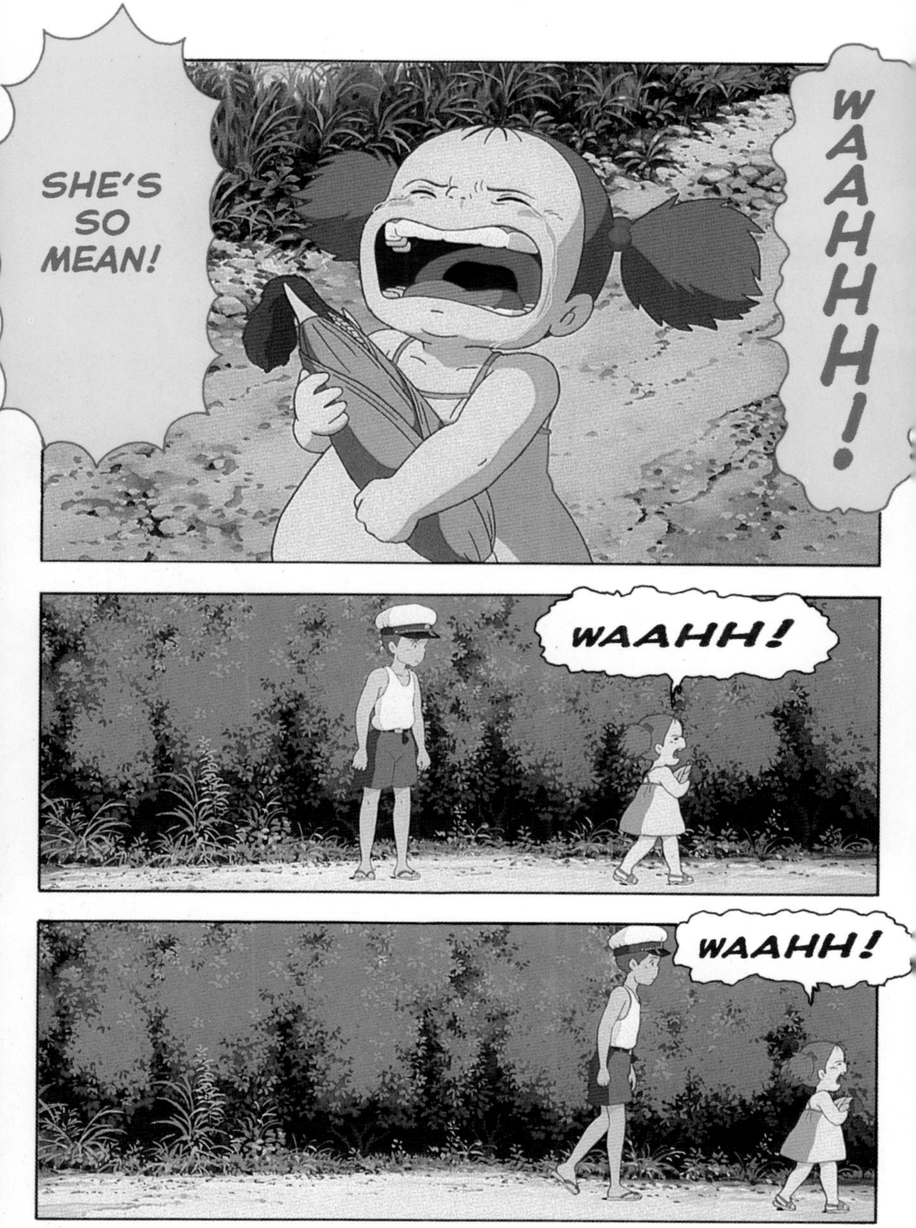
WAAHHH!
SHE'S SO MEAN!
WAAHH!
WAAHH!

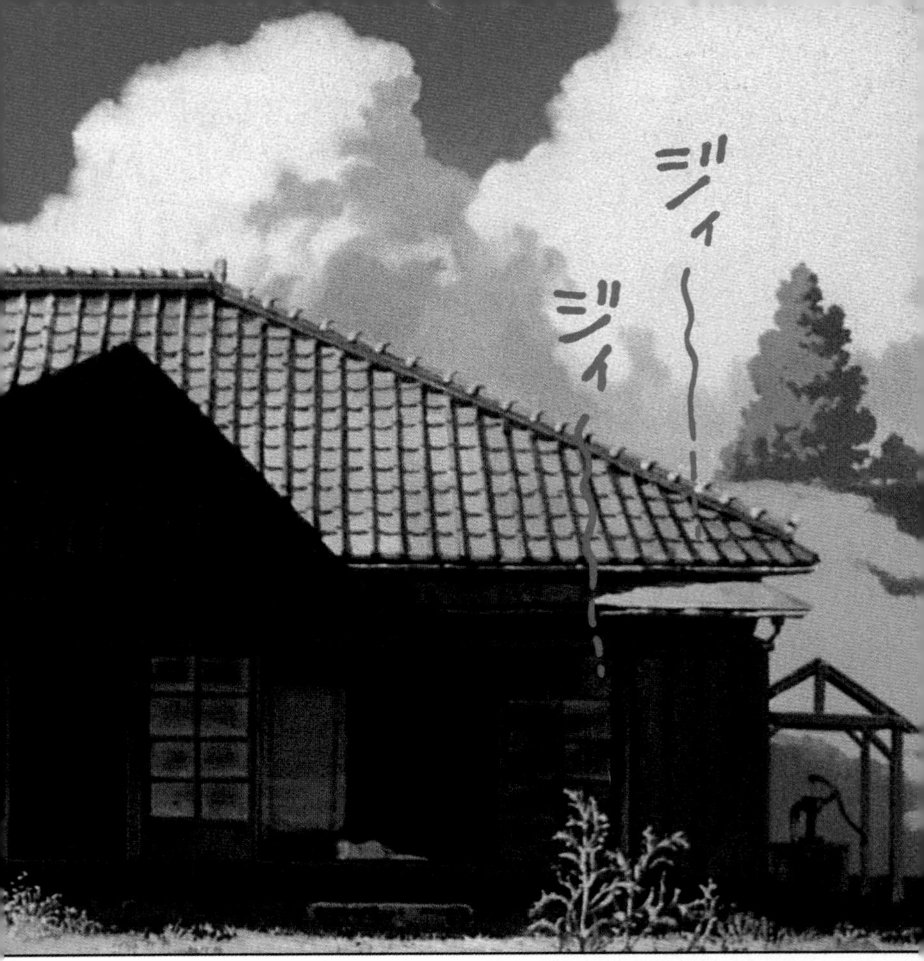
ジィ～～…
ジィ～～…
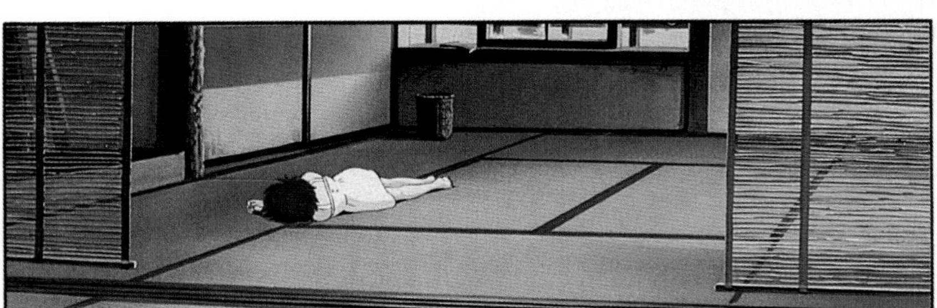

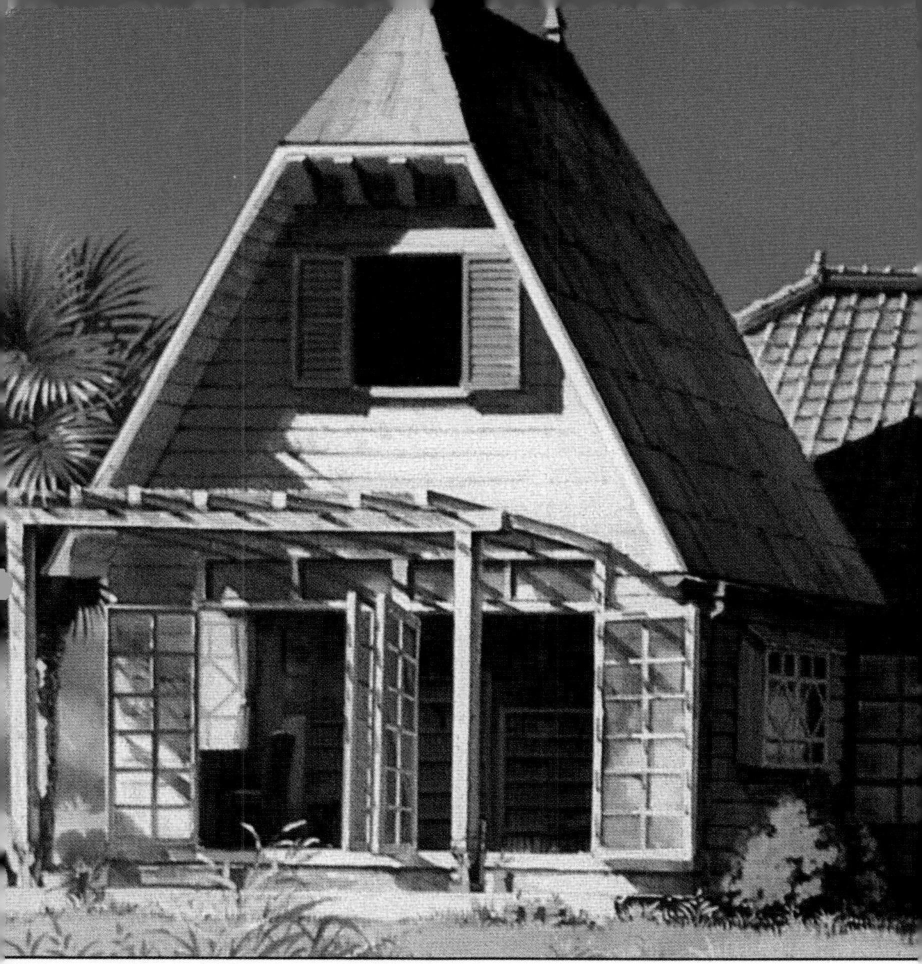

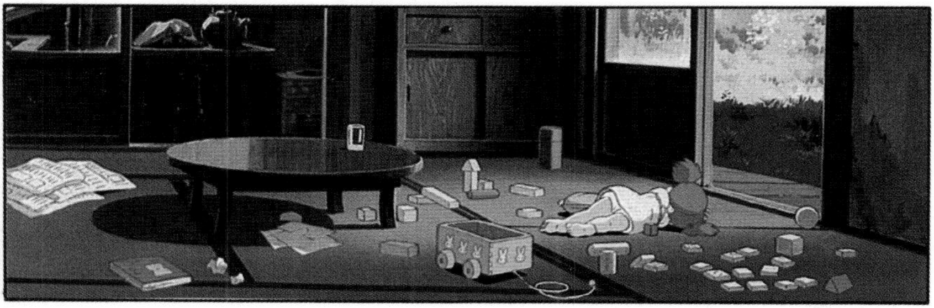

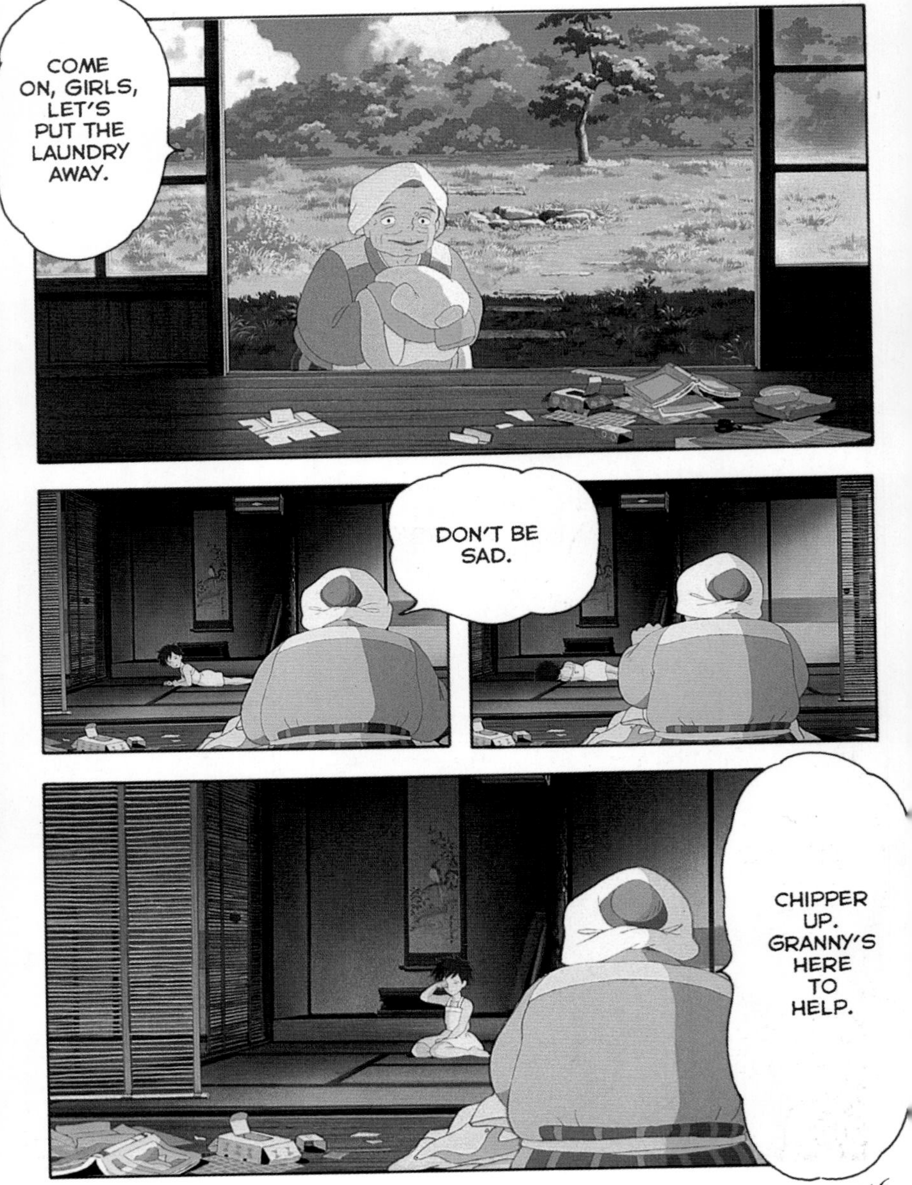
COME ON, GIRLS, LET'S PUT THE LAUNDRY AWAY.
DON'T BE SAD.
CHIPPER UP. GRANNY'S HERE TO HELP.

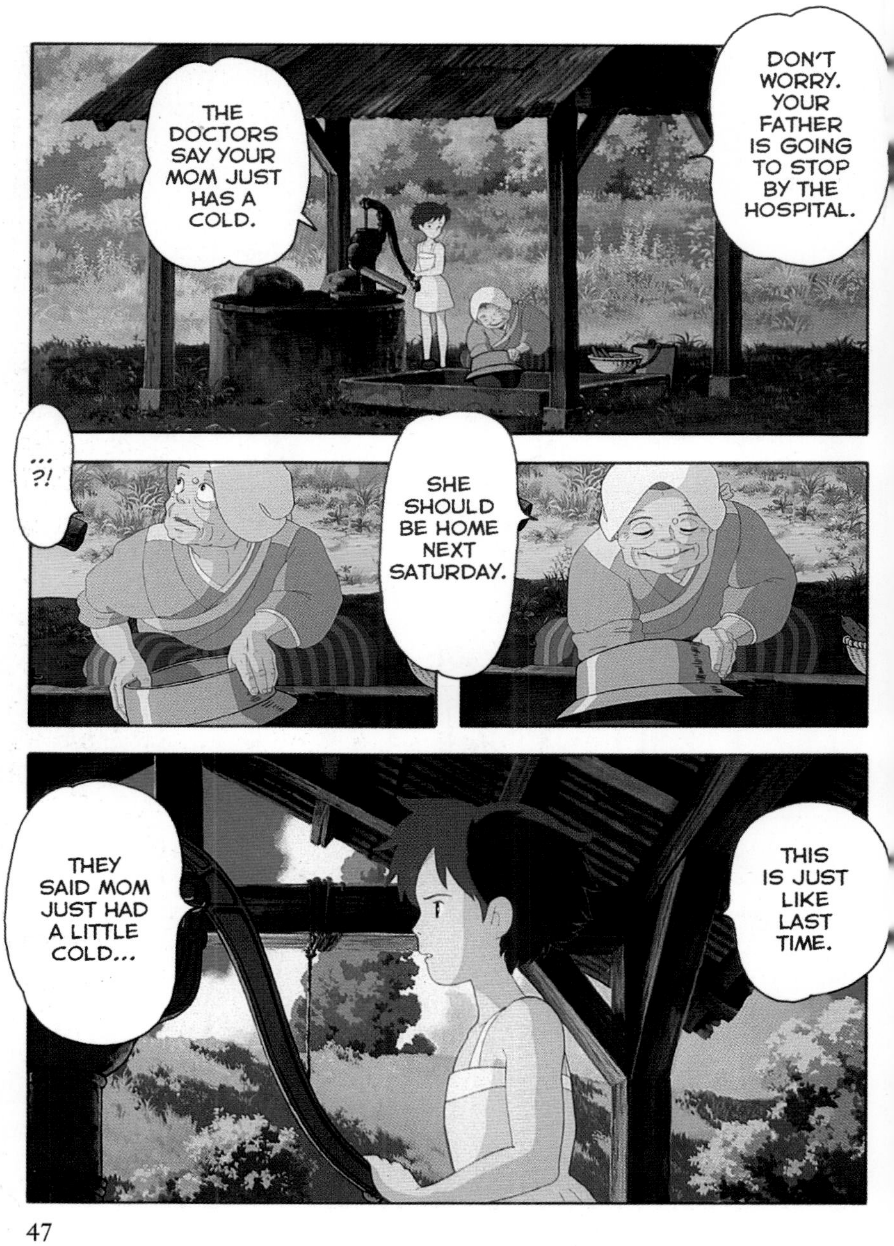
DON'T WORRY. YOUR FATHER IS GOING TO STOP BY THE HOSPITAL.
THE DOCTORS SAY YOUR MOM JUST HAS A COLD.
SHE SHOULD BE HOME NEXT SATURDAY.
...?!
THIS IS JUST LIKE LAST TIME.
THEY SAID MOM JUST HAD A LITTLE COLD...

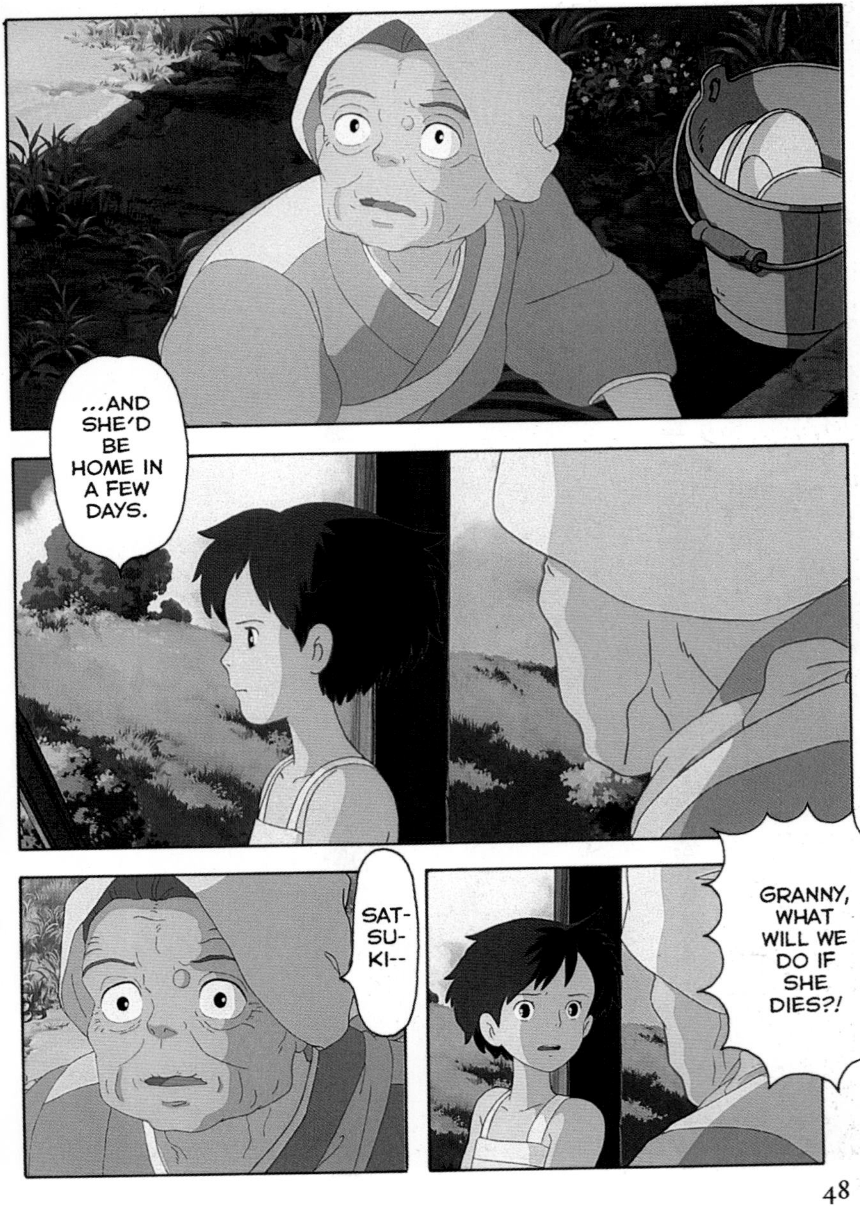
...AND SHE'D BE HOME IN A FEW DAYS.
GRANNY, WHAT WILL WE DO IF SHE DIES?!
SAT-SU-KI--

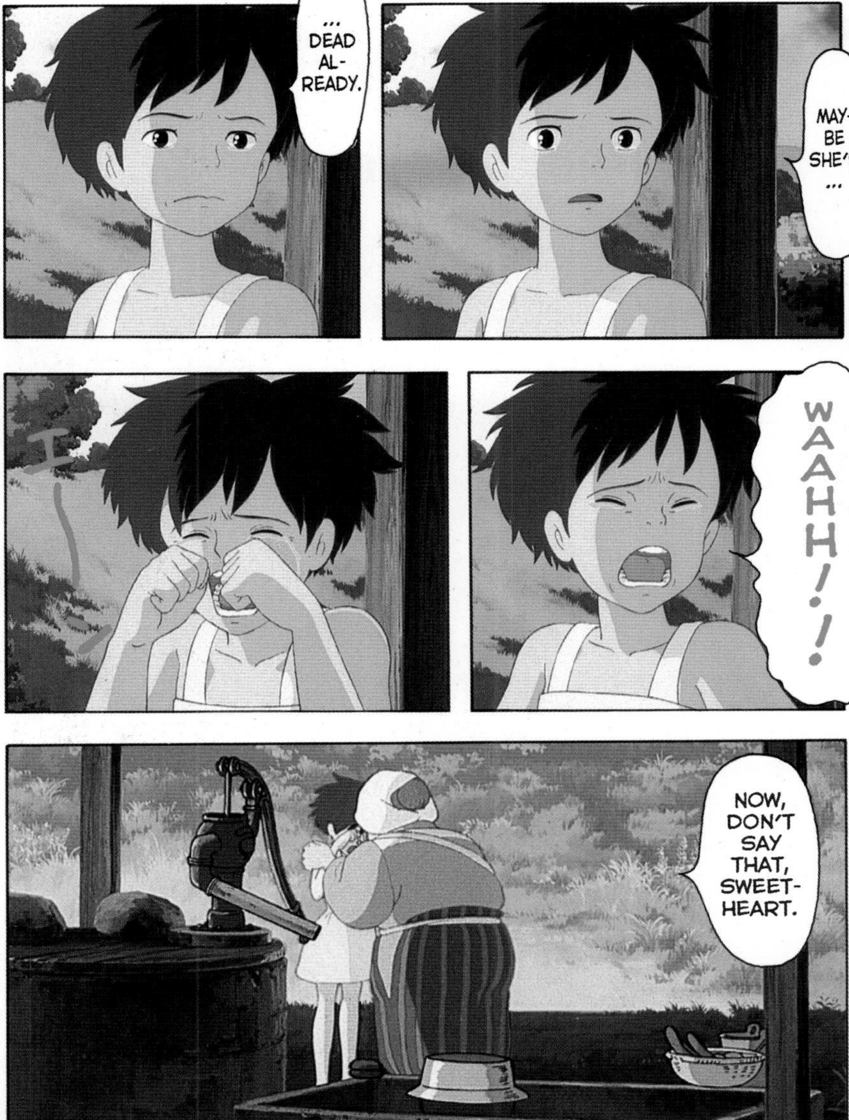
MAY-BE SHE'S ...
... DEAD AL-READY.
WAAHH!!
NOW, DON'T SAY THAT, SWEET-HEART.

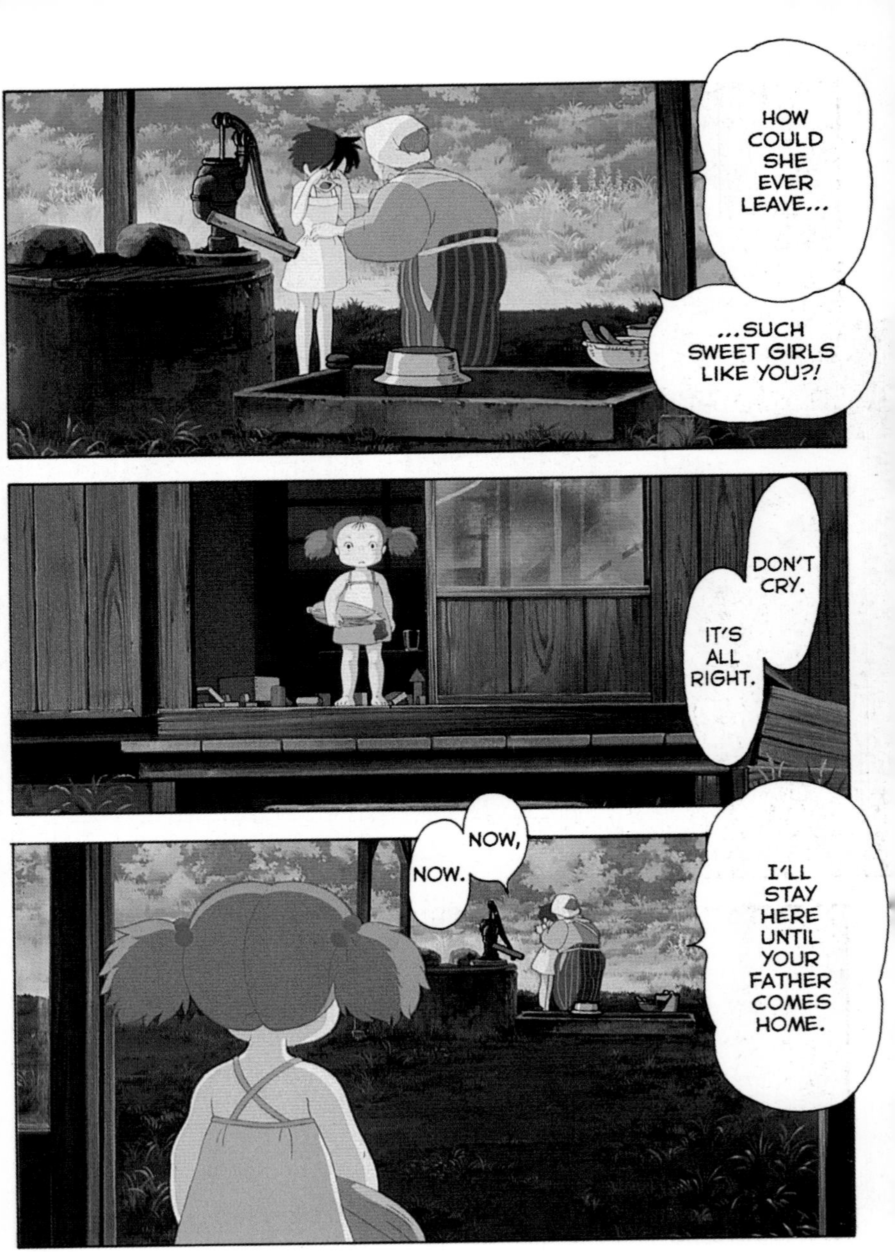
HOW COULD SHE EVER LEAVE...
...SUCH SWEET GIRLS LIKE YOU?!
DON'T CRY.
IT'S ALL RIGHT.
I'LL STAY HERE UNTIL YOUR FATHER COMES HOME.
NOW,
NOW.

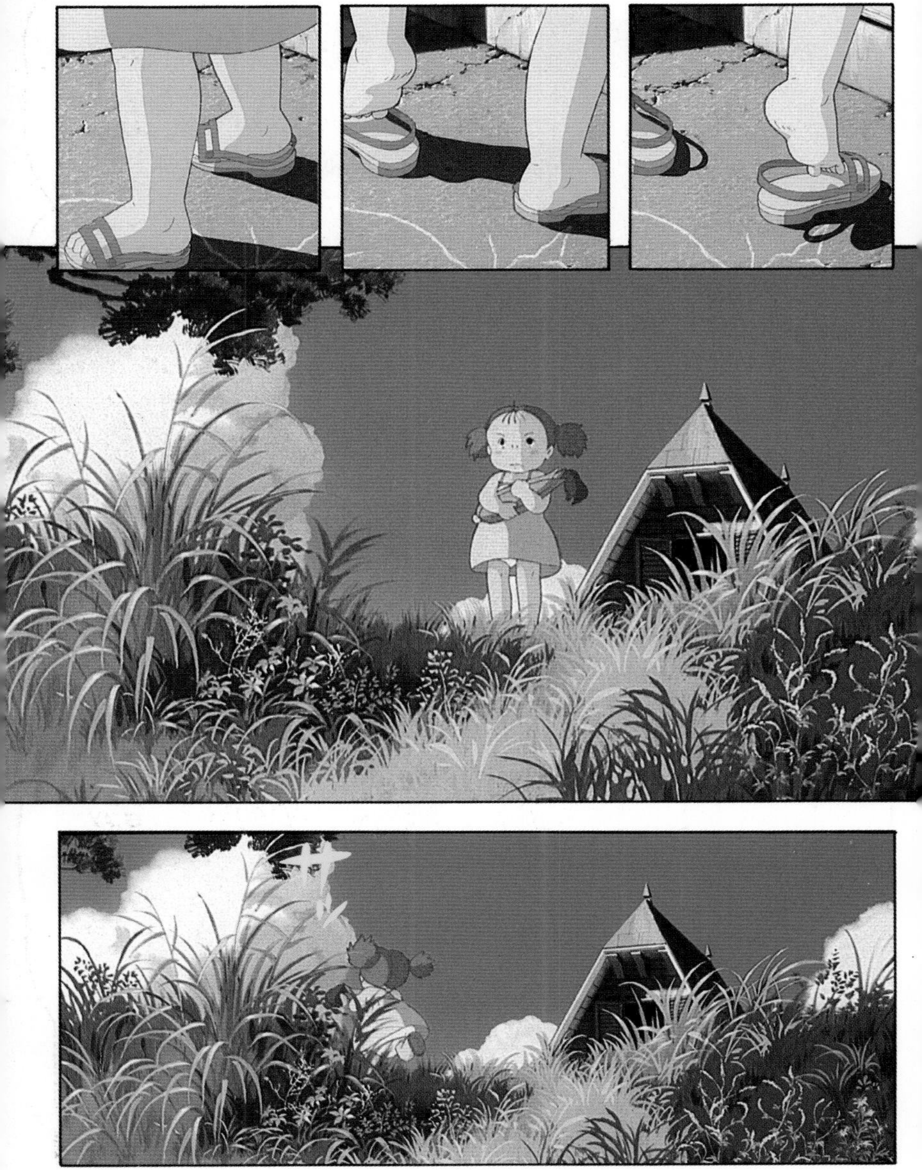
サッ

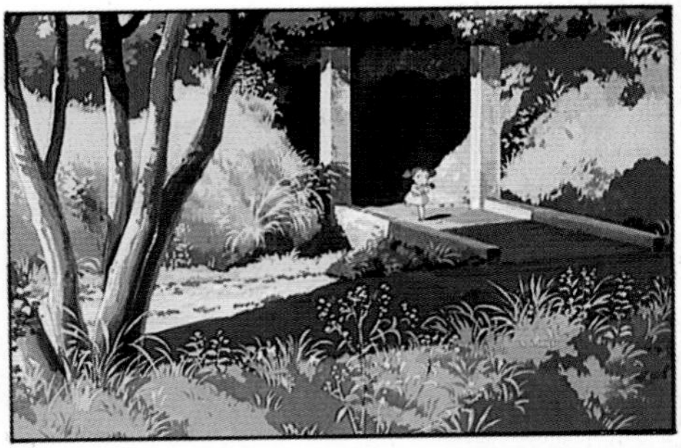

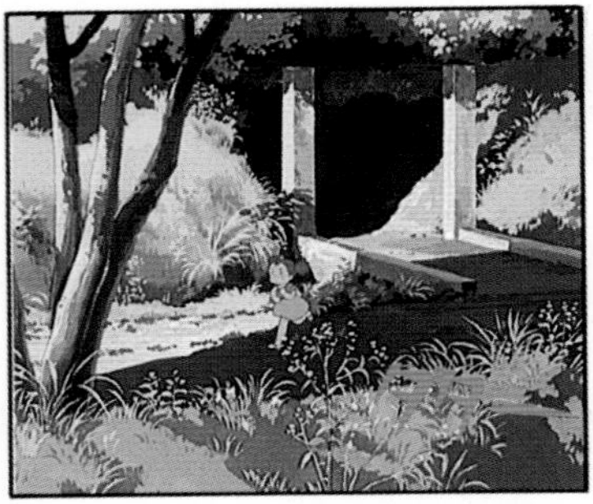

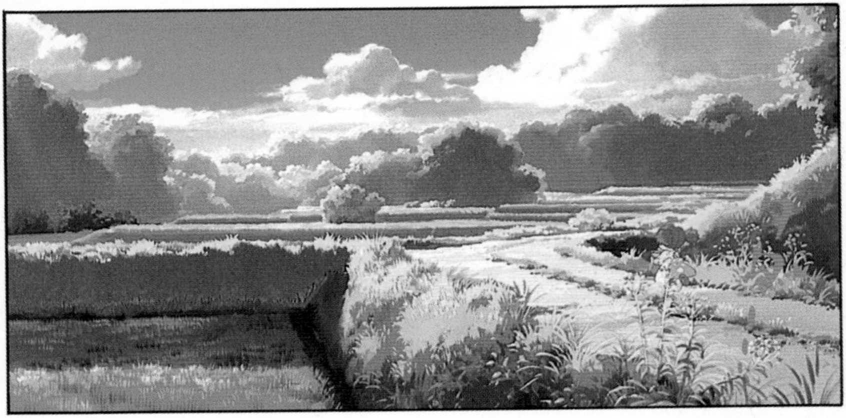

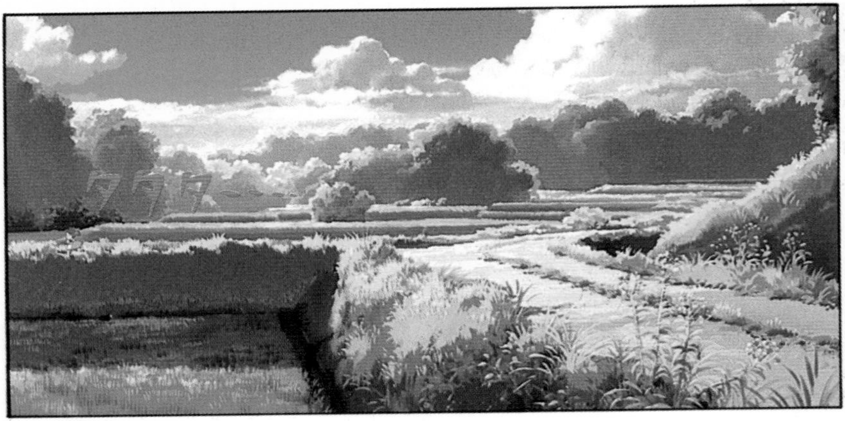
タタタ――――

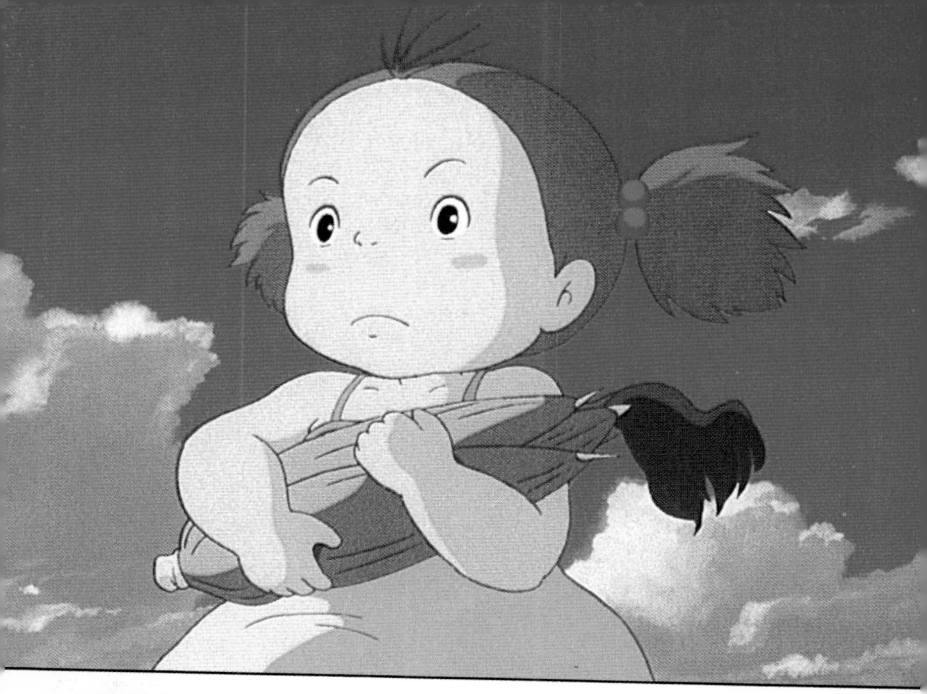

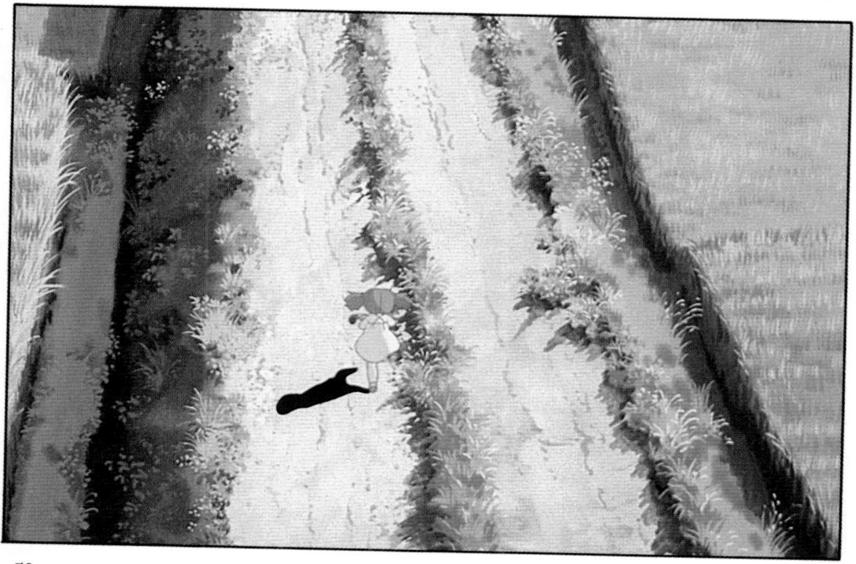

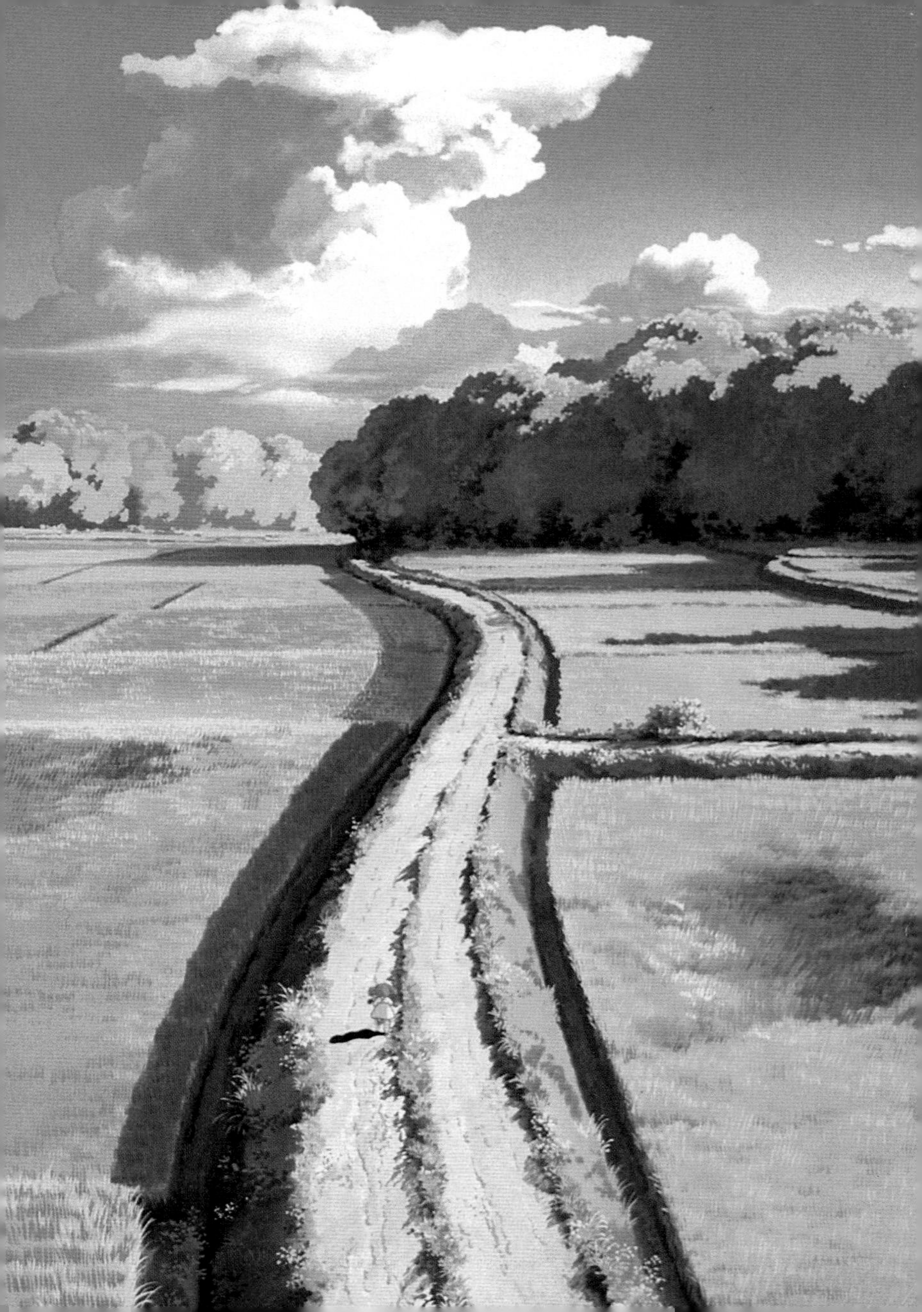

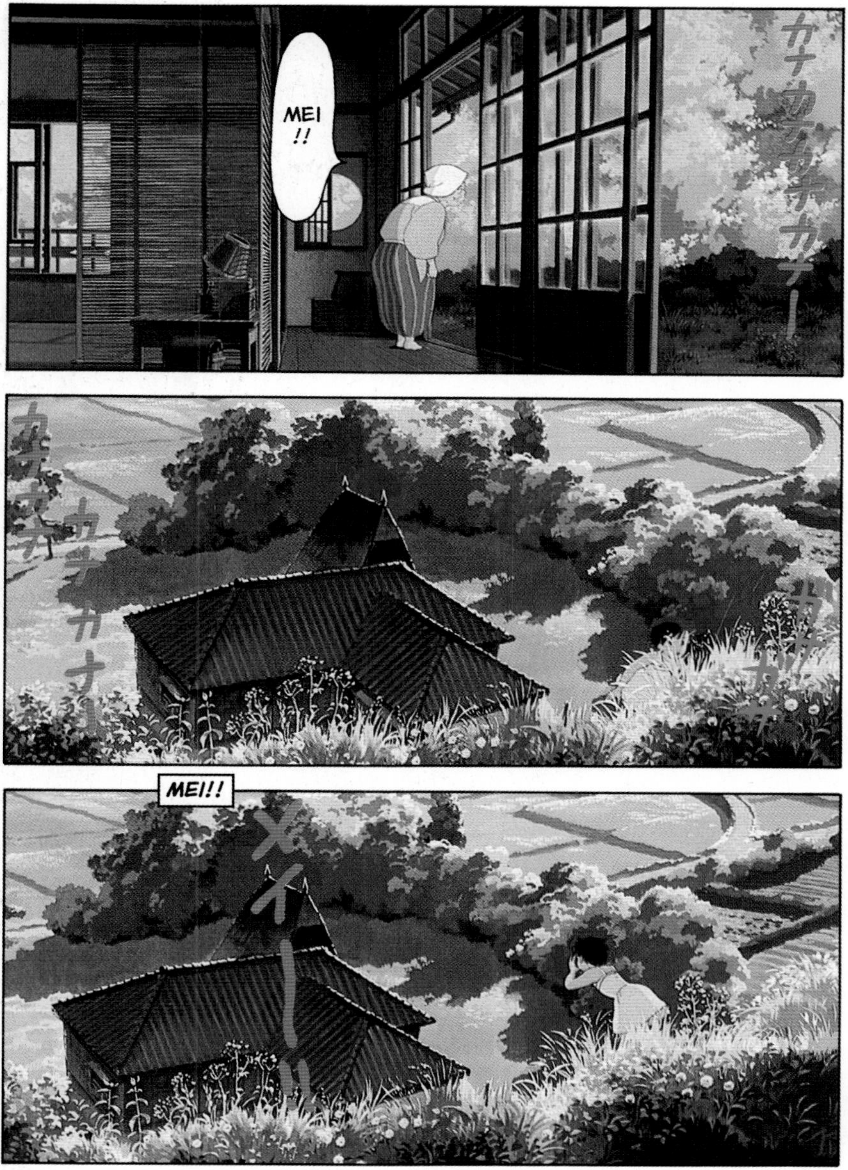
MEI !!
MEI!!
メイー

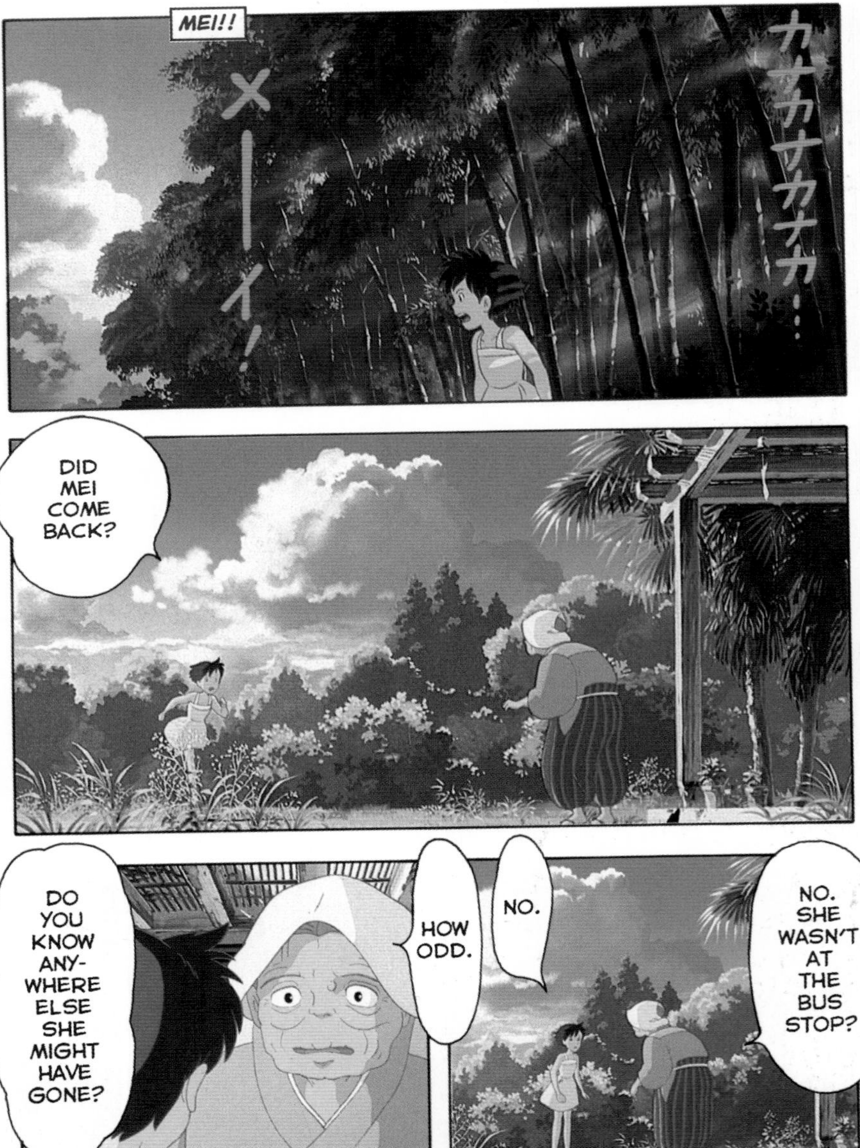
カナカナカナカ…
MEI!!
メーイ!
DID MEI COME BACK?
NO. SHE WASN'T AT THE BUS STOP?
NO.
HOW ODD.
DO YOU KNOW ANYWHERE ELSE SHE MIGHT HAVE GONE?

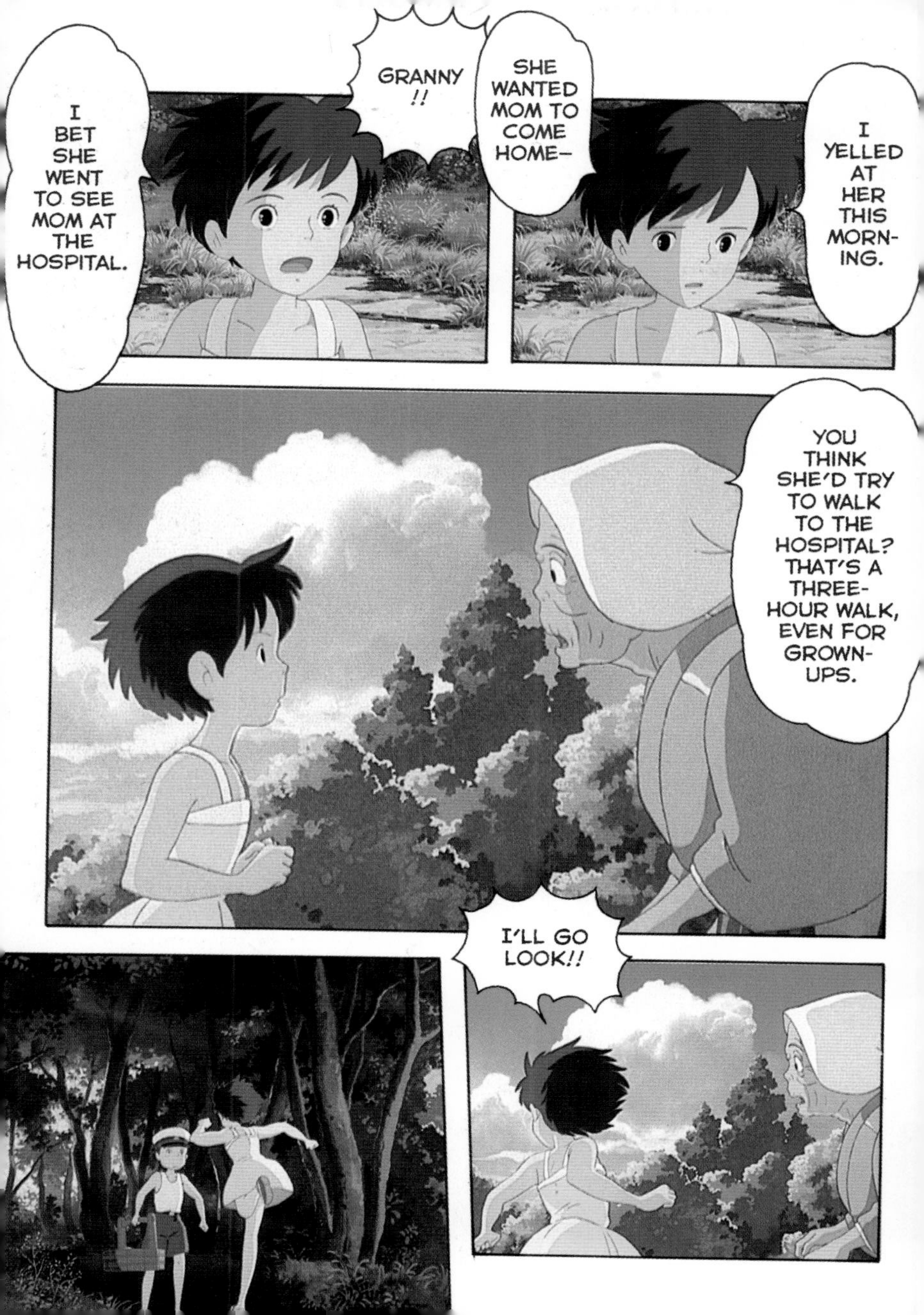
I YELLED AT HER THIS MORNING.
SHE WANTED MOM TO COME HOME–
GRANNY!!
I BET SHE WENT TO SEE MOM AT THE HOSPITAL.
YOU THINK SHE'D TRY TO WALK TO THE HOSPITAL? THAT'S A THREE-HOUR WALK, EVEN FOR GROWN-UPS.
I'LL GO LOOK!!

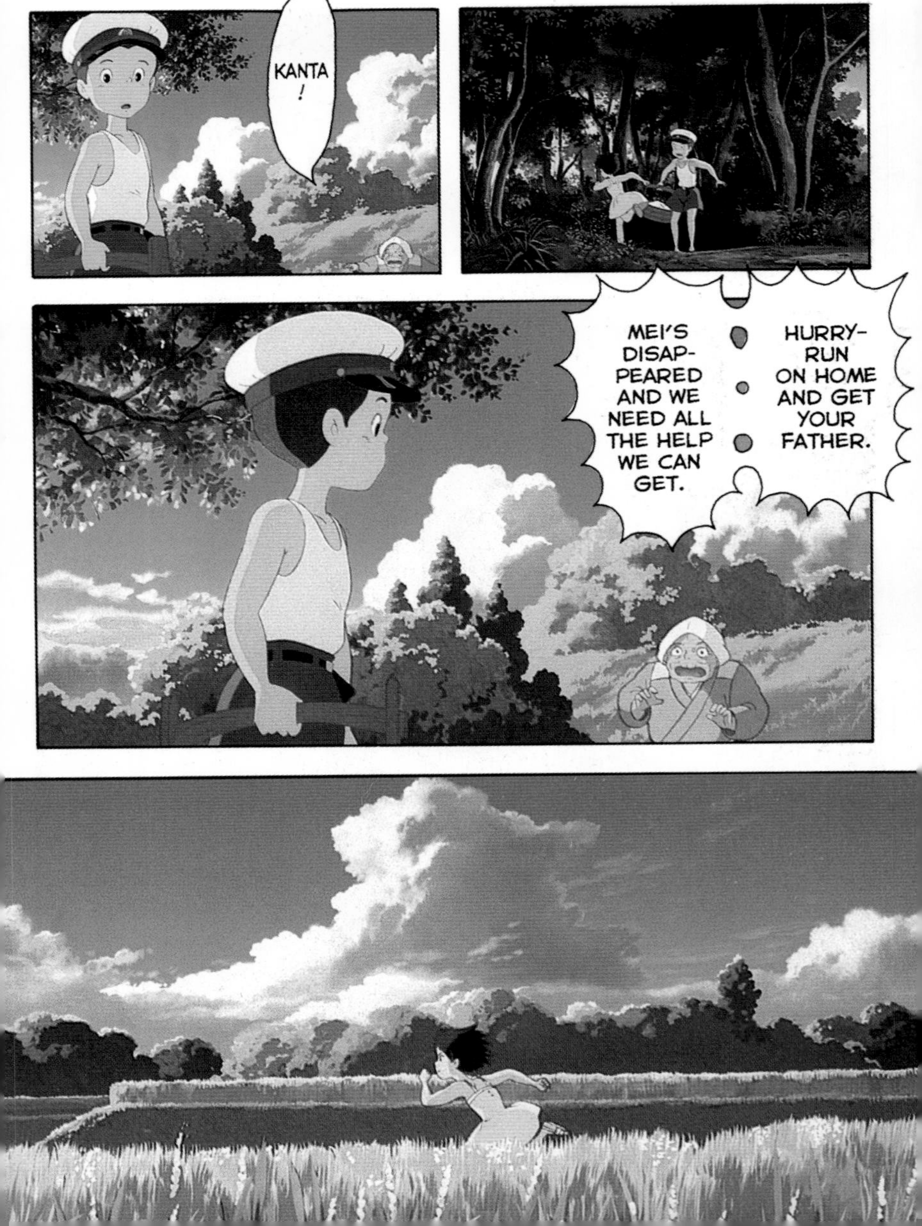
KANTA!
MEI'S DISAPPEARED AND WE NEED ALL THE HELP WE CAN GET.
HURRY—RUN ON HOME AND GET YOUR FATHER.

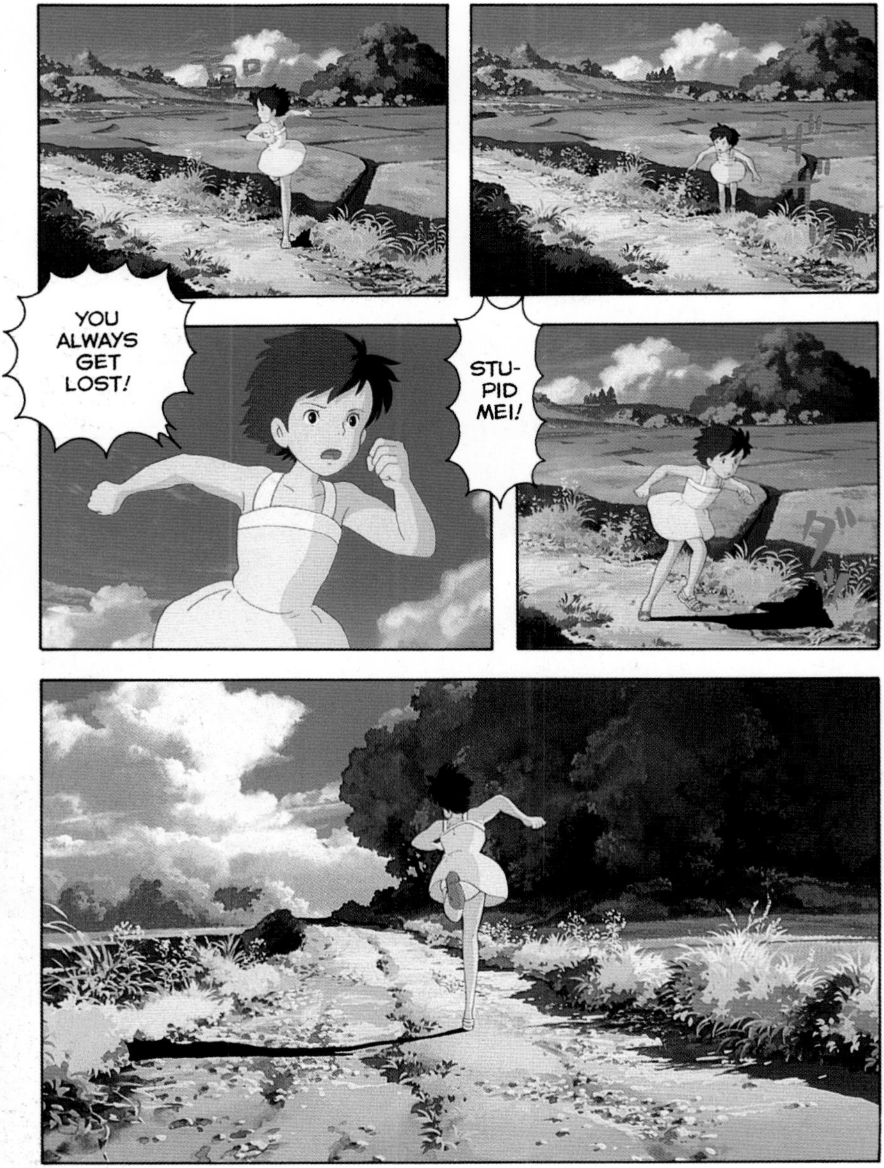
STU-PID MEI!
YOU ALWAYS GET LOST!

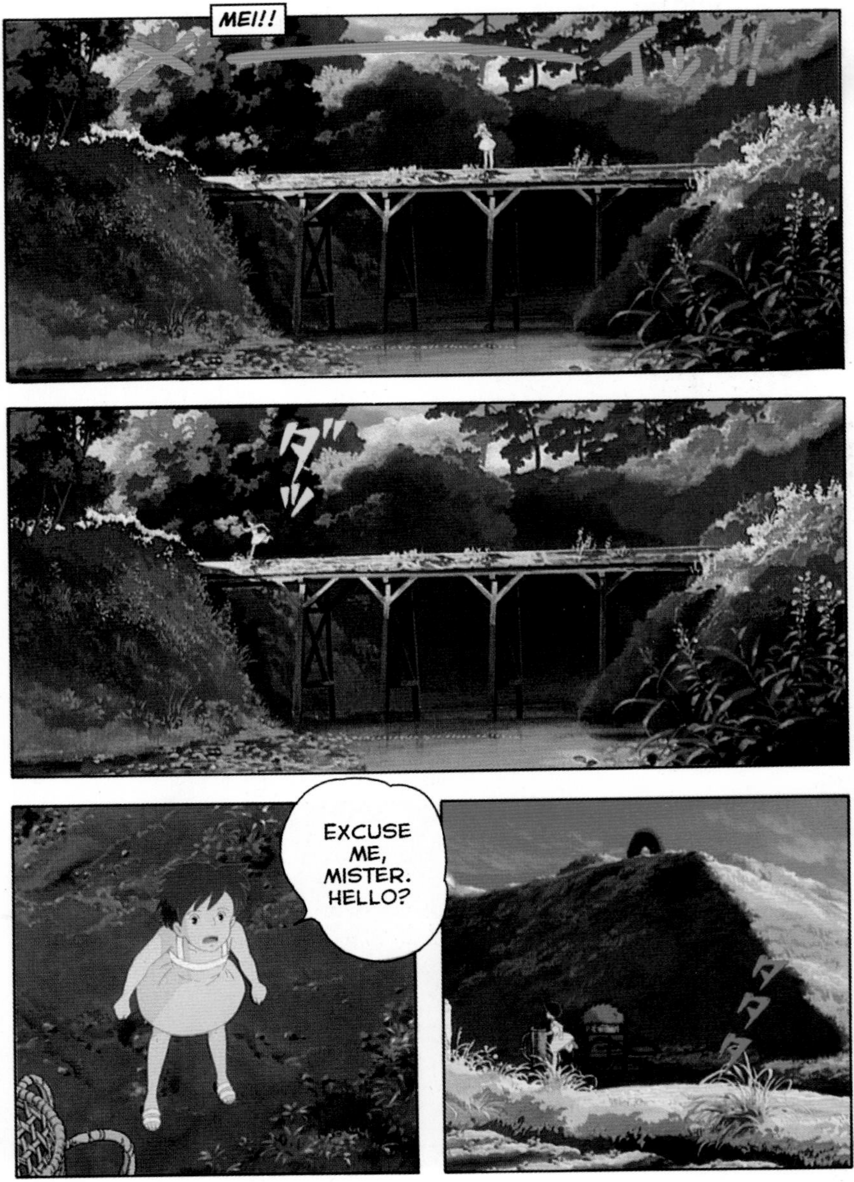
MEI!!
ダッ
タタタ
EXCUSE ME, MISTER. HELLO?

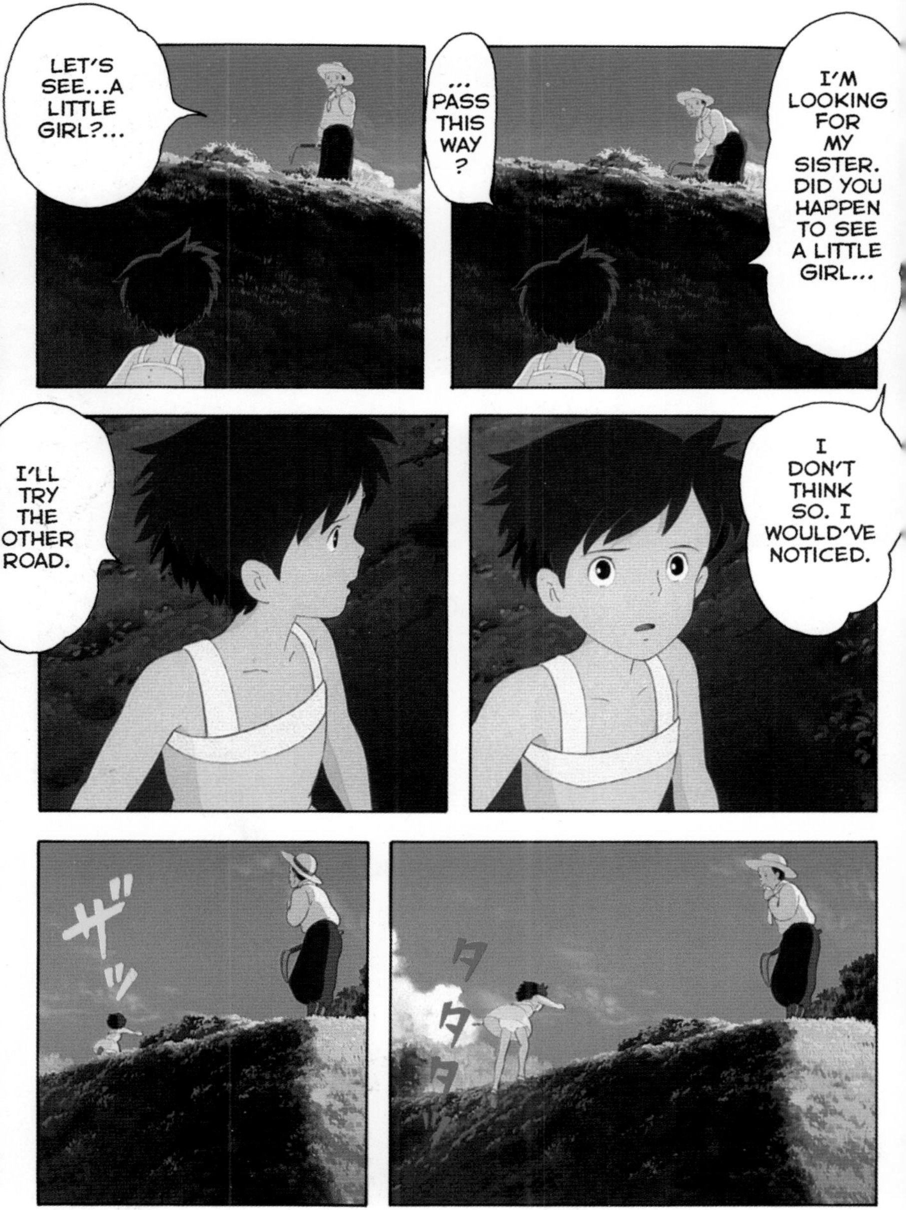
I'M LOOKING FOR MY SISTER. DID YOU HAPPEN TO SEE A LITTLE GIRL...
...PASS THIS WAY?
LET'S SEE...A LITTLE GIRL?...
I DON'T THINK SO. I WOULD'VE NOTICED.
I'LL TRY THE OTHER ROAD.
タタタ
ザッ

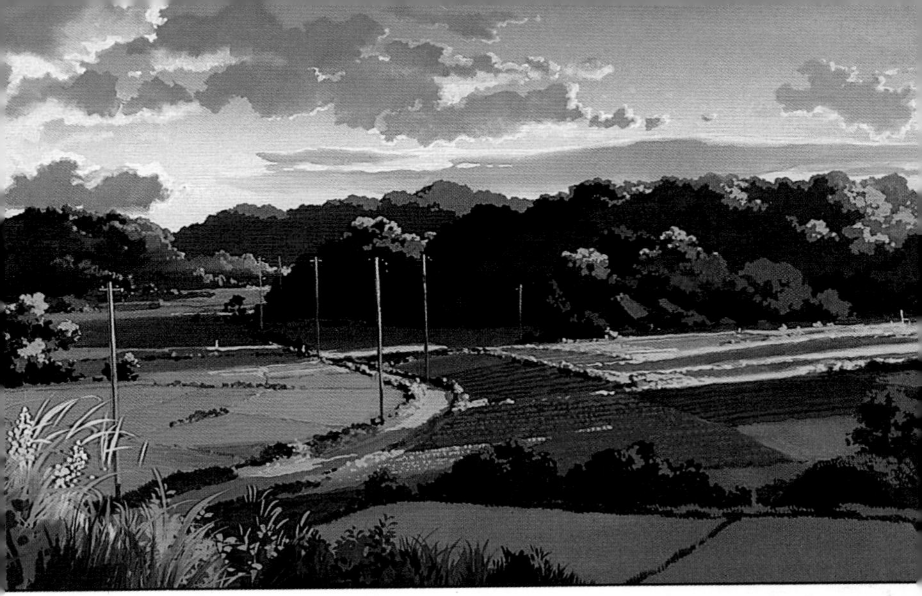

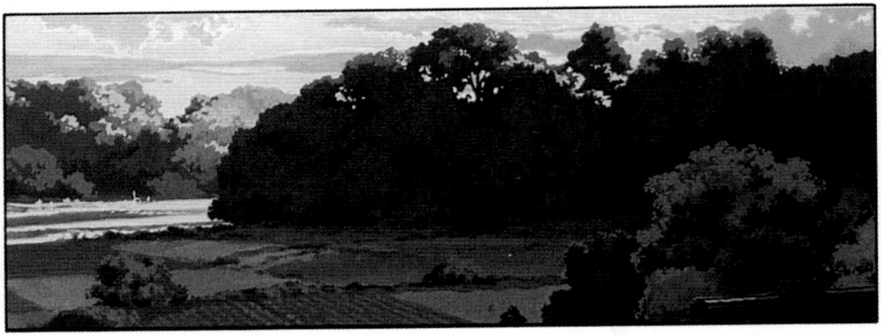

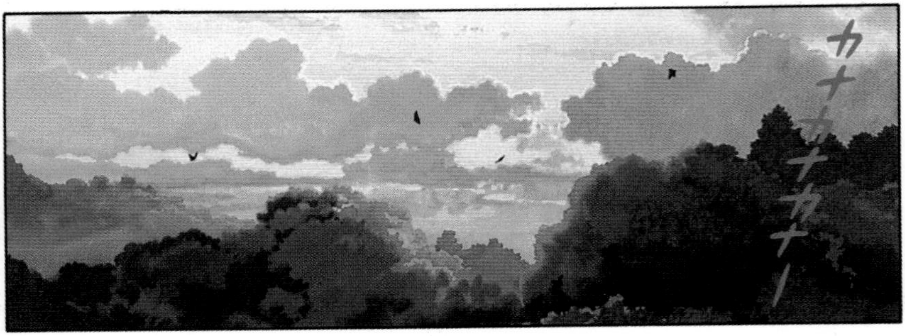
カナカナカナー

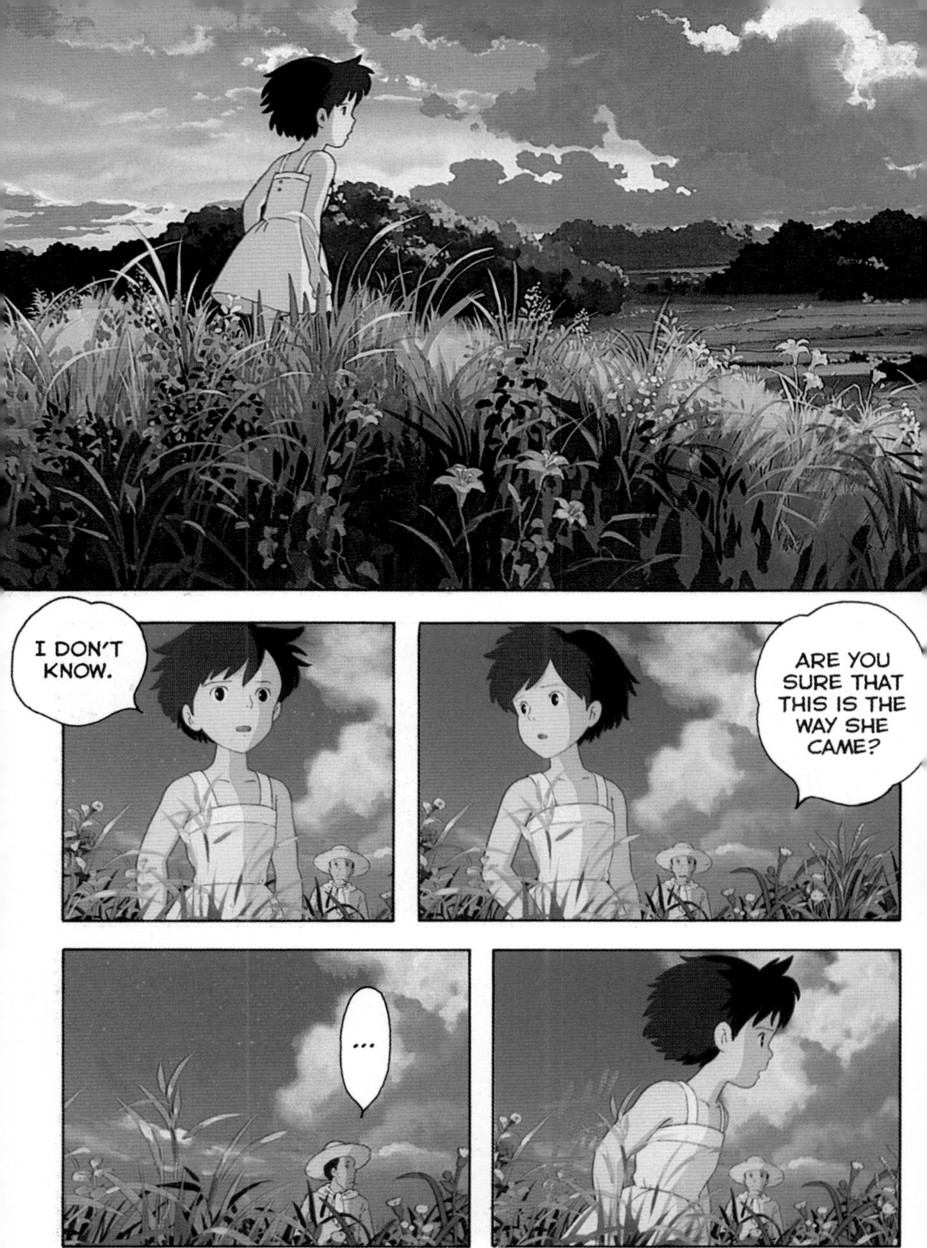
ARE YOU SURE THAT THIS IS THE WAY SHE CAME?
I DON'T KNOW.
...

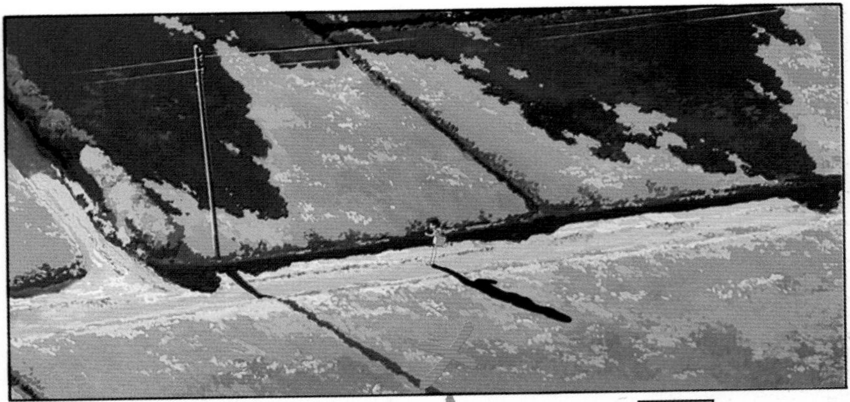

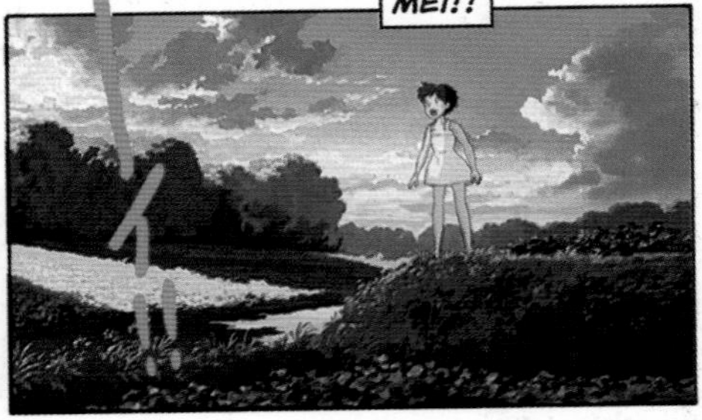
MEI!!
ーイ!!

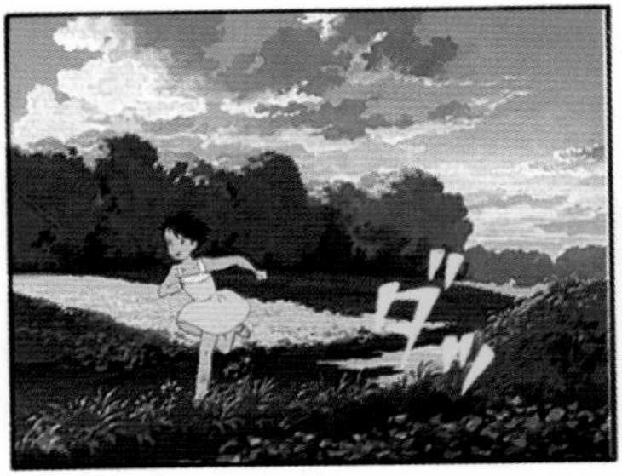
ダッ

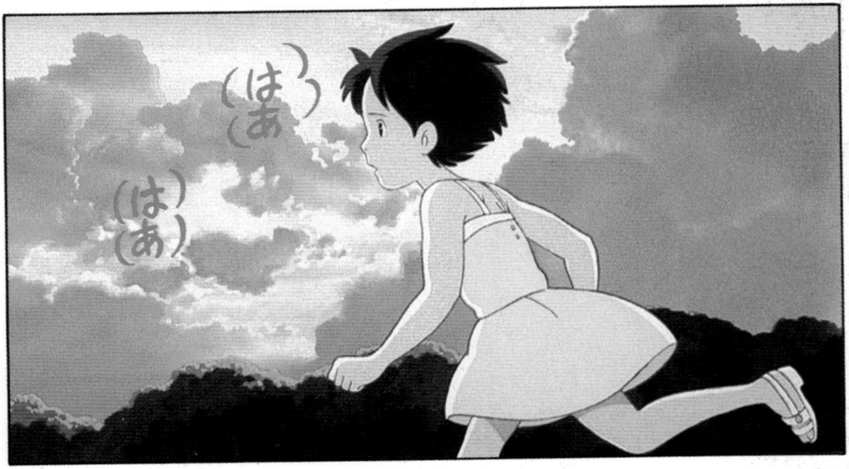
はぁ
はぁ

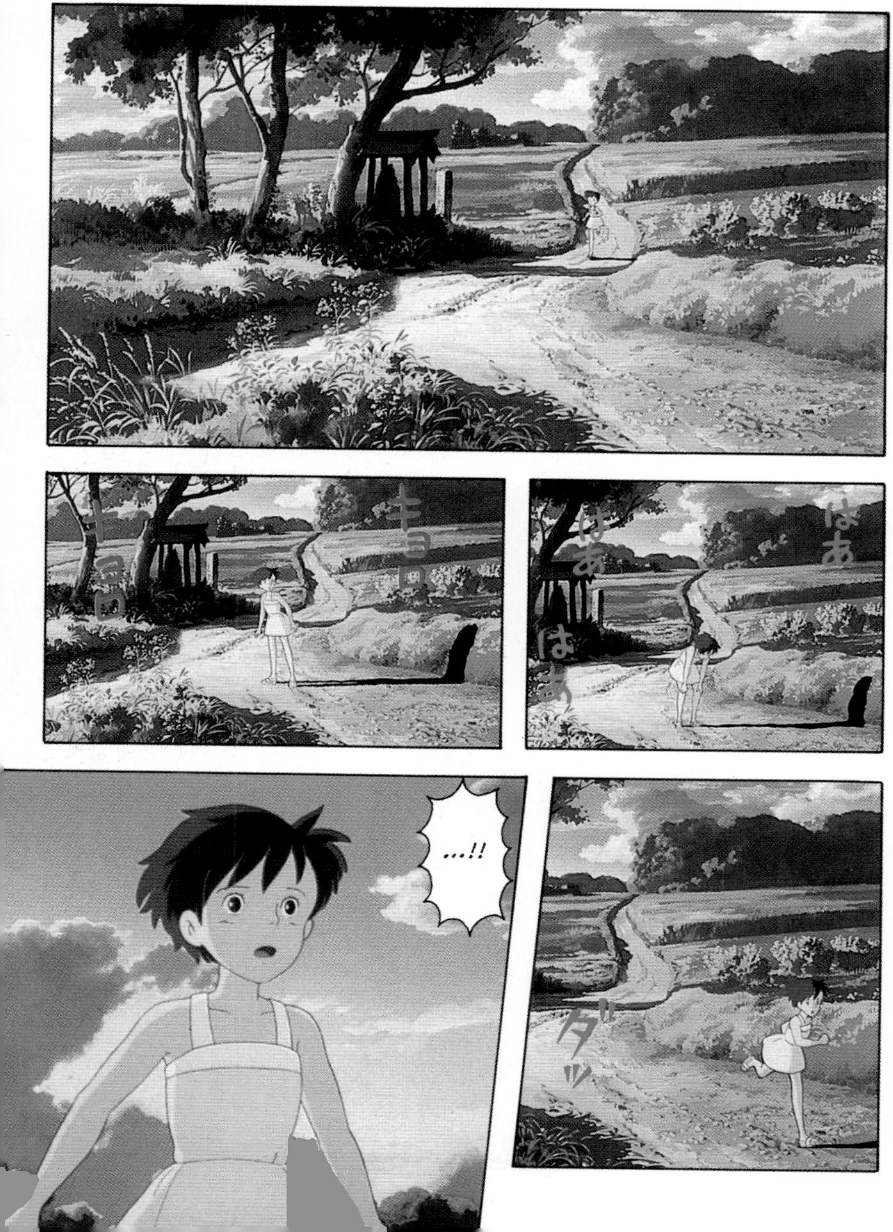
はぁ
はぁ はぁ
キョロ
キョロ
ダッ
...!!

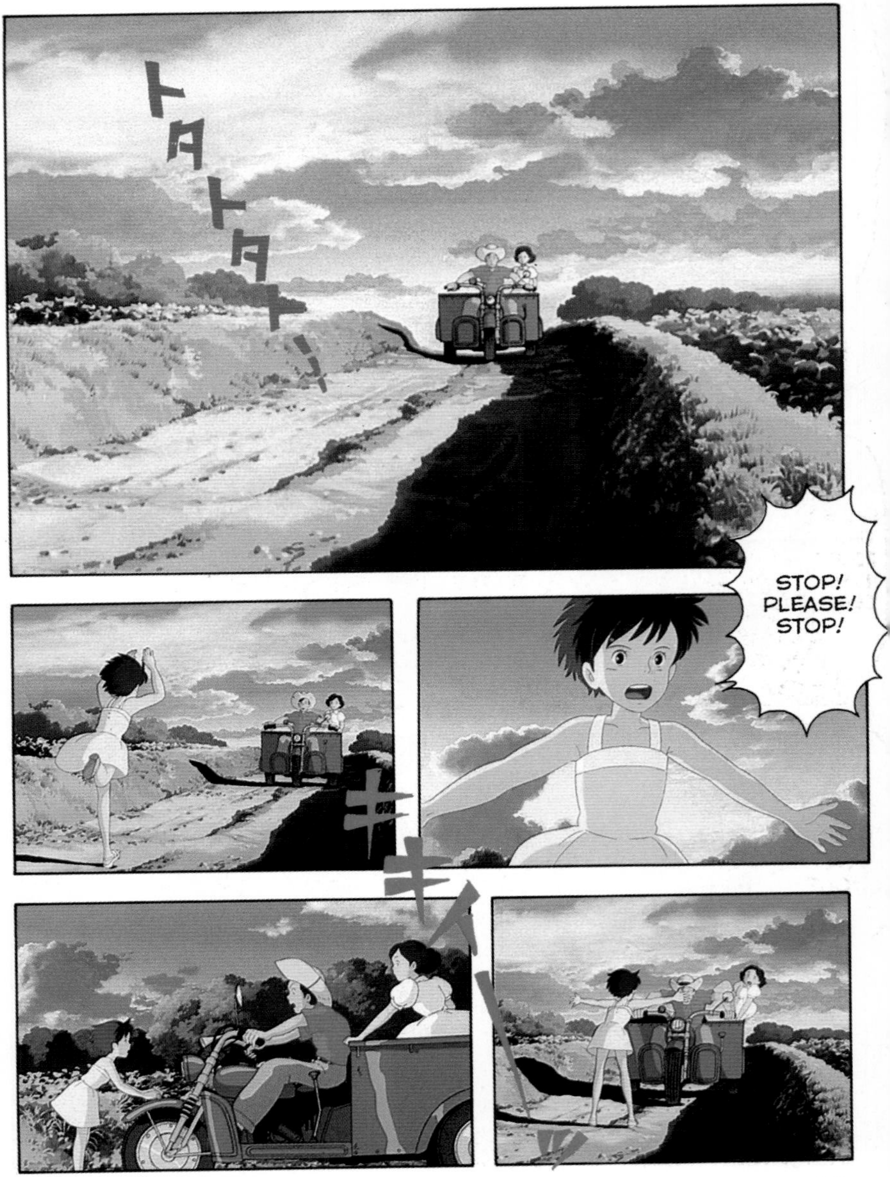
トタトタト
STOP! PLEASE! STOP!

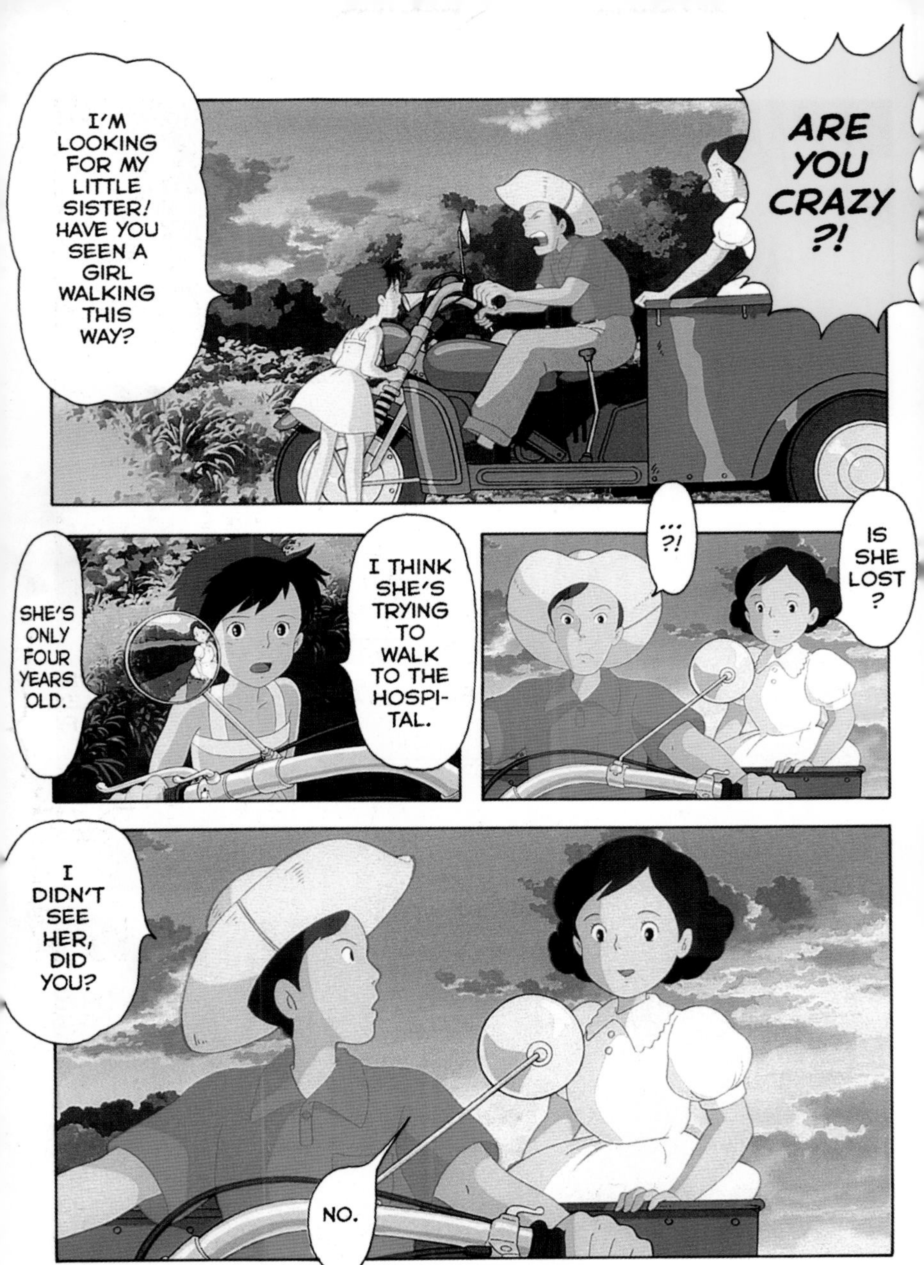
ARE YOU CRAZY?!
I'M LOOKING FOR MY LITTLE SISTER! HAVE YOU SEEN A GIRL WALKING THIS WAY?
IS SHE LOST?
...?!
I THINK SHE'S TRYING TO WALK TO THE HOSPI-TAL.
SHE'S ONLY FOUR YEARS OLD.
I DIDN'T SEE HER, DID YOU?
NO.

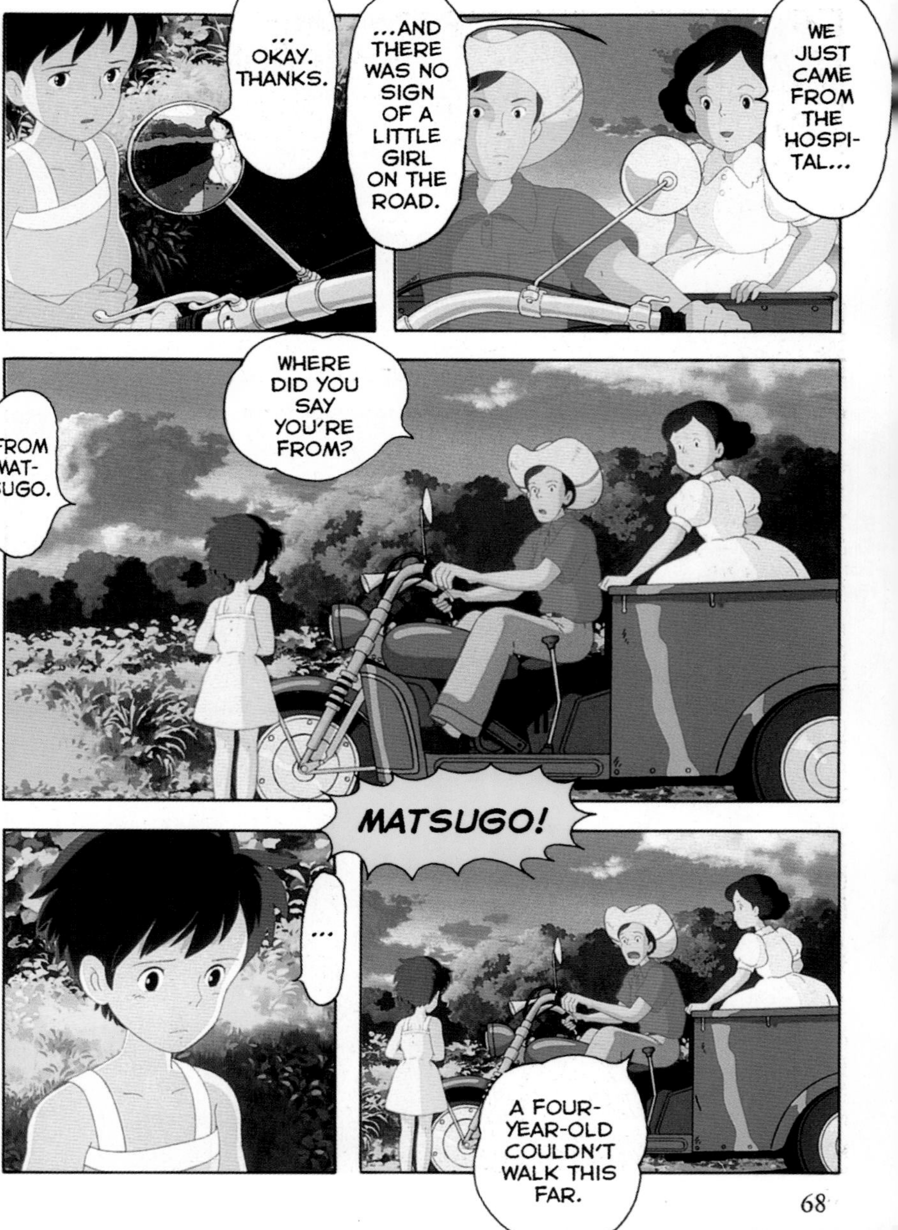
WE JUST CAME FROM THE HOSPI-TAL...
...AND THERE WAS NO SIGN OF A LITTLE GIRL ON THE ROAD.
... OKAY. THANKS.
WHERE DID YOU SAY YOU'RE FROM?
FROM MAT-SUGO.
MATSUGO!
A FOUR-YEAR-OLD COULDN'T WALK THIS FAR.
...

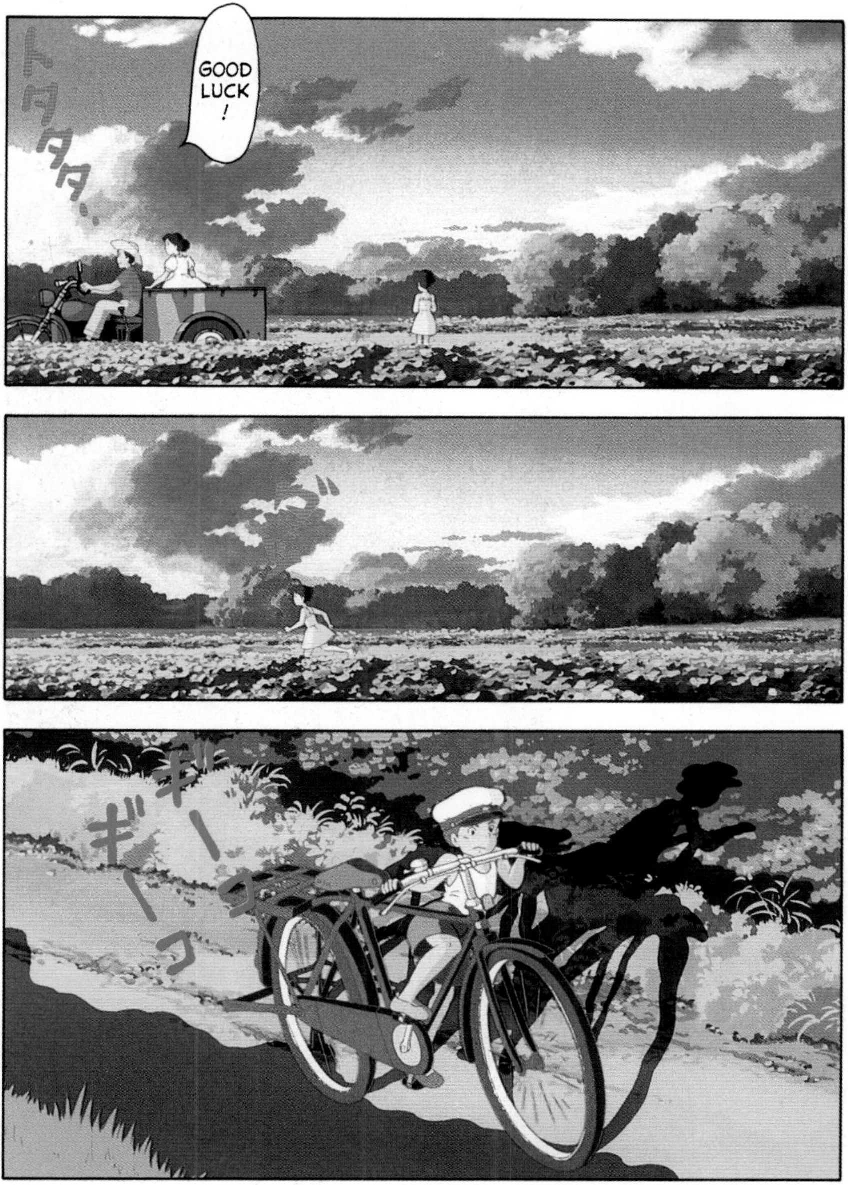
GOOD LUCK!
トタタタ
ギーコ
ギーコ

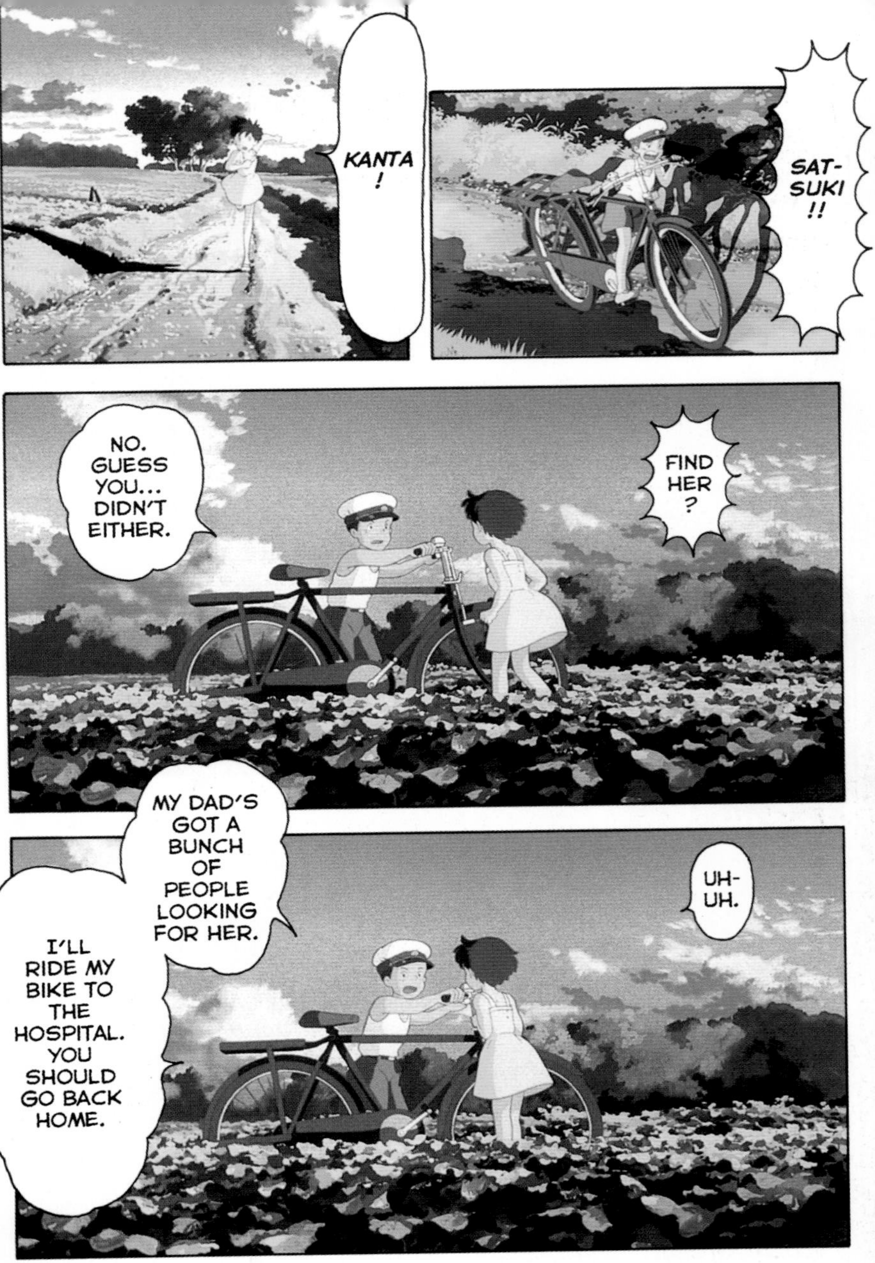
SAT-SUKI !!
KANTA !
FIND HER ?
NO. GUESS YOU... DIDN'T EITHER.
UH-UH.
MY DAD'S GOT A BUNCH OF PEOPLE LOOKING FOR HER.
I'LL RIDE MY BIKE TO THE HOSPITAL. YOU SHOULD GO BACK HOME.

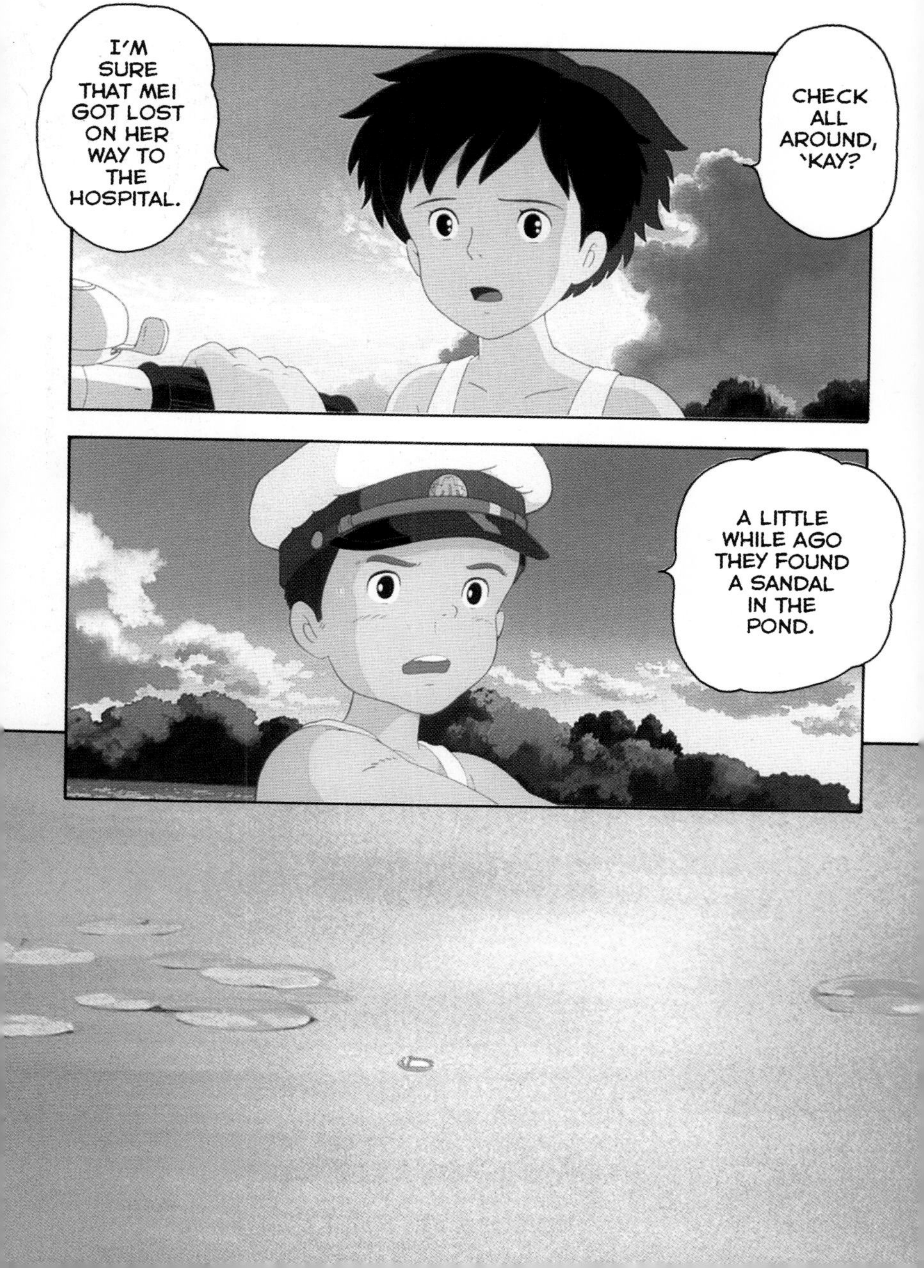
CHECK ALL AROUND, `KAY?
I'M SURE THAT MEI GOT LOST ON HER WAY TO THE HOSPITAL.
A LITTLE WHILE AGO THEY FOUND A SANDAL IN THE POND.

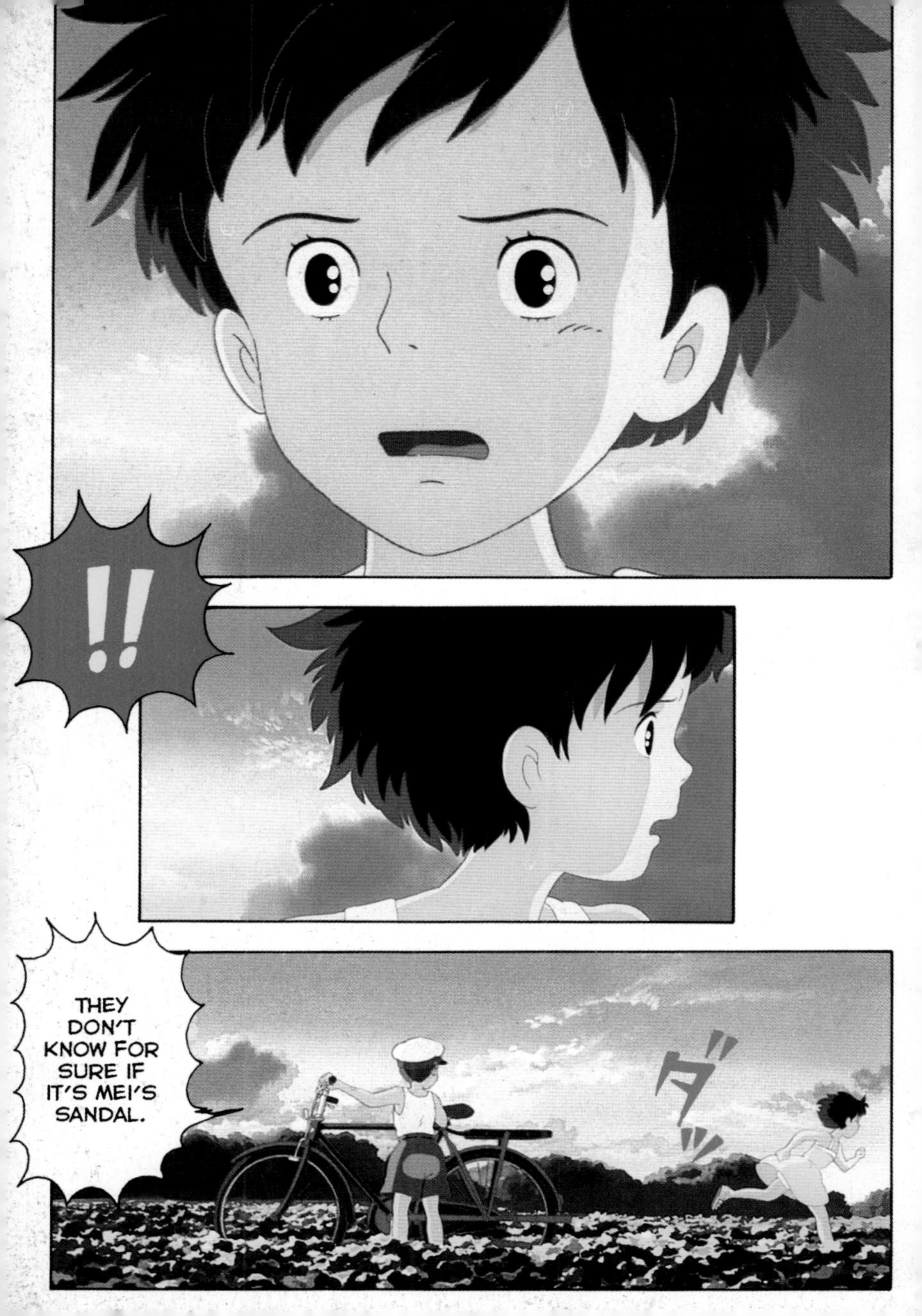
!!
THEY DON'T KNOW FOR SURE IF IT'S MEI'S SANDAL.
ダダッ

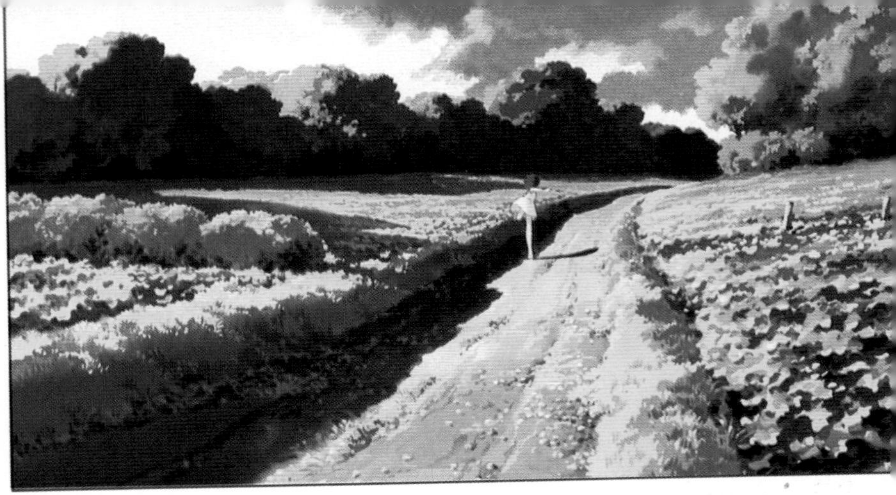
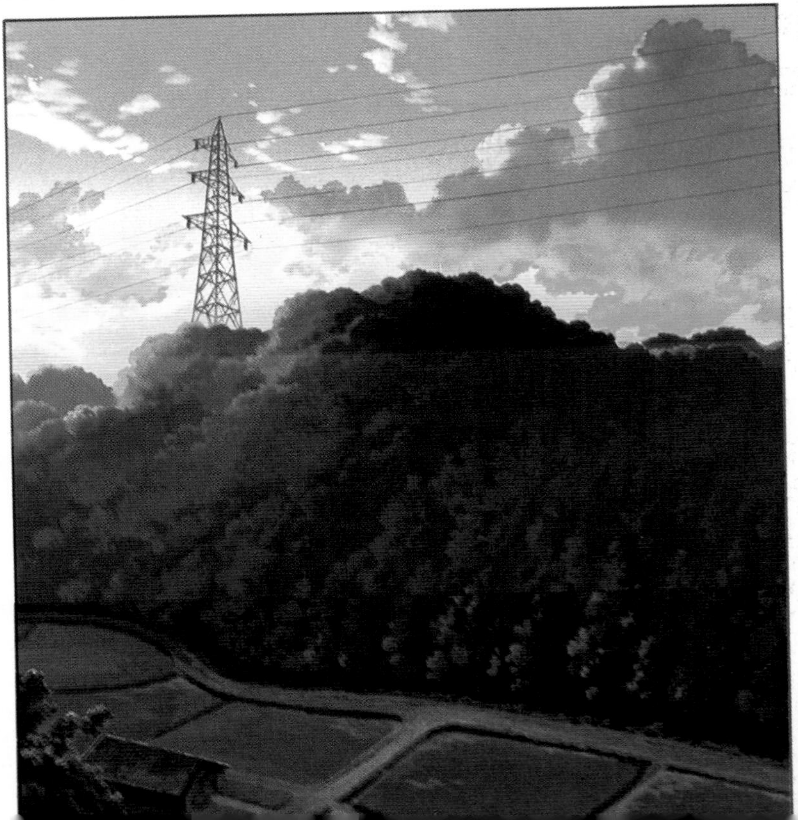

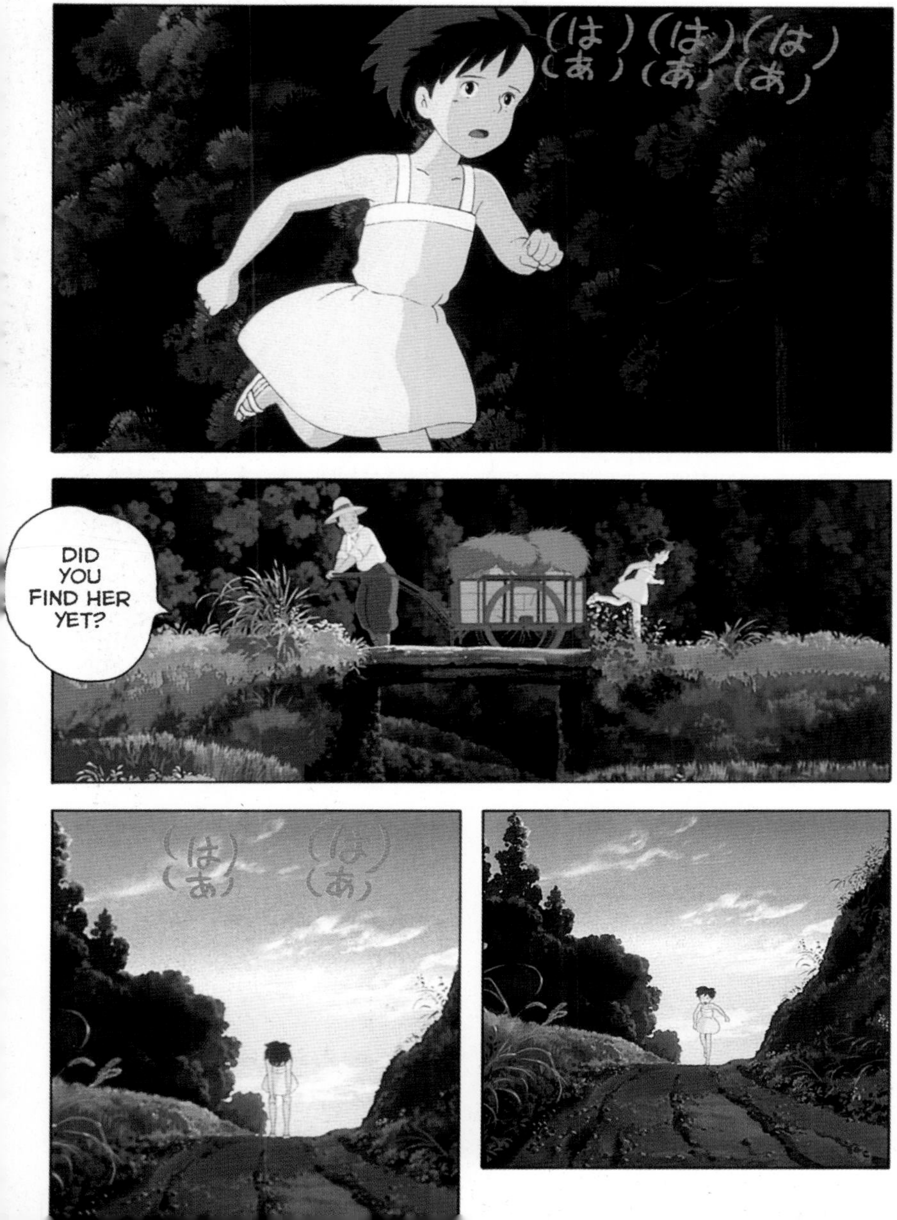
はあ はあ はあ
DID YOU FIND HER YET?
はあ はあ

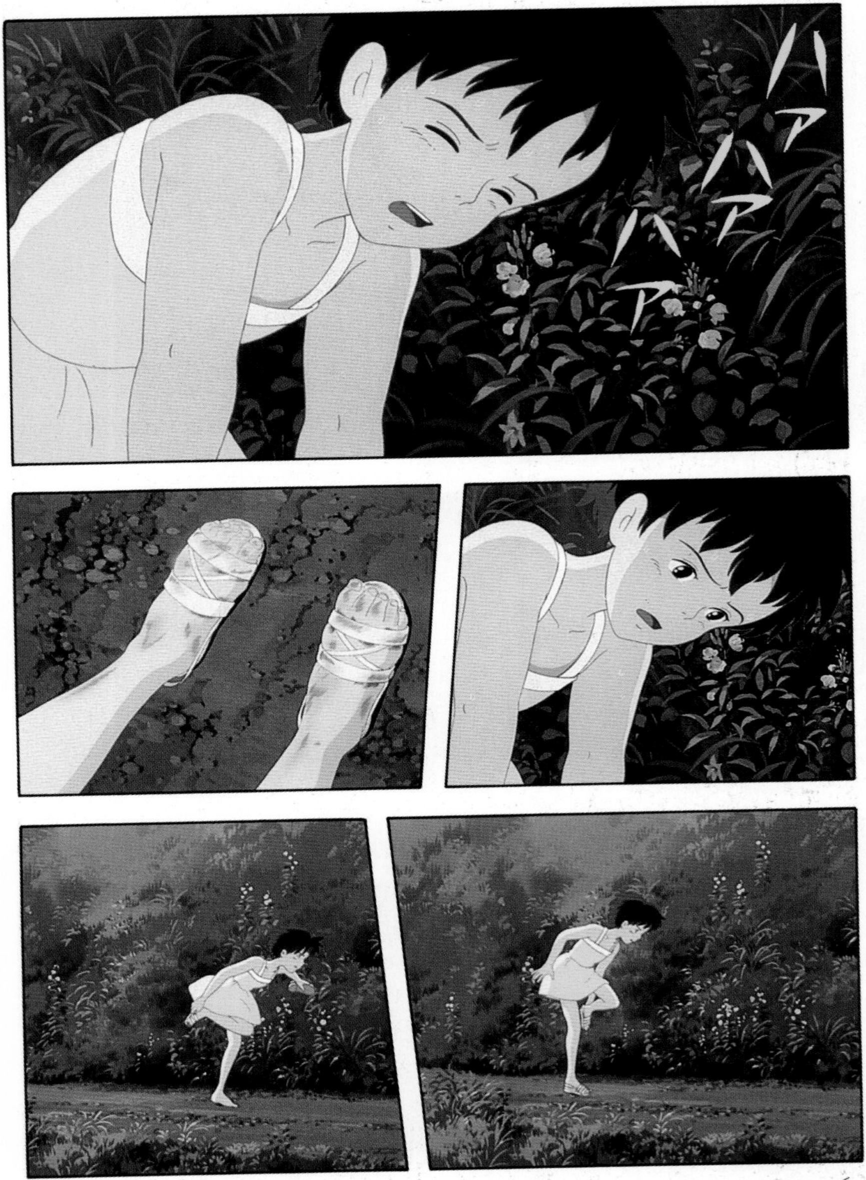
ハアハアハア

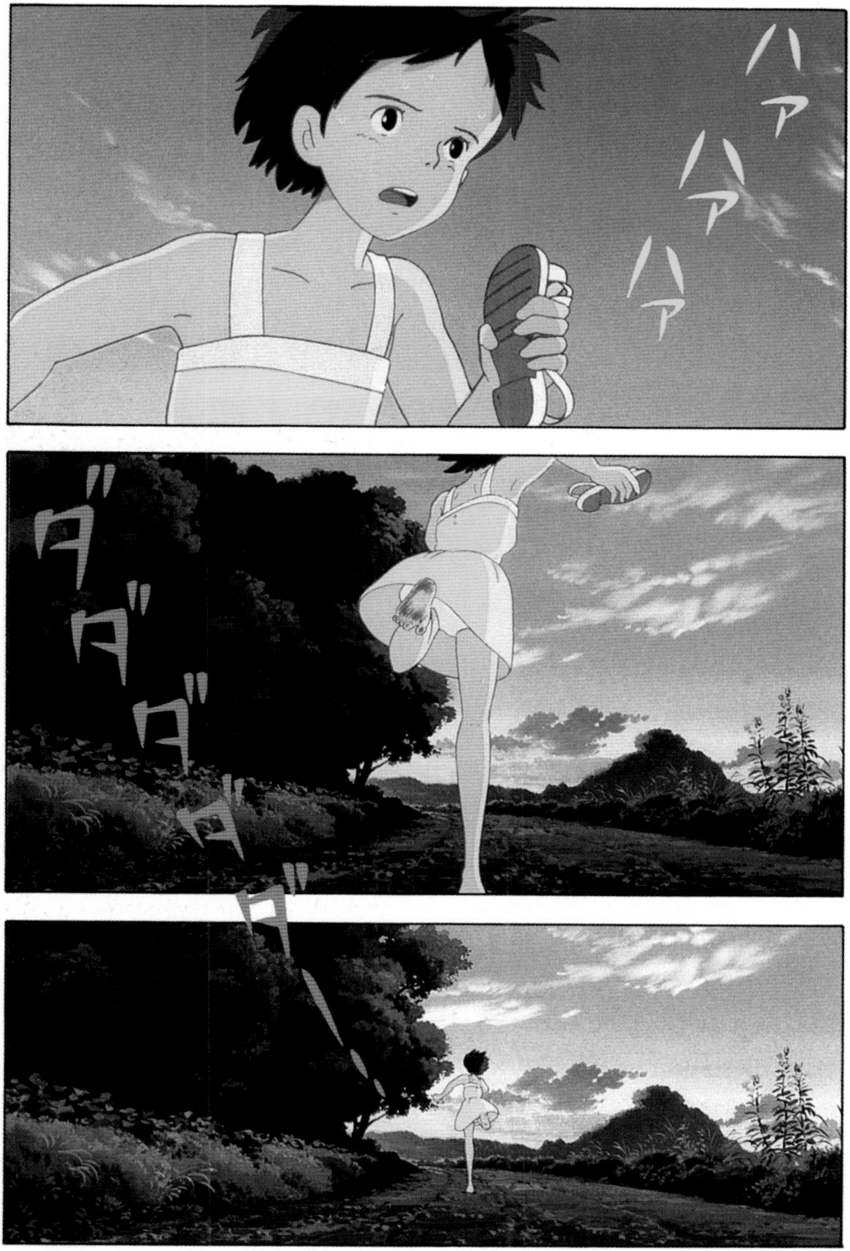
ハァハァハァ
ダダダダダダ

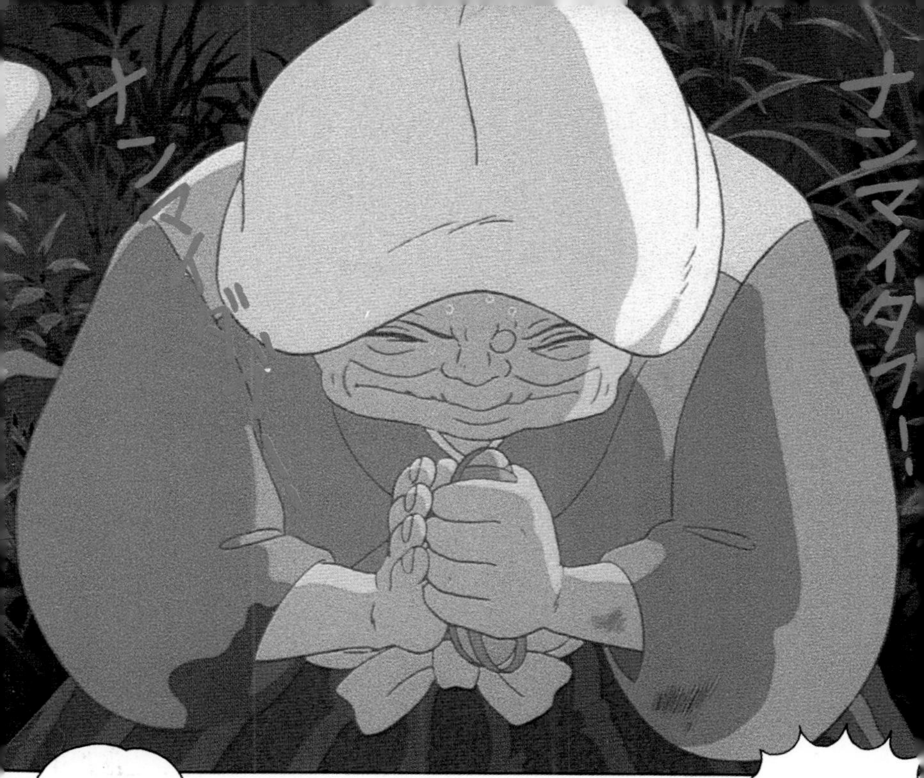
ナンマイダブ!!

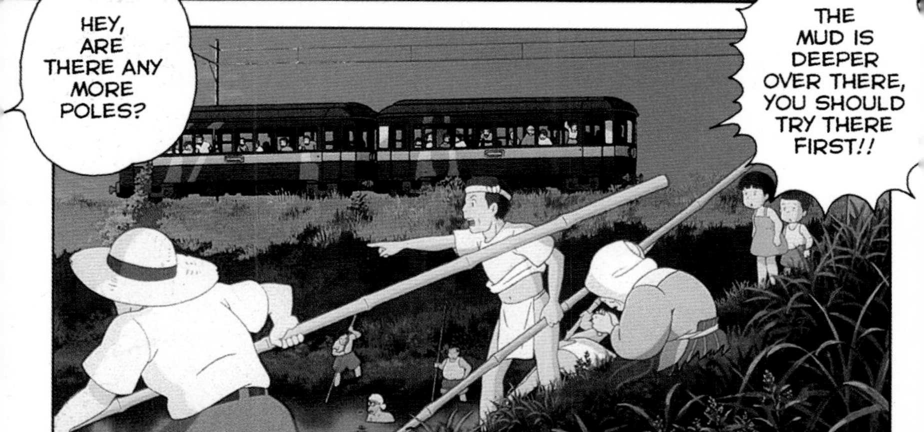
THE MUD IS DEEPER OVER THERE, YOU SHOULD TRY THERE FIRST!!
HEY, ARE THERE ANY MORE POLES?

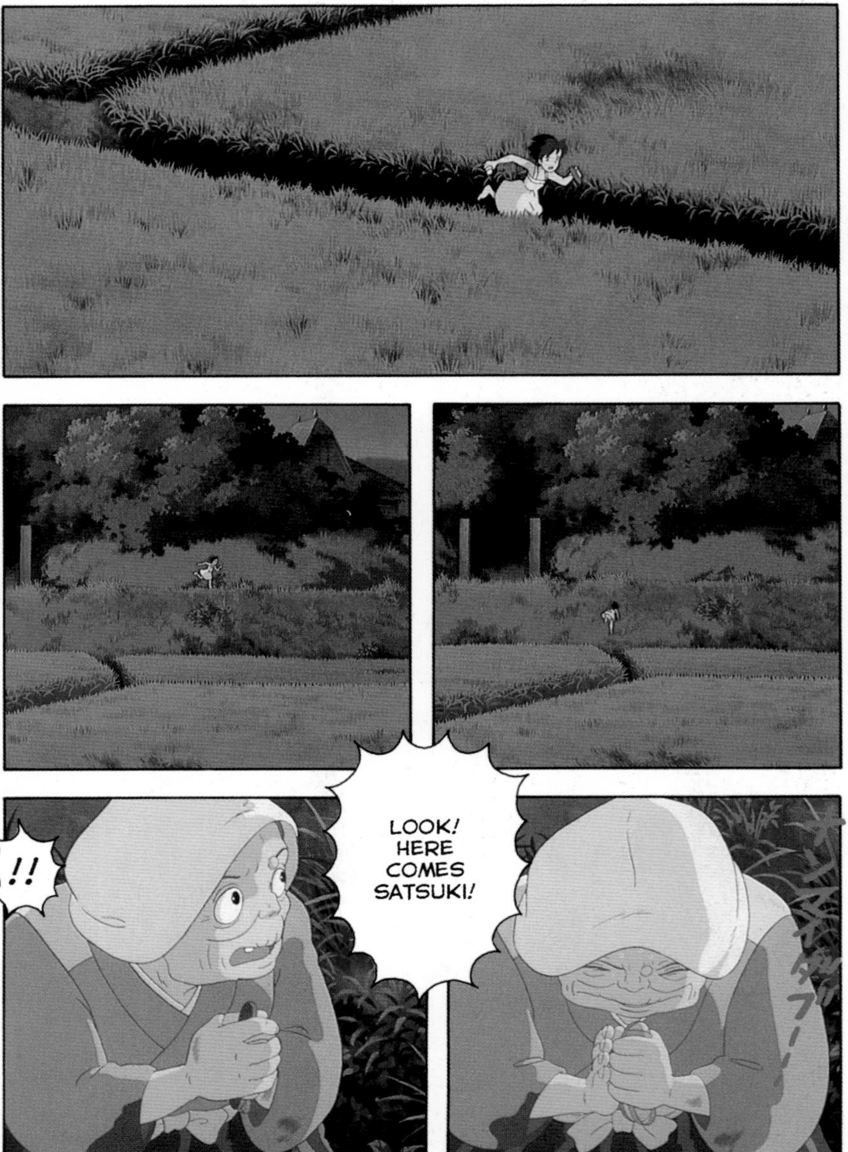
LOOK! HERE COMES SATSUKI!
!!

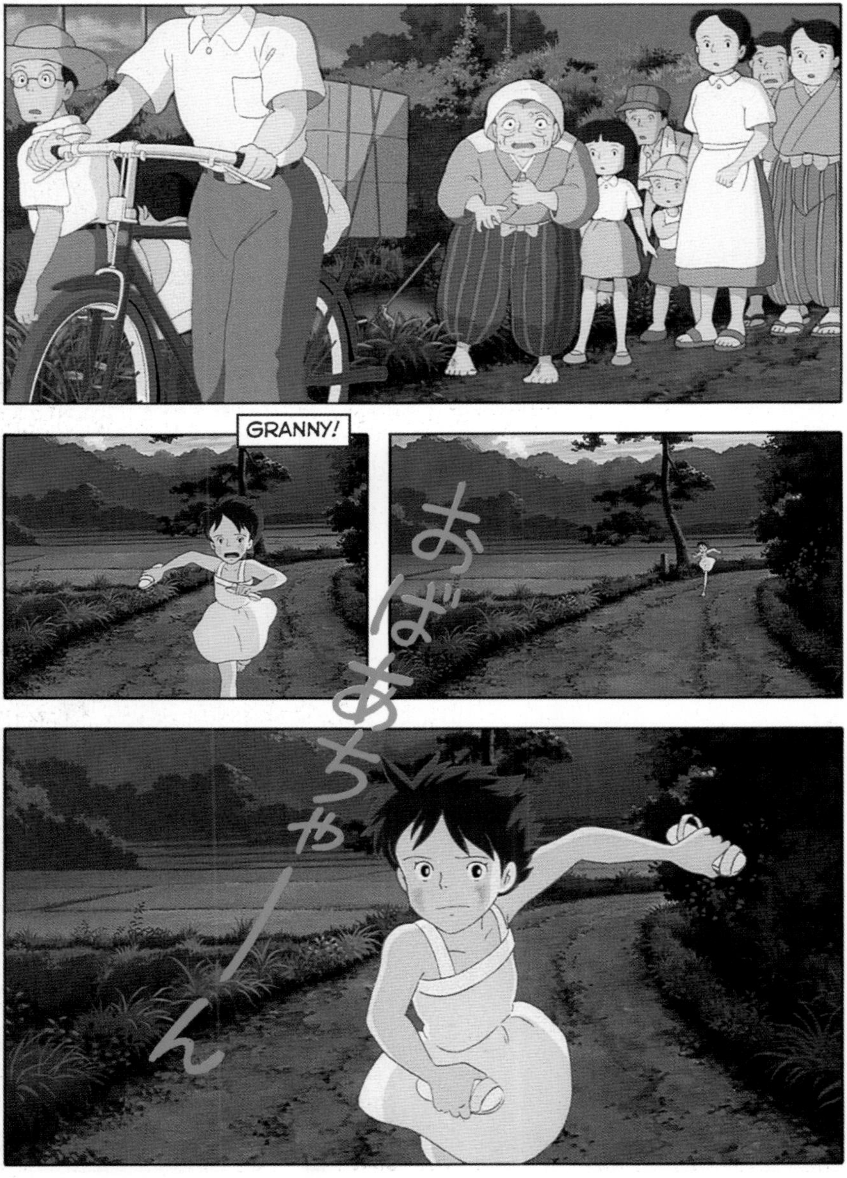
おばあちゃーん
GRANNY!

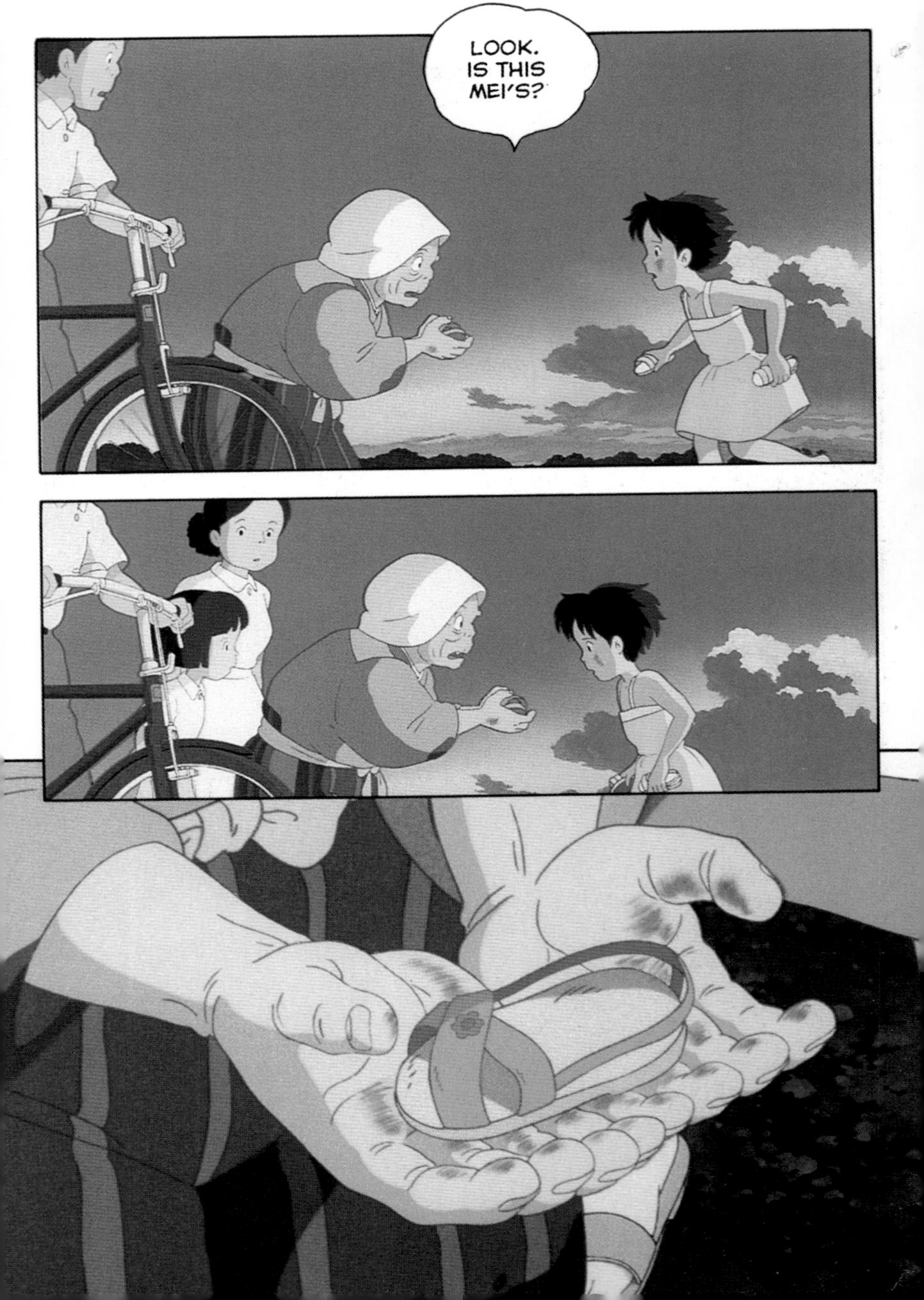
LOOK. IS THIS MEI'S?

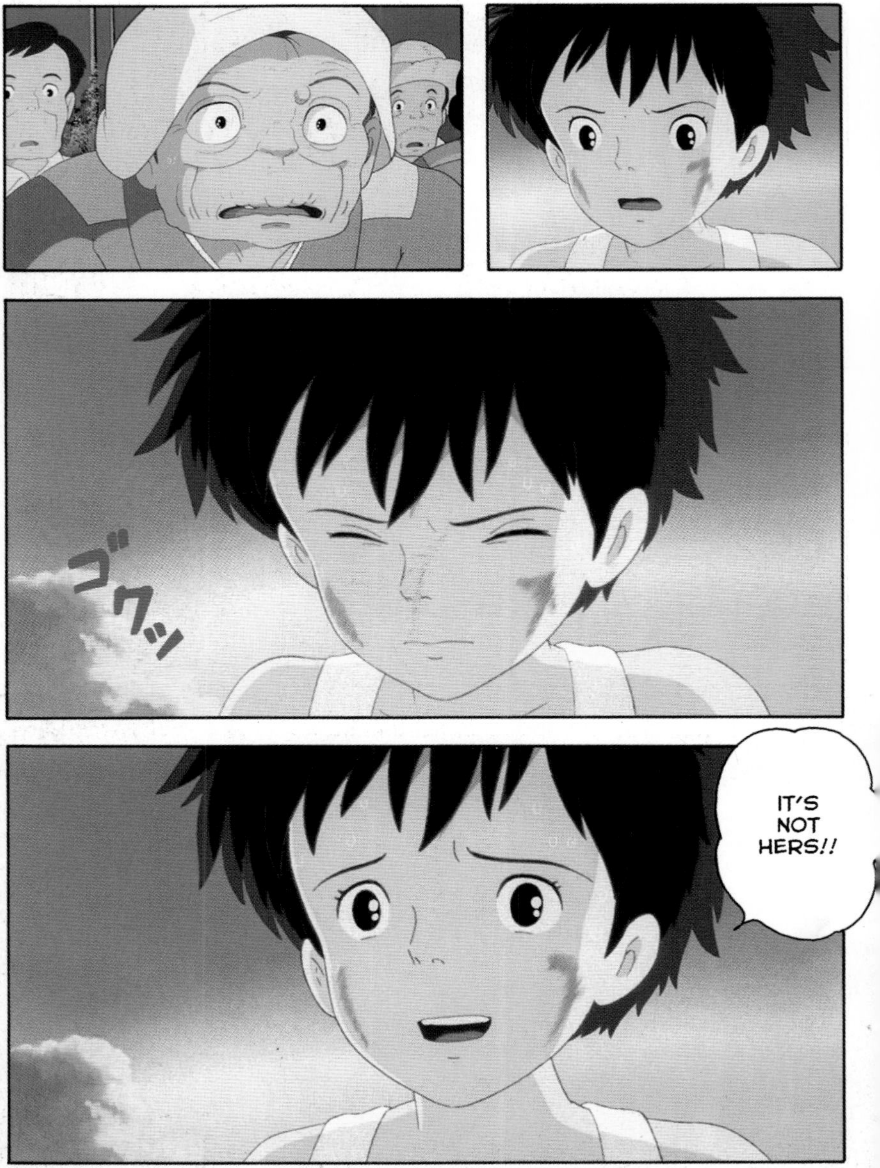
ゴクッ
IT'S NOT HERS!!

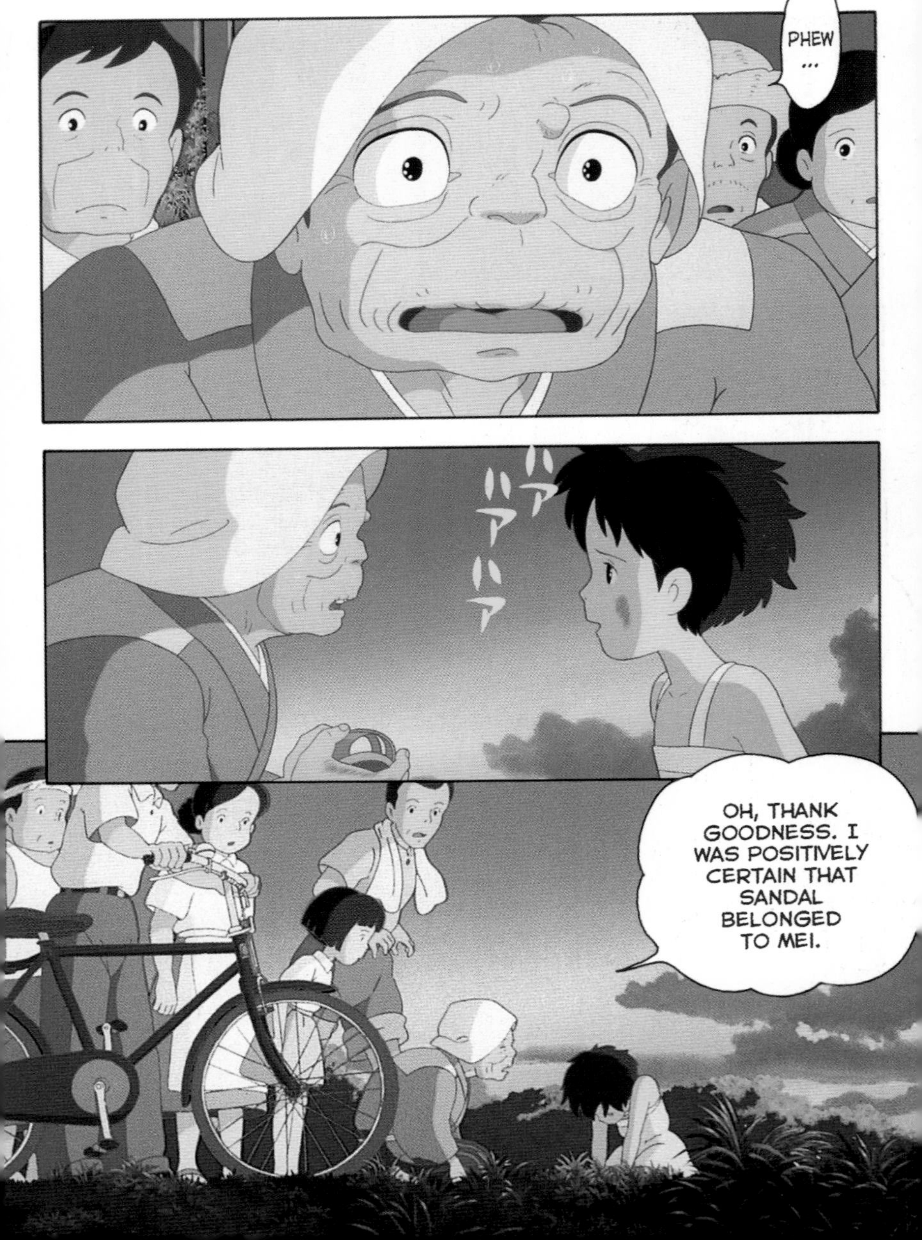
PHEW ...
ハア
ハアハア
OH, THANK GOODNESS. I WAS POSITIVELY CERTAIN THAT SANDAL BELONGED TO MEI.

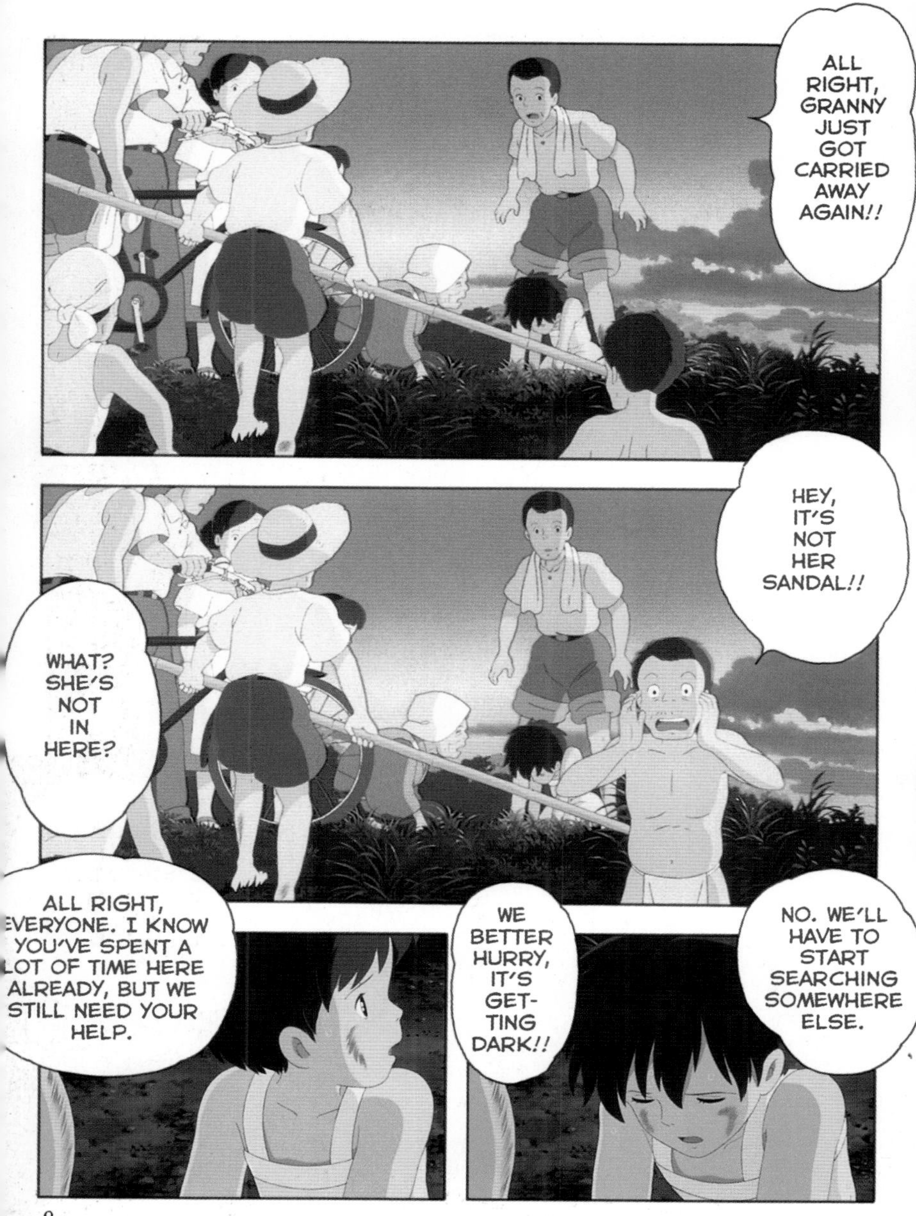
ALL RIGHT, GRANNY JUST GOT CARRIED AWAY AGAIN!!
HEY, IT'S NOT HER SANDAL!!
WHAT? SHE'S NOT IN HERE?
NO. WE'LL HAVE TO START SEARCHING SOMEWHERE ELSE.
WE BETTER HURRY, IT'S GET- TING DARK!!
ALL RIGHT, EVERYONE. I KNOW YOU'VE SPENT A LOT OF TIME HERE ALREADY, BUT WE STILL NEED YOUR HELP.

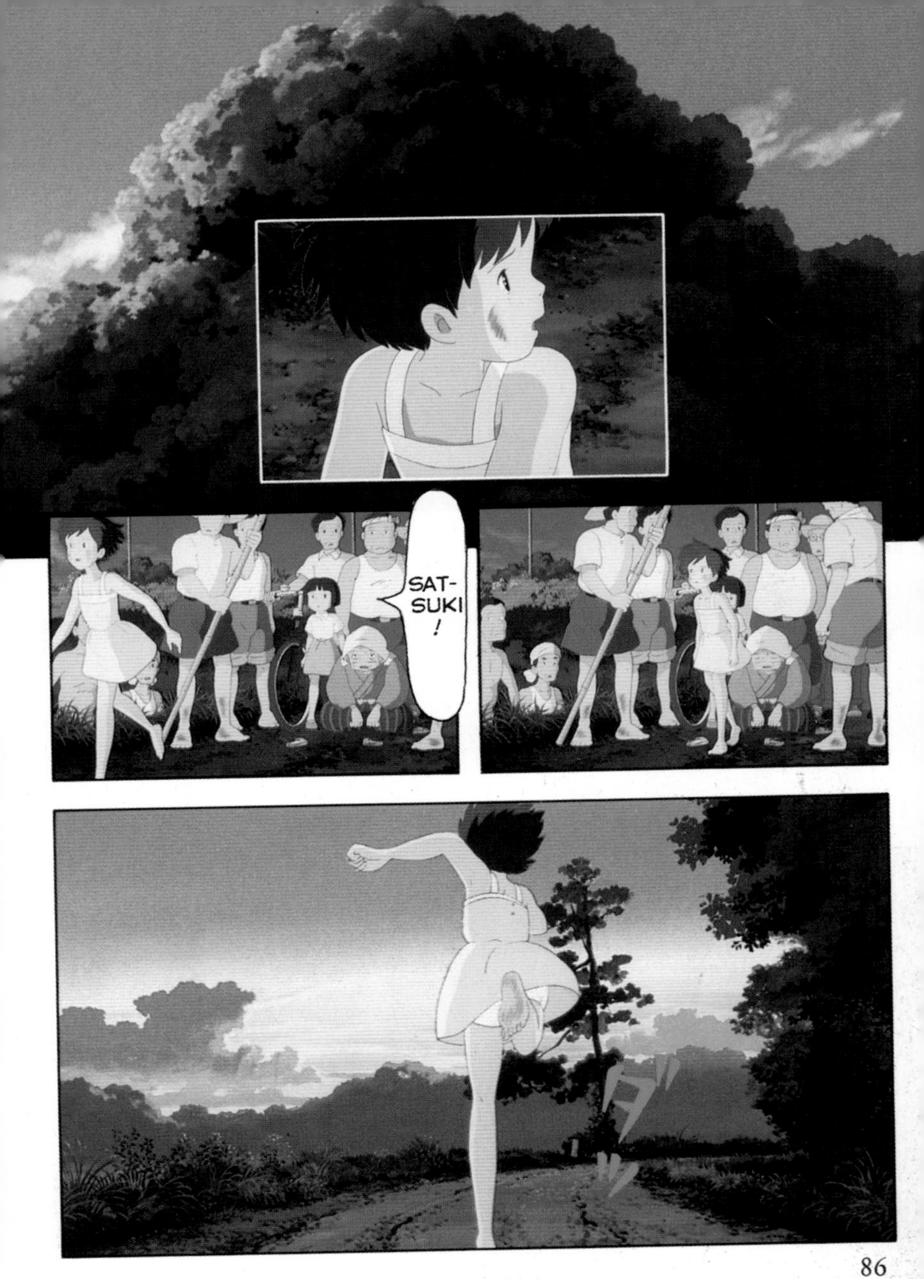
SAT-SUKI!
ダッ

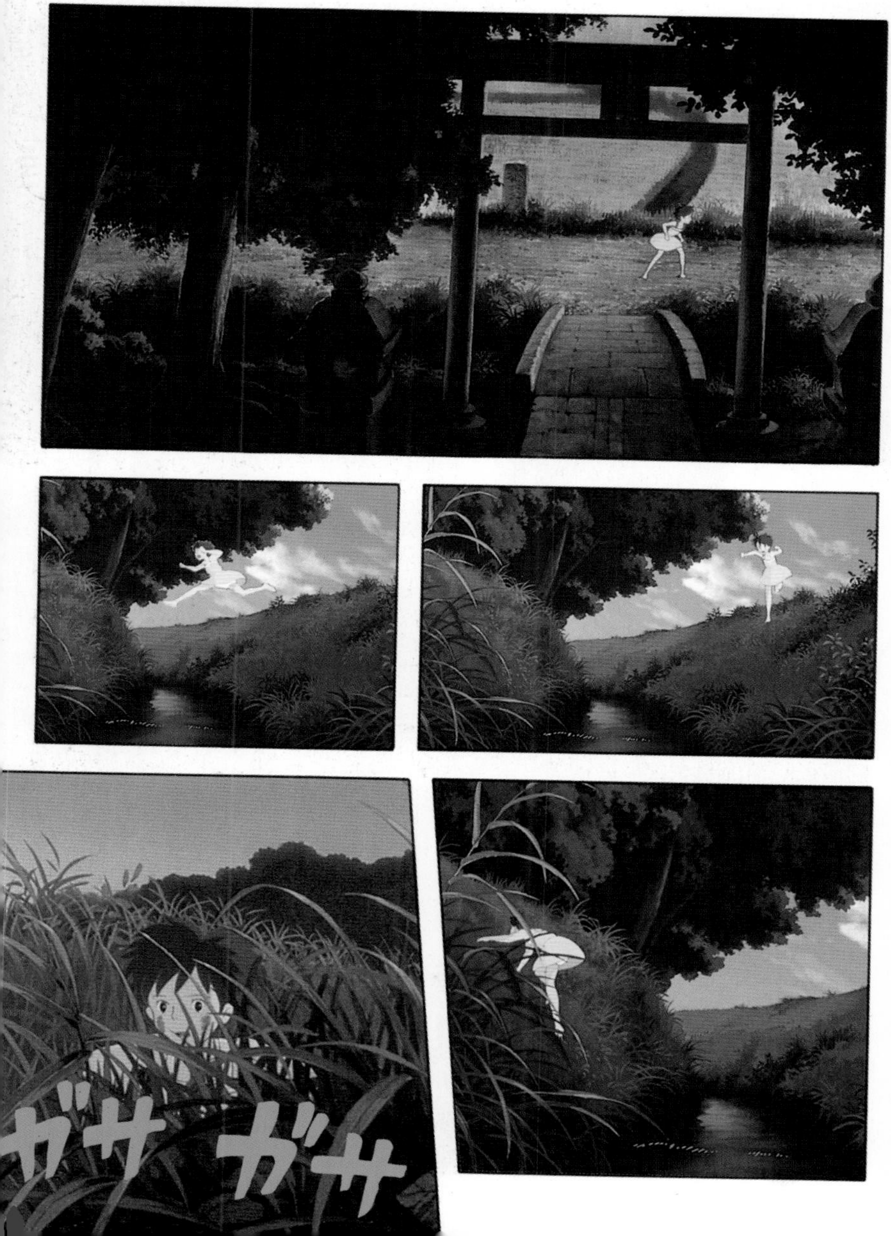
ガサ ガサ

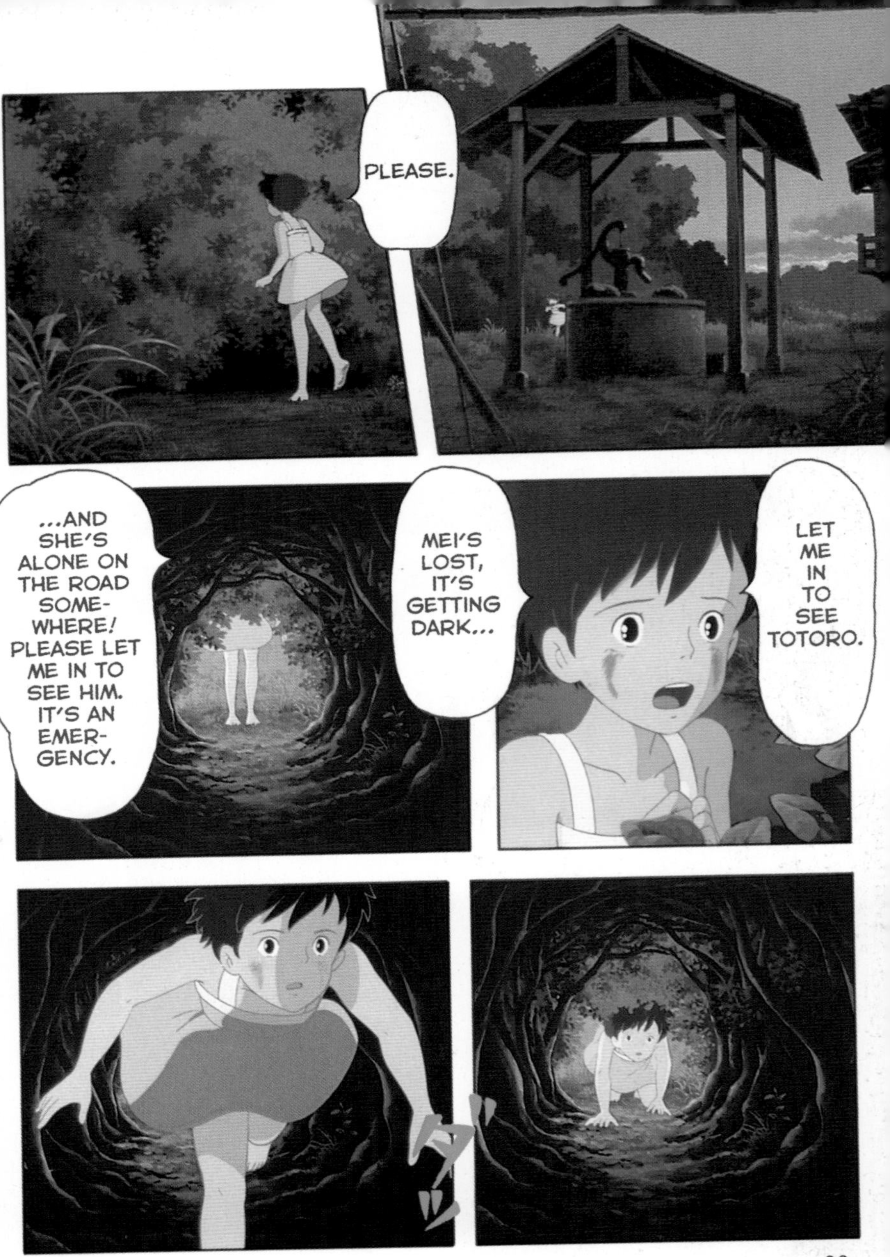
PLEASE.
LET ME IN TO SEE TOTORO.
MEI'S LOST, IT'S GETTING DARK...
...AND SHE'S ALONE ON THE ROAD SOME-WHERE! PLEASE LET ME IN TO SEE HIM. IT'S AN EMER-GENCY.

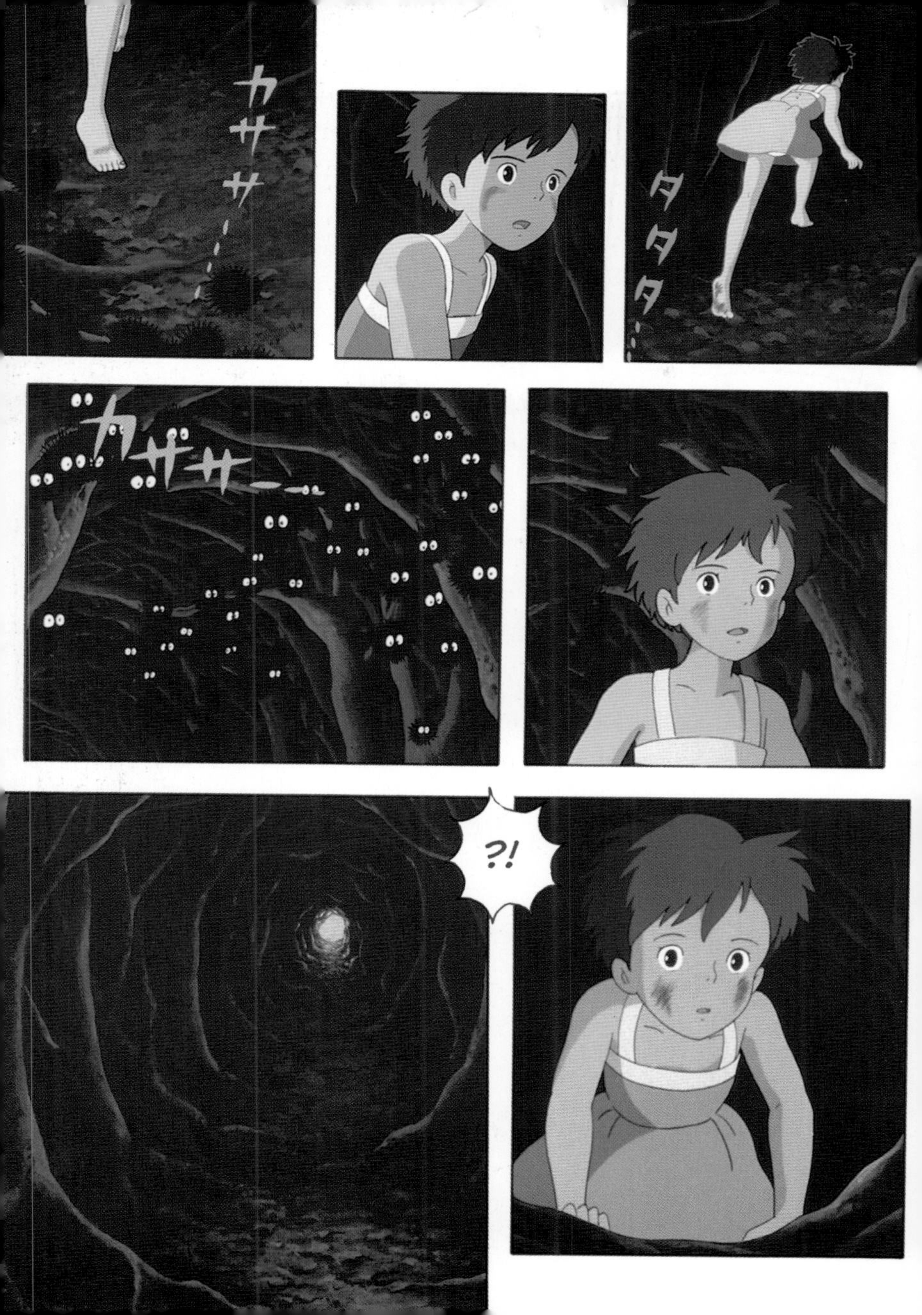

タタタタ
カササ
カササー
?!

ダッ
AHH!
ガッ

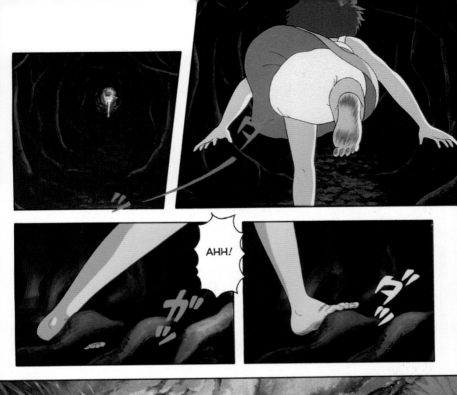

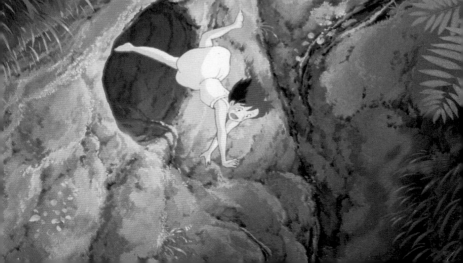

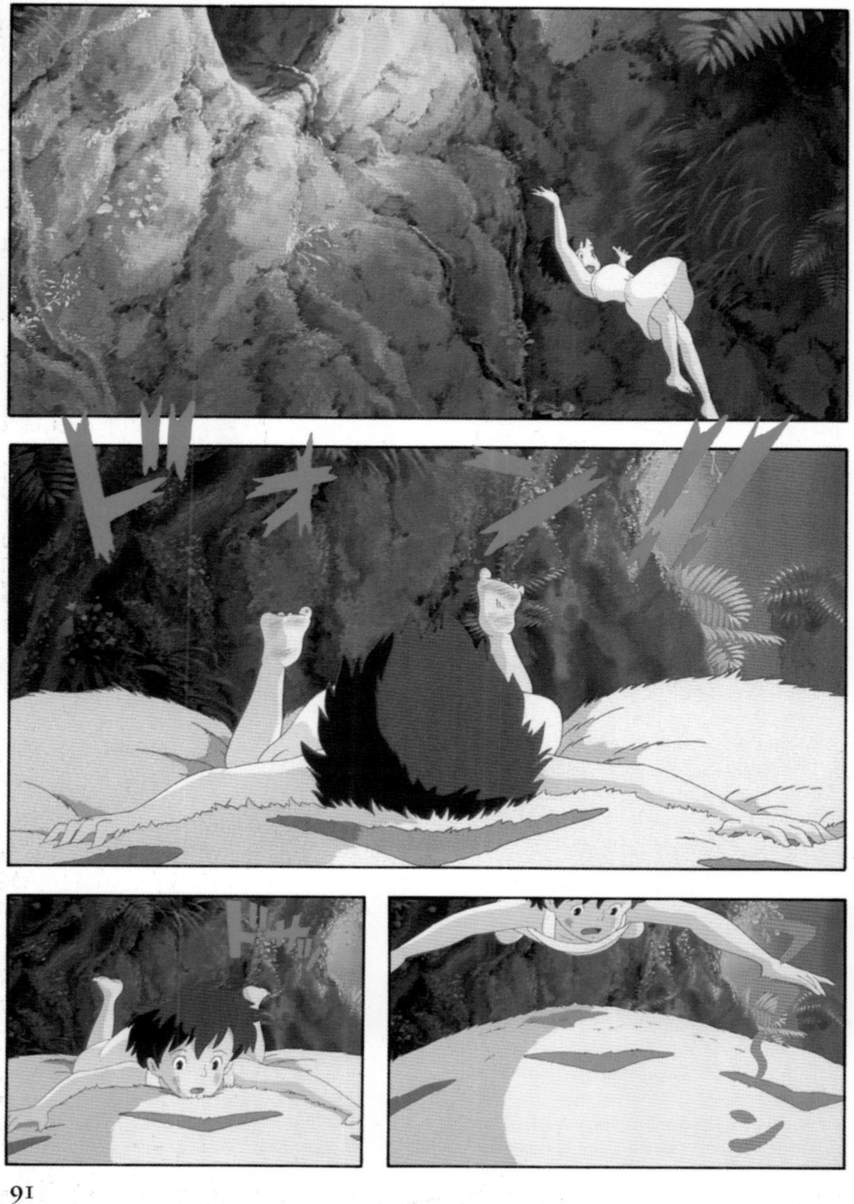
ドォーン

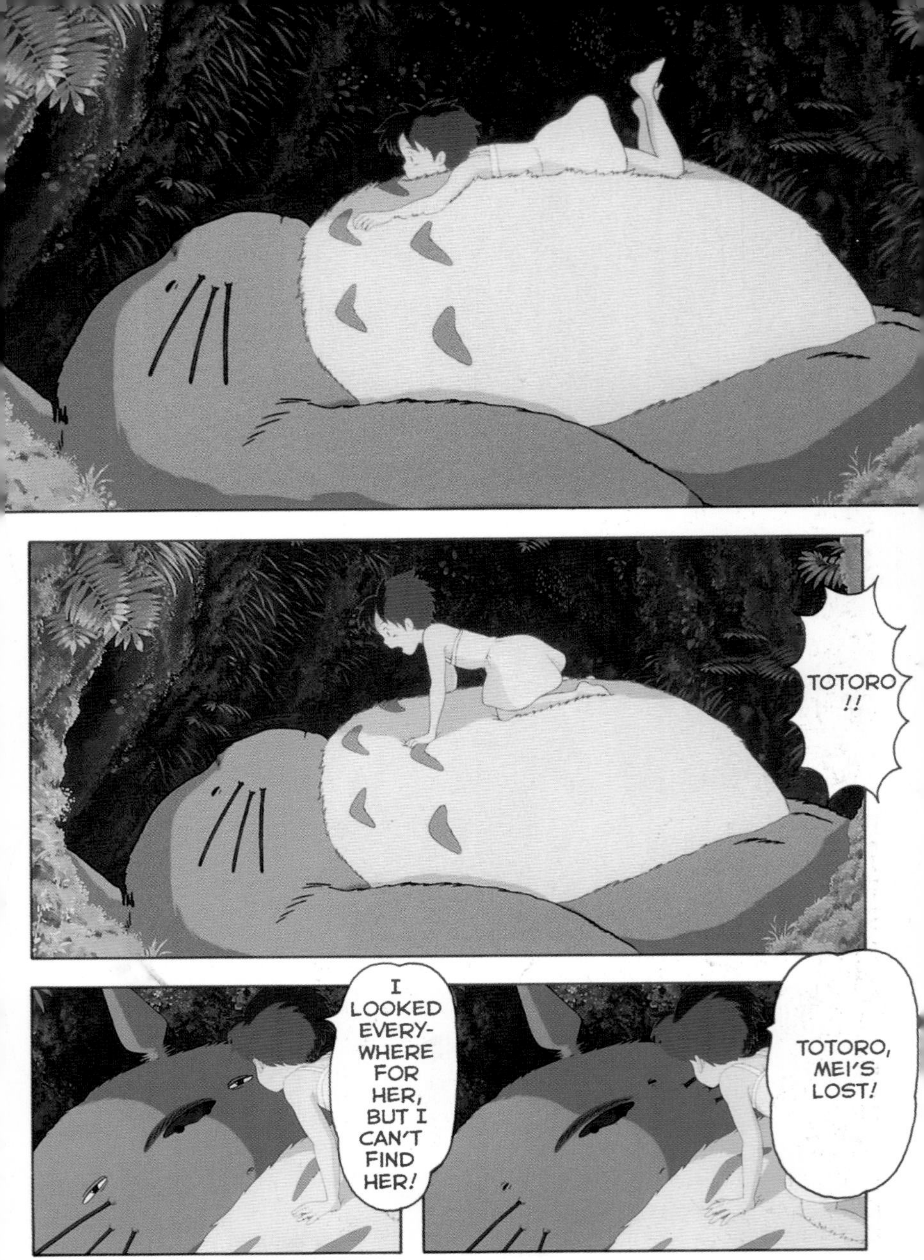
TOTORO !!
TOTORO, MEI'S LOST!
I LOOKED EVERY-WHERE FOR HER, BUT I CAN'T FIND HER!

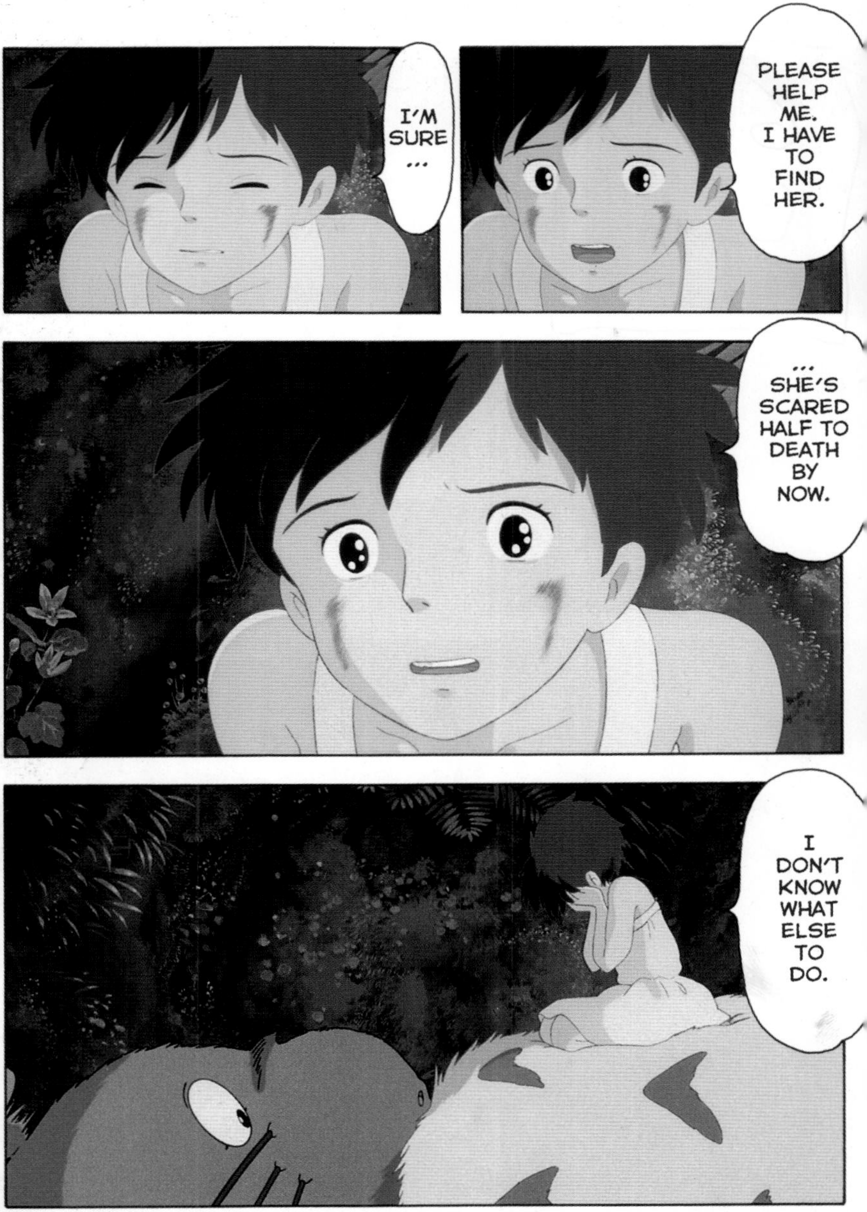
PLEASE HELP ME. I HAVE TO FIND HER.
I'M SURE ...
... SHE'S SCARED HALF TO DEATH BY NOW.
I DON'T KNOW WHAT ELSE TO DO.

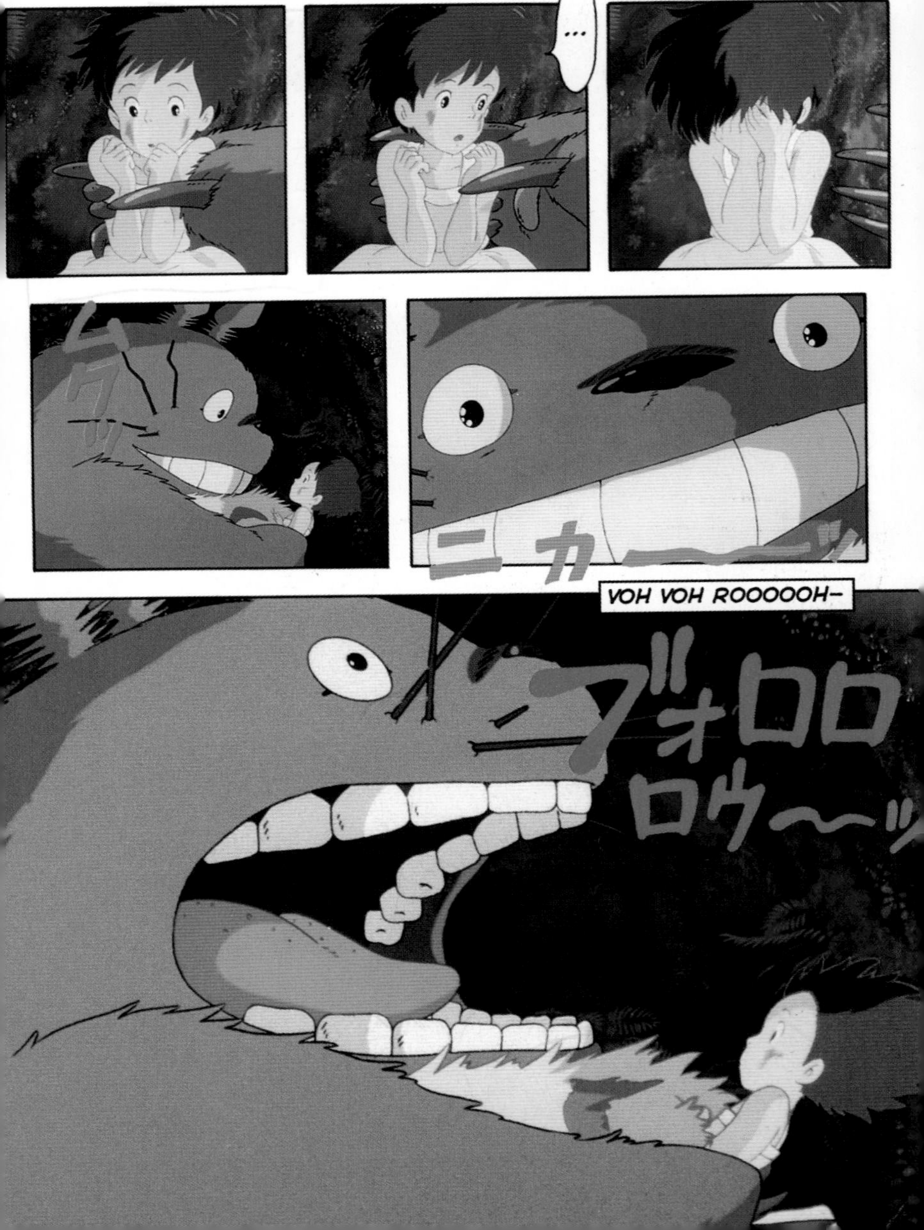
...
ニカーーッ
ムクッ
VOH VOH ROOOOOH-
ブォロロ
ロウ〜〜ッ

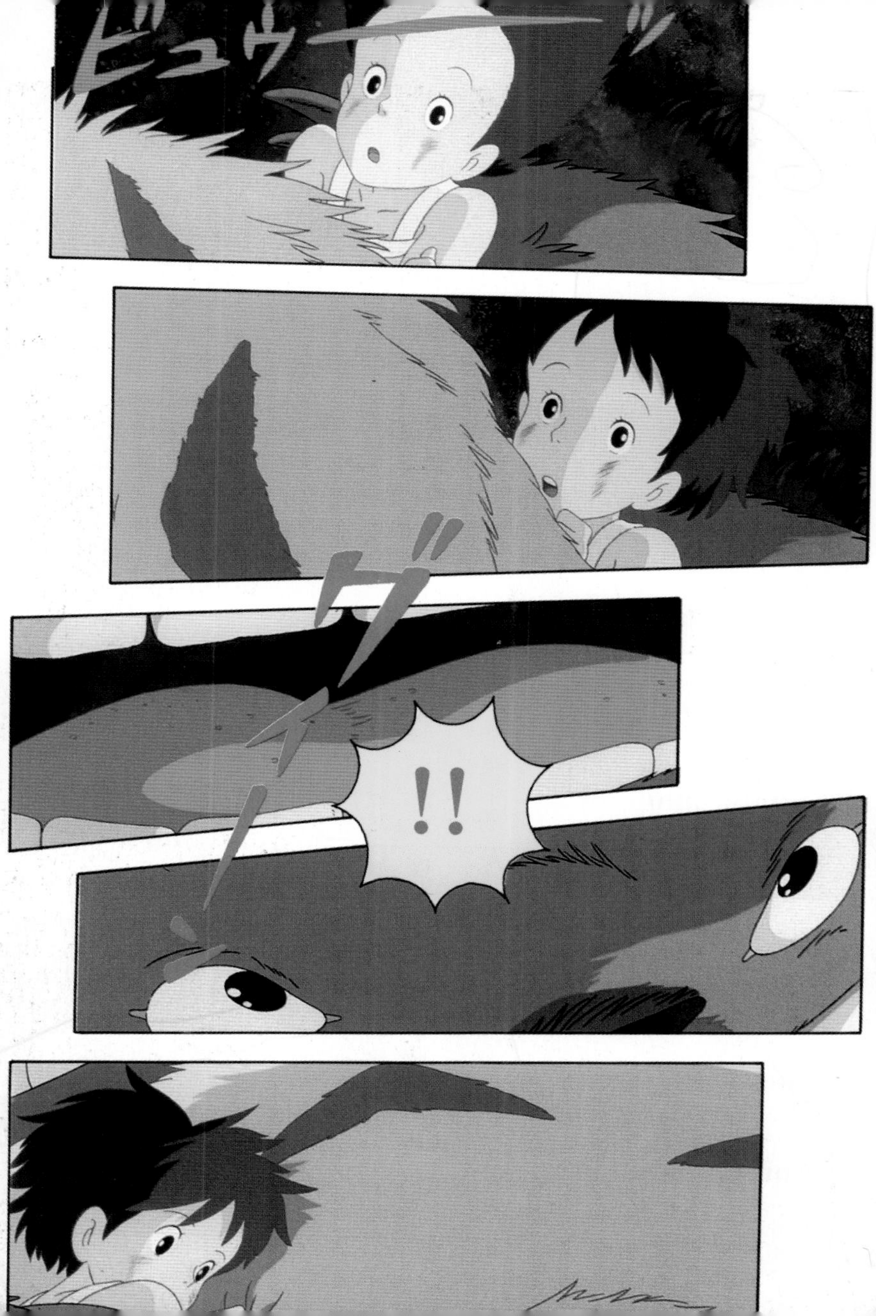
ビュウ
ヴォー
!!

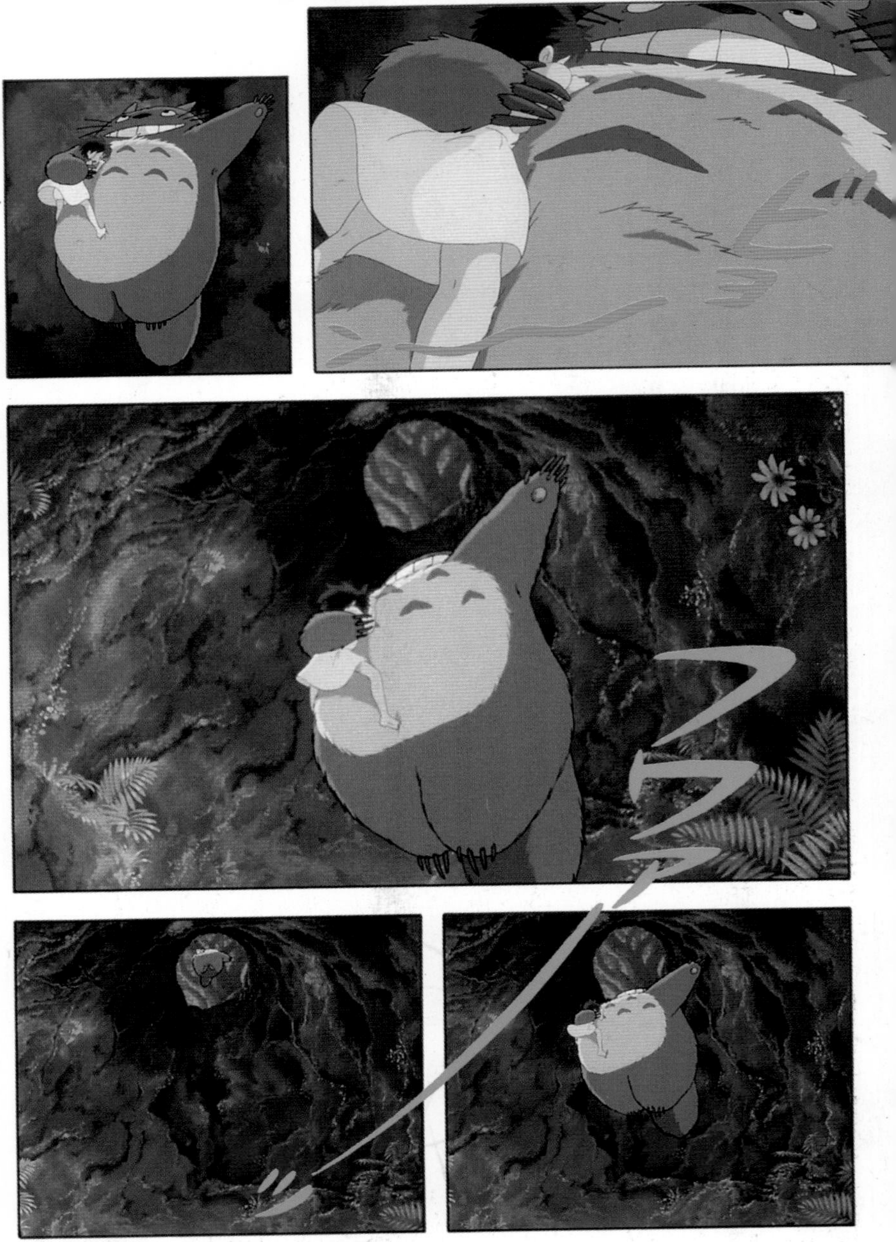
フワァッ

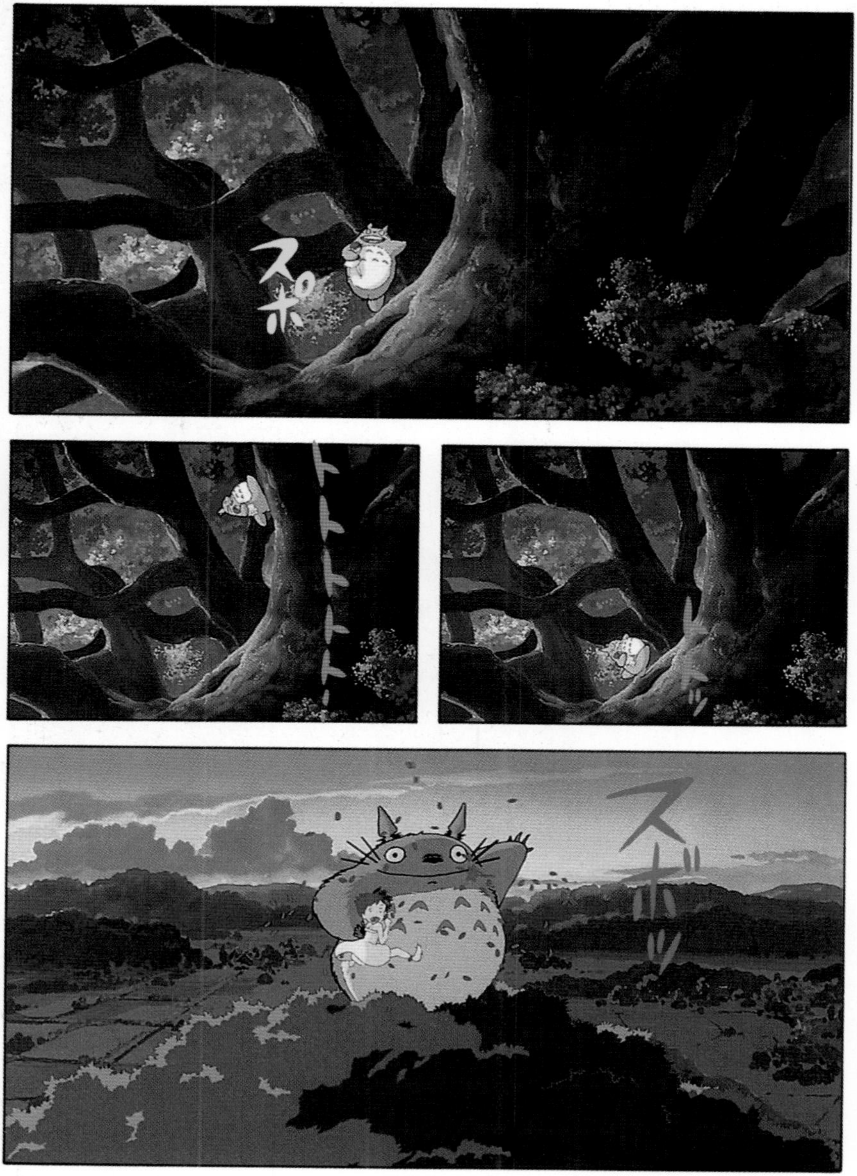
スポポ
トトッ
トトトトト
ズボッ

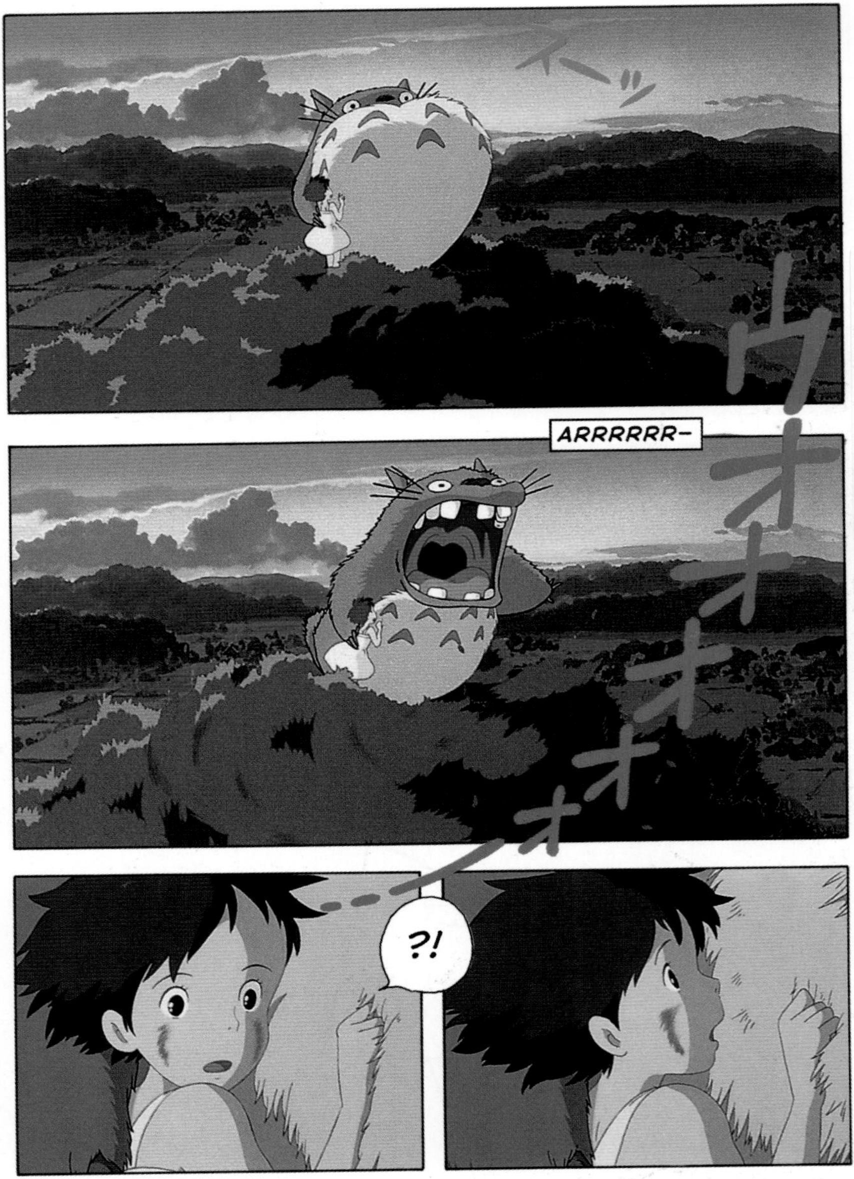
ARRRRRR–
?!

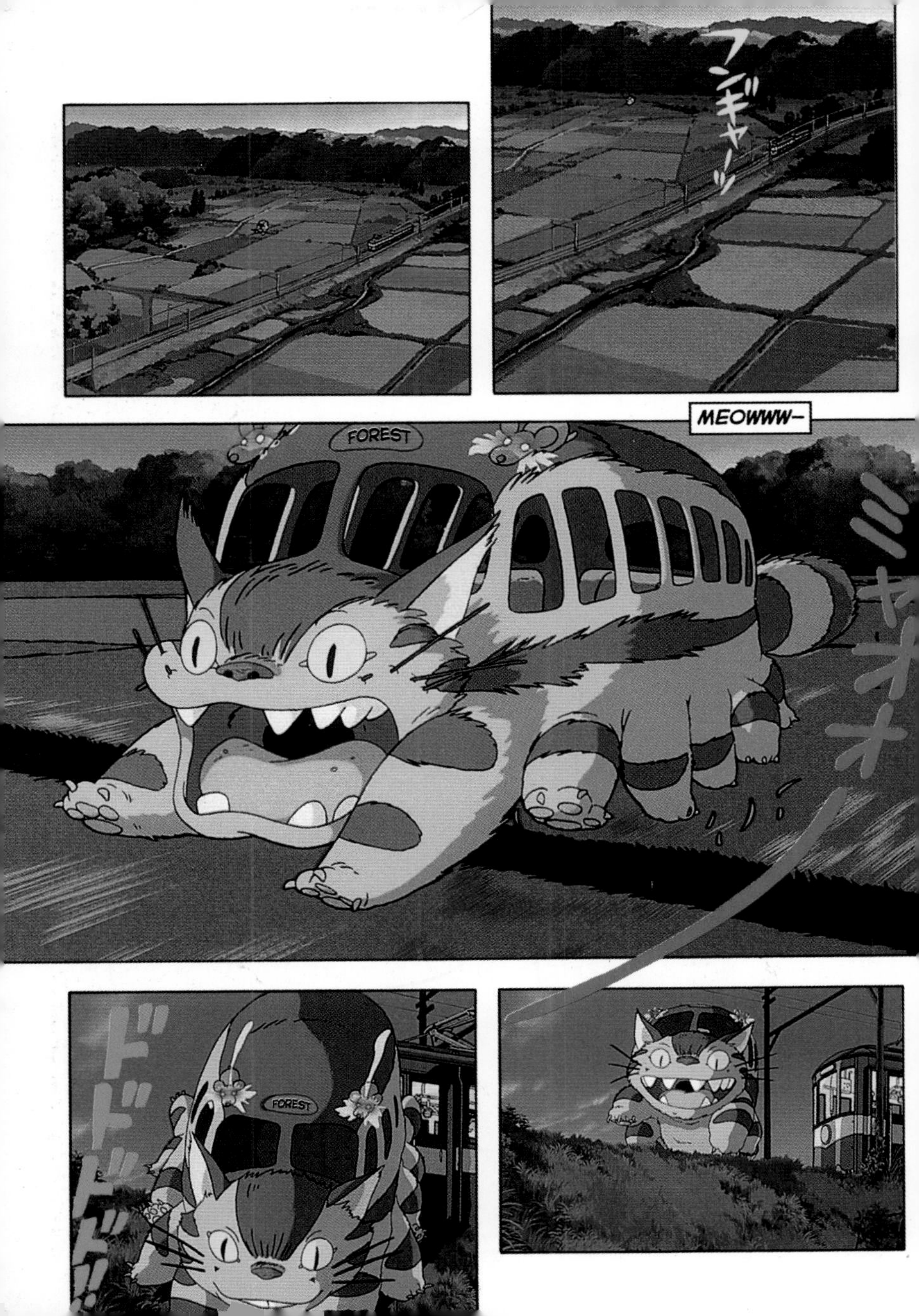
MEOWWW–
FOREST
FOREST

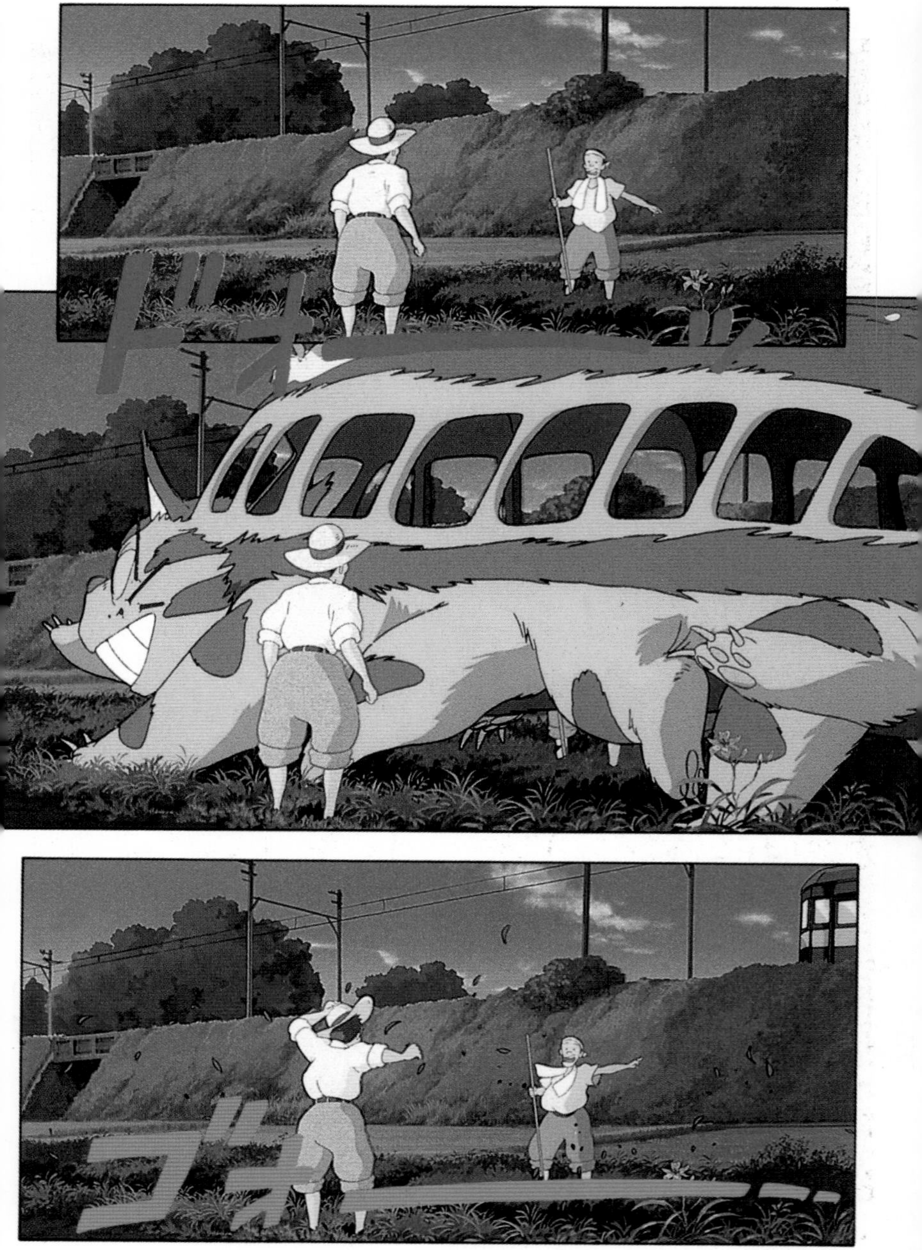
ドオーーッ
ゴオーー…

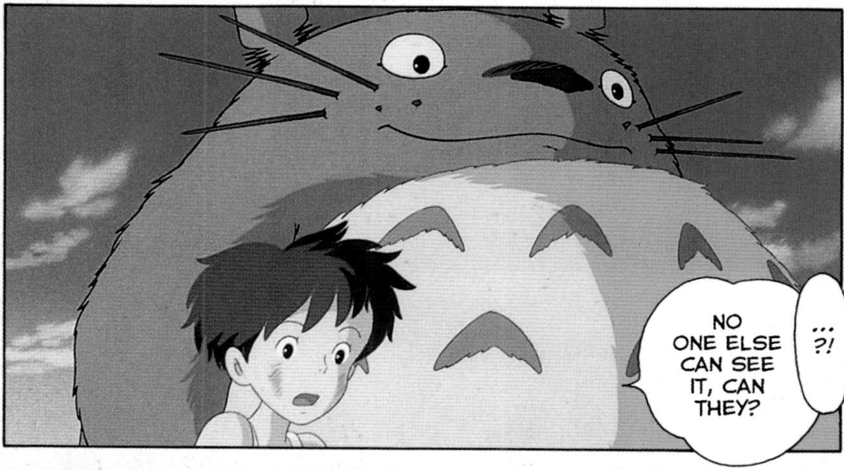
...?!
NO ONE ELSE CAN SEE IT, CAN THEY?
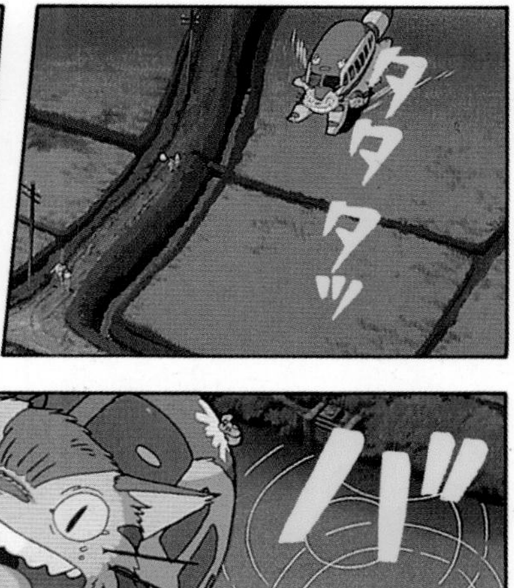
タタタッ
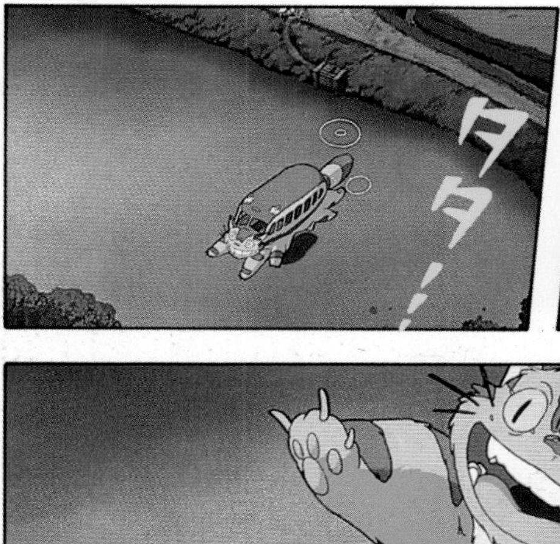
タタ!!
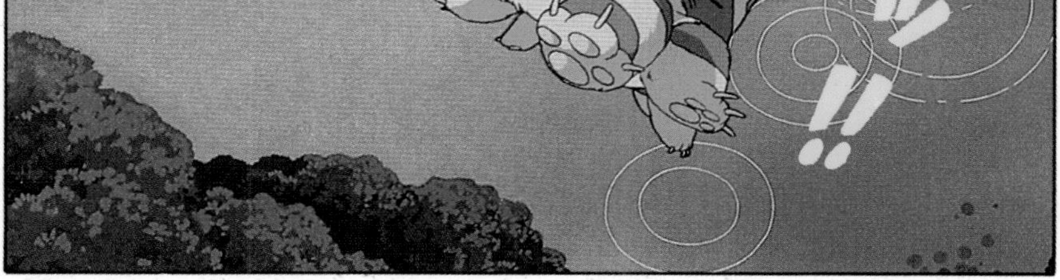
バッ!!

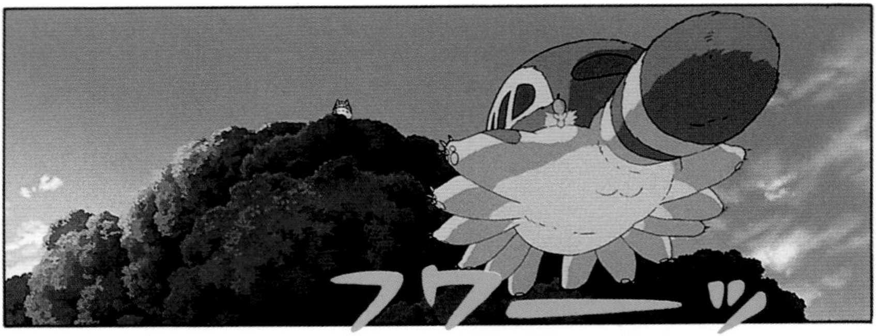
フワーーッ
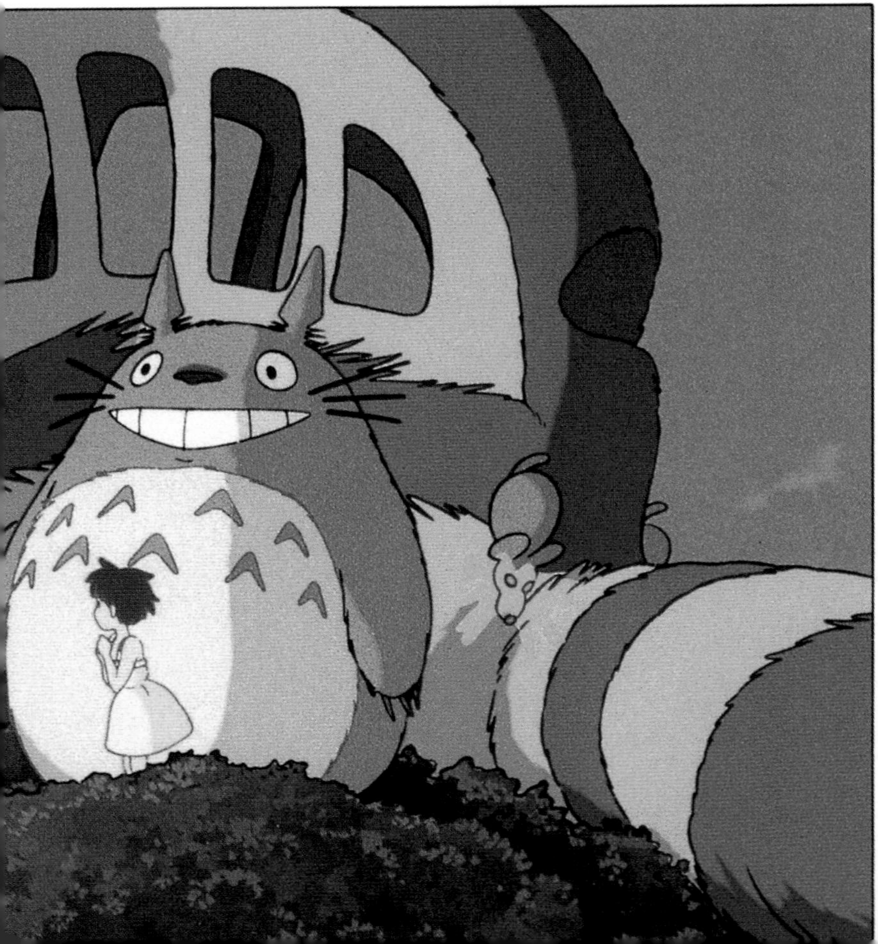

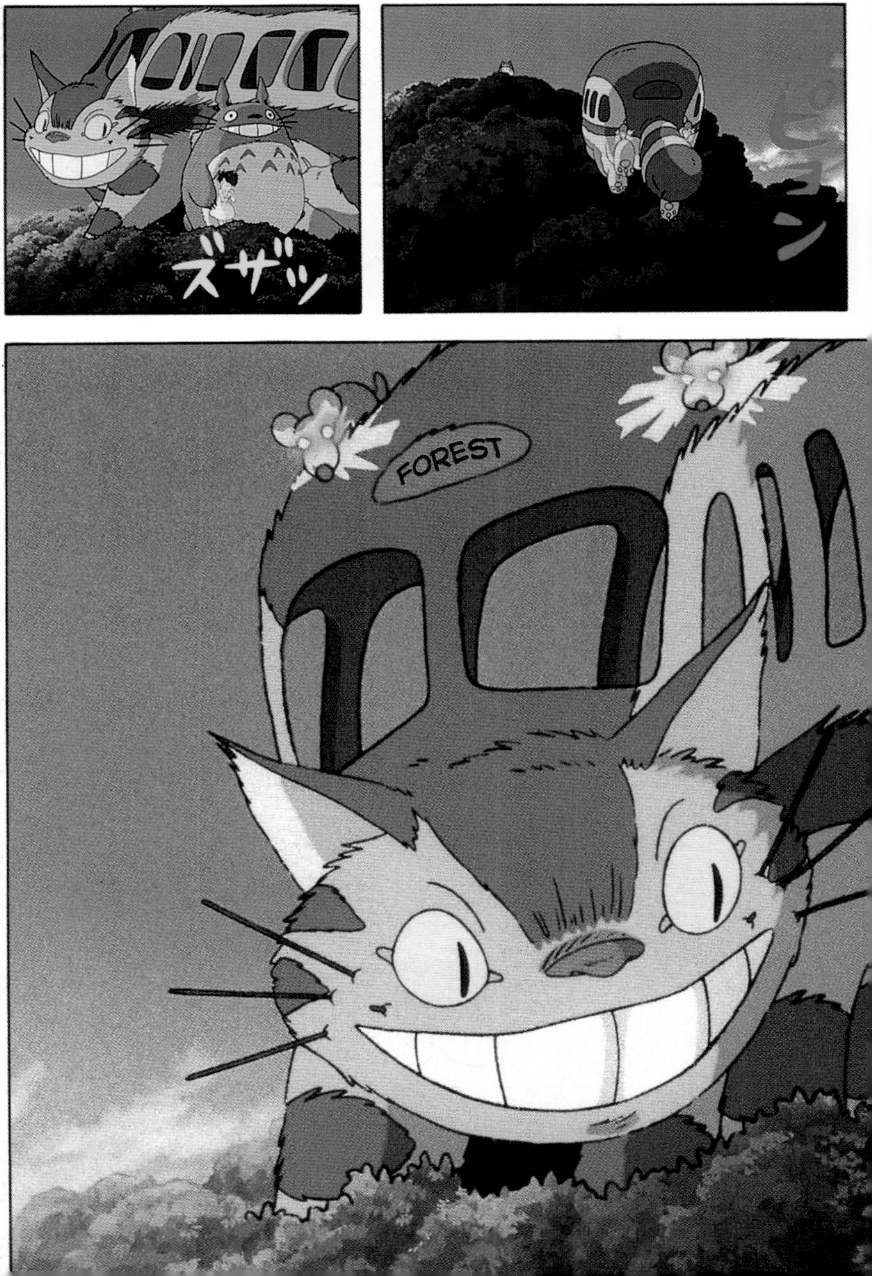
ピョン
ズザッ
FOREST

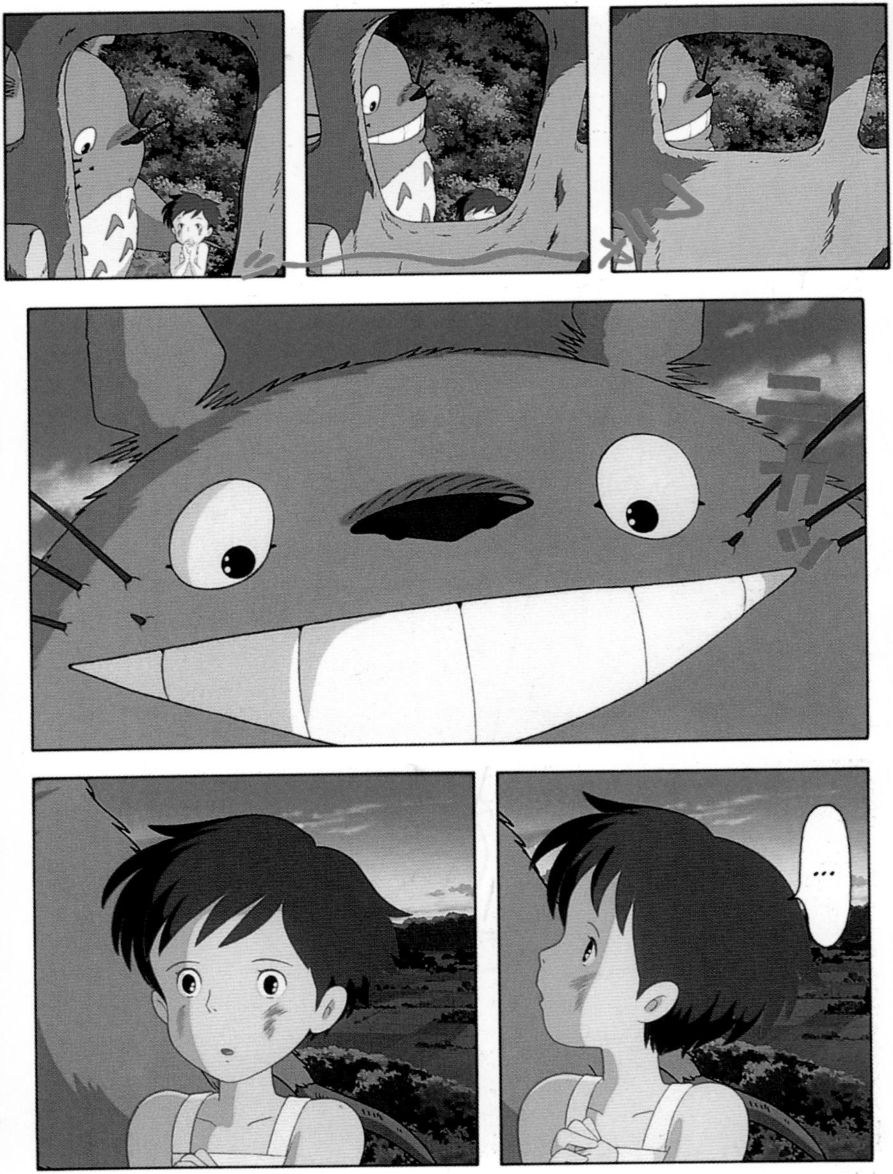
ニカッ
…

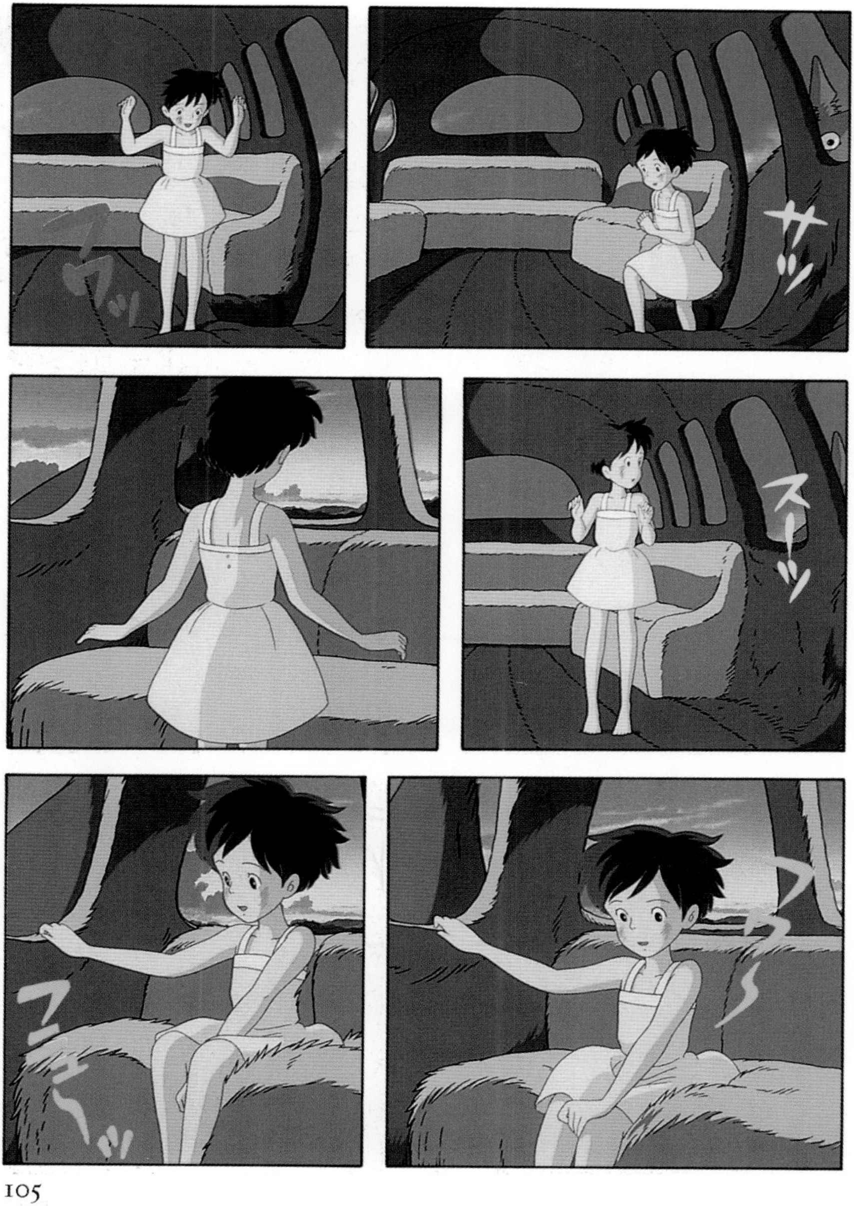
サッ
フワッ
スーッ
フワ〜
フニュ〜ッ

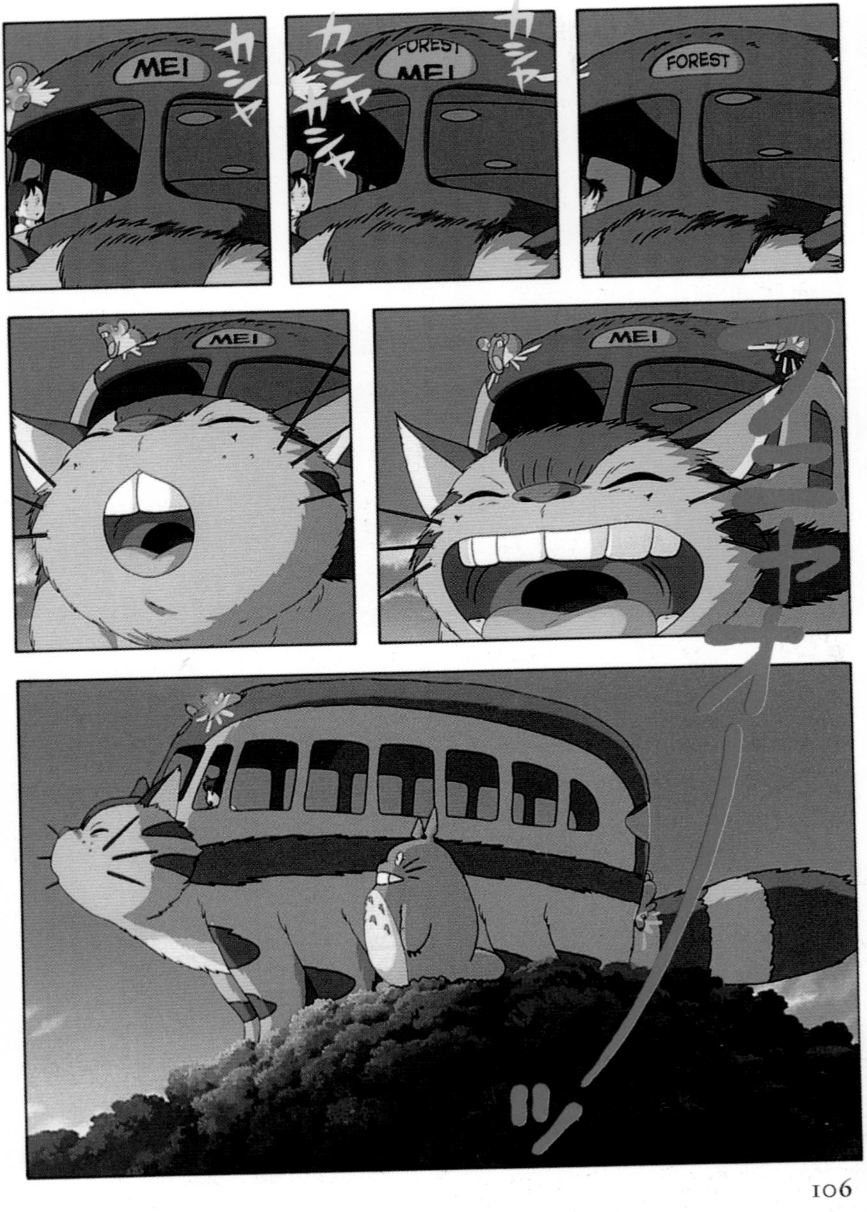
FOREST
カシャー
FOREST
MEI
カシャ
カシャ
カシャ
MEI
カシャ
MEI
フニャオーン
MEI

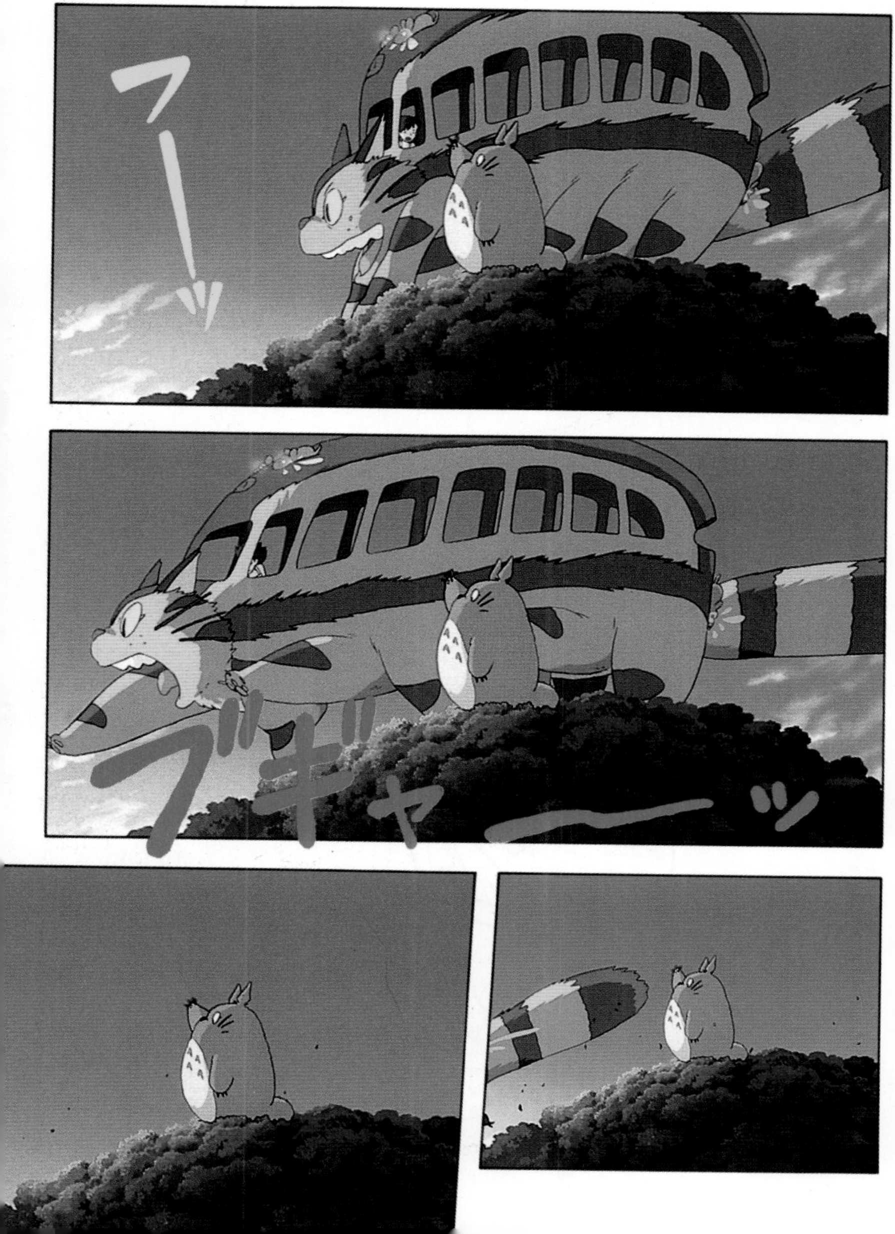
フーッ
ブギャーッ

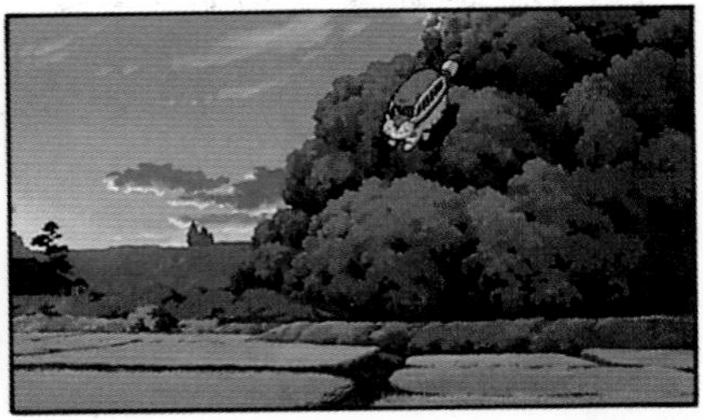

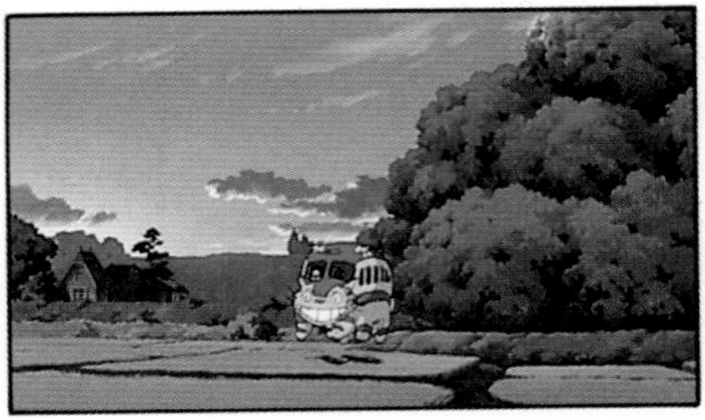

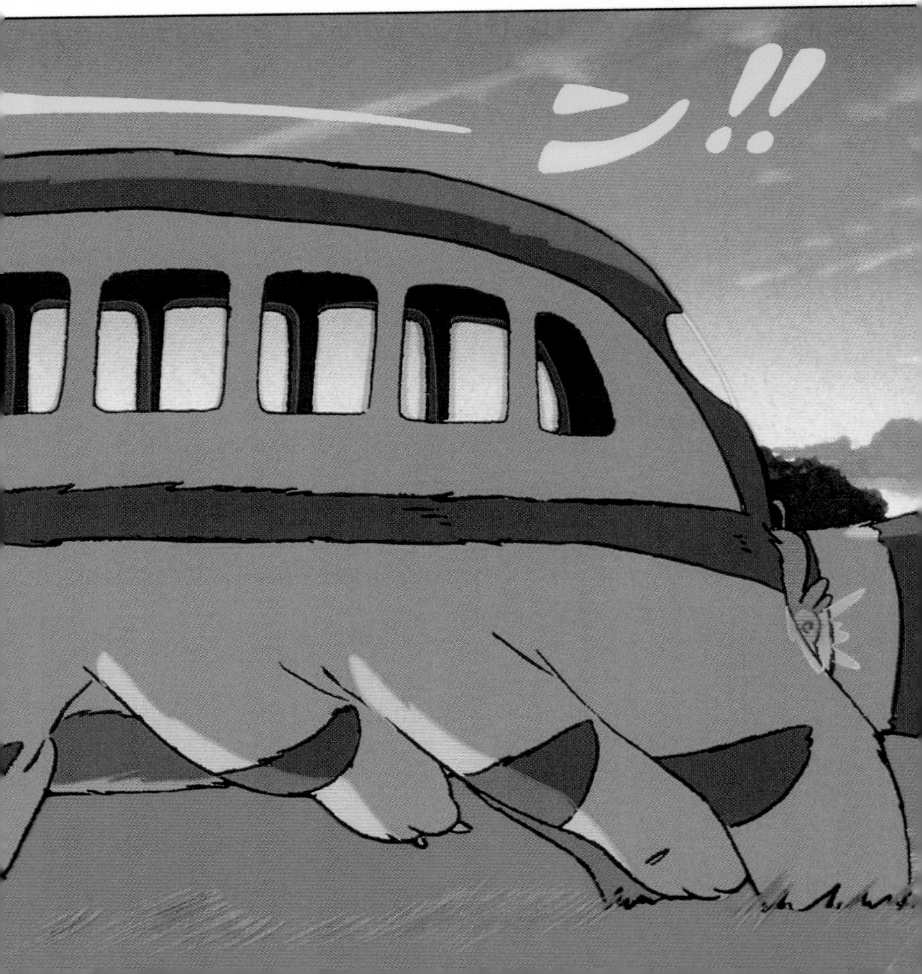
ーン!!

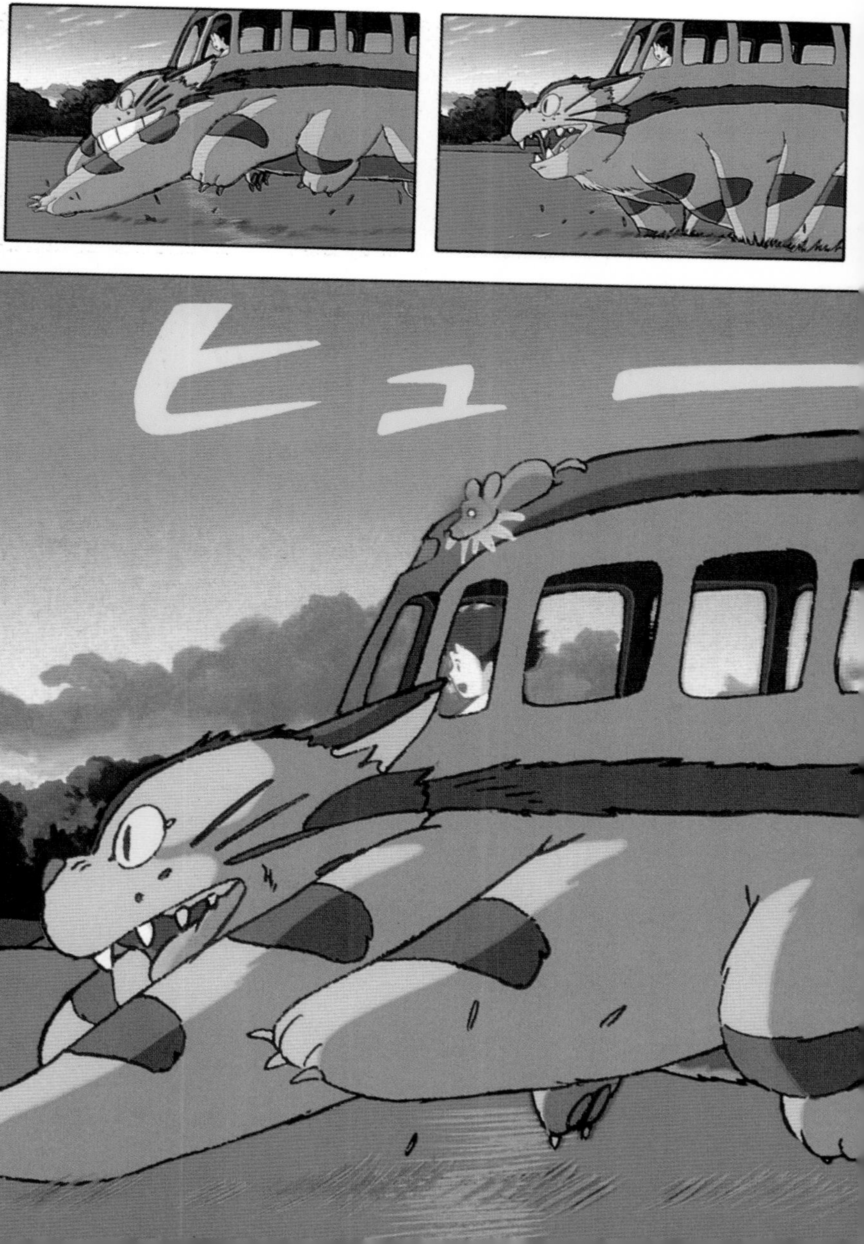
ヒュー

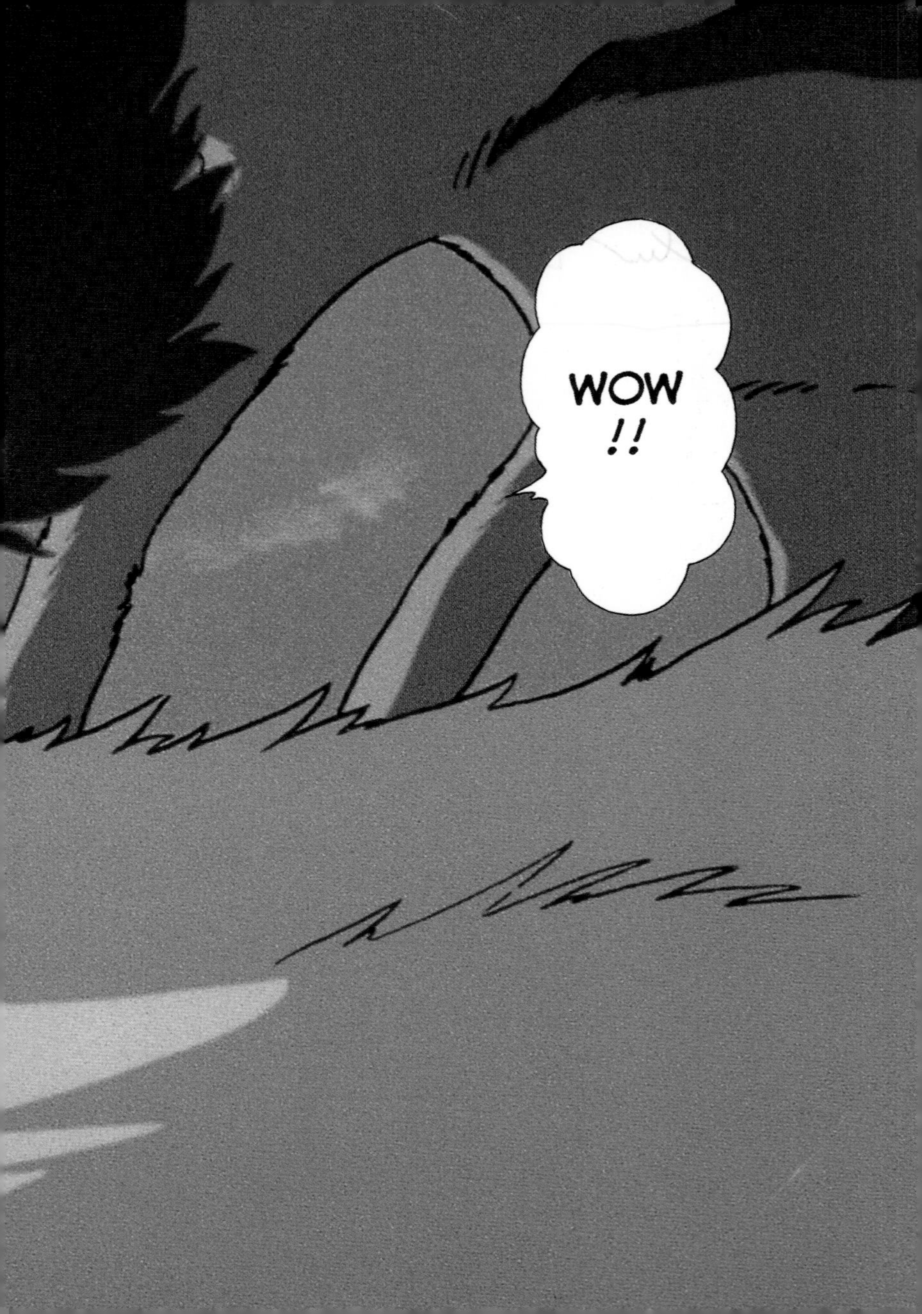
WOW !!

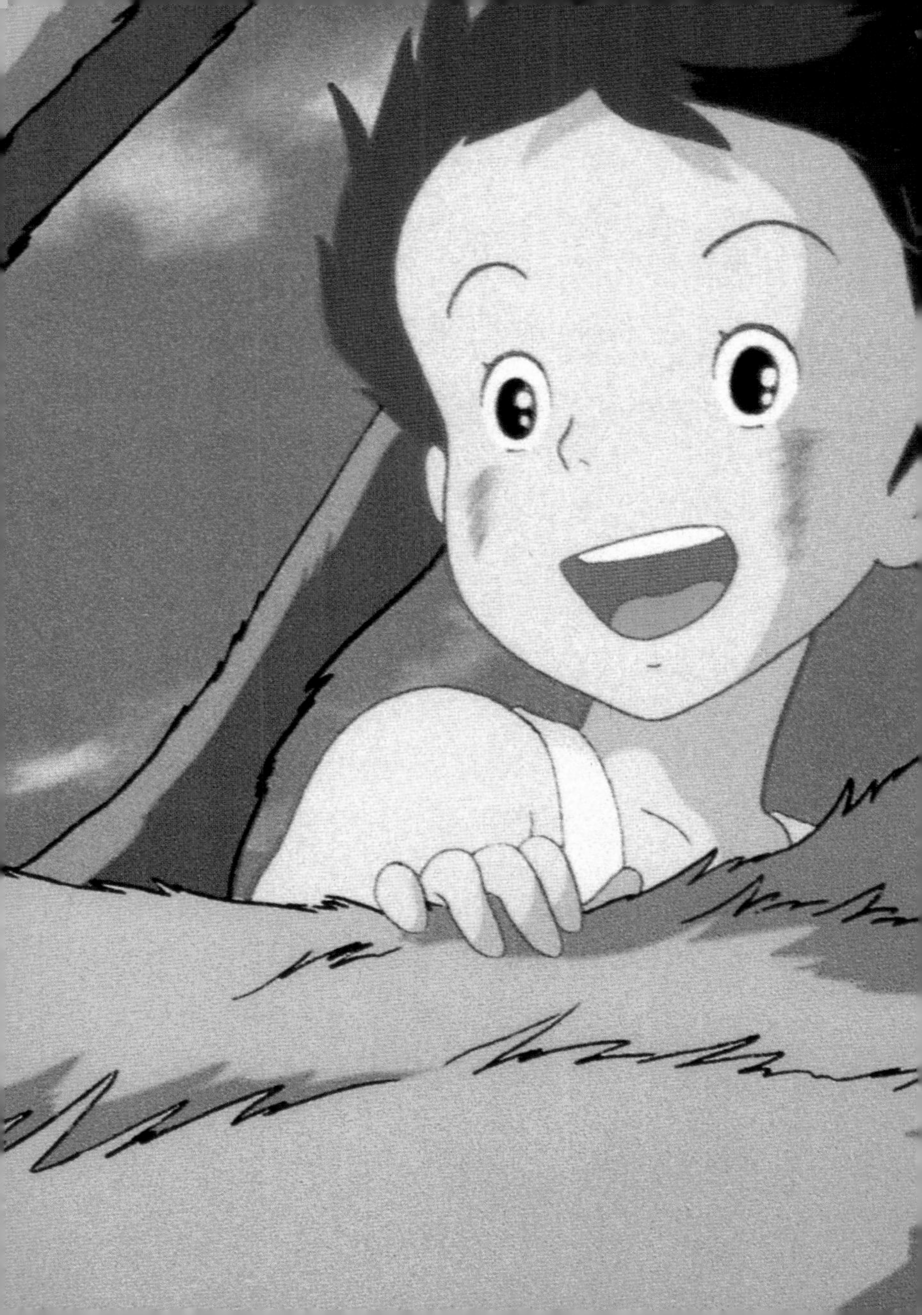

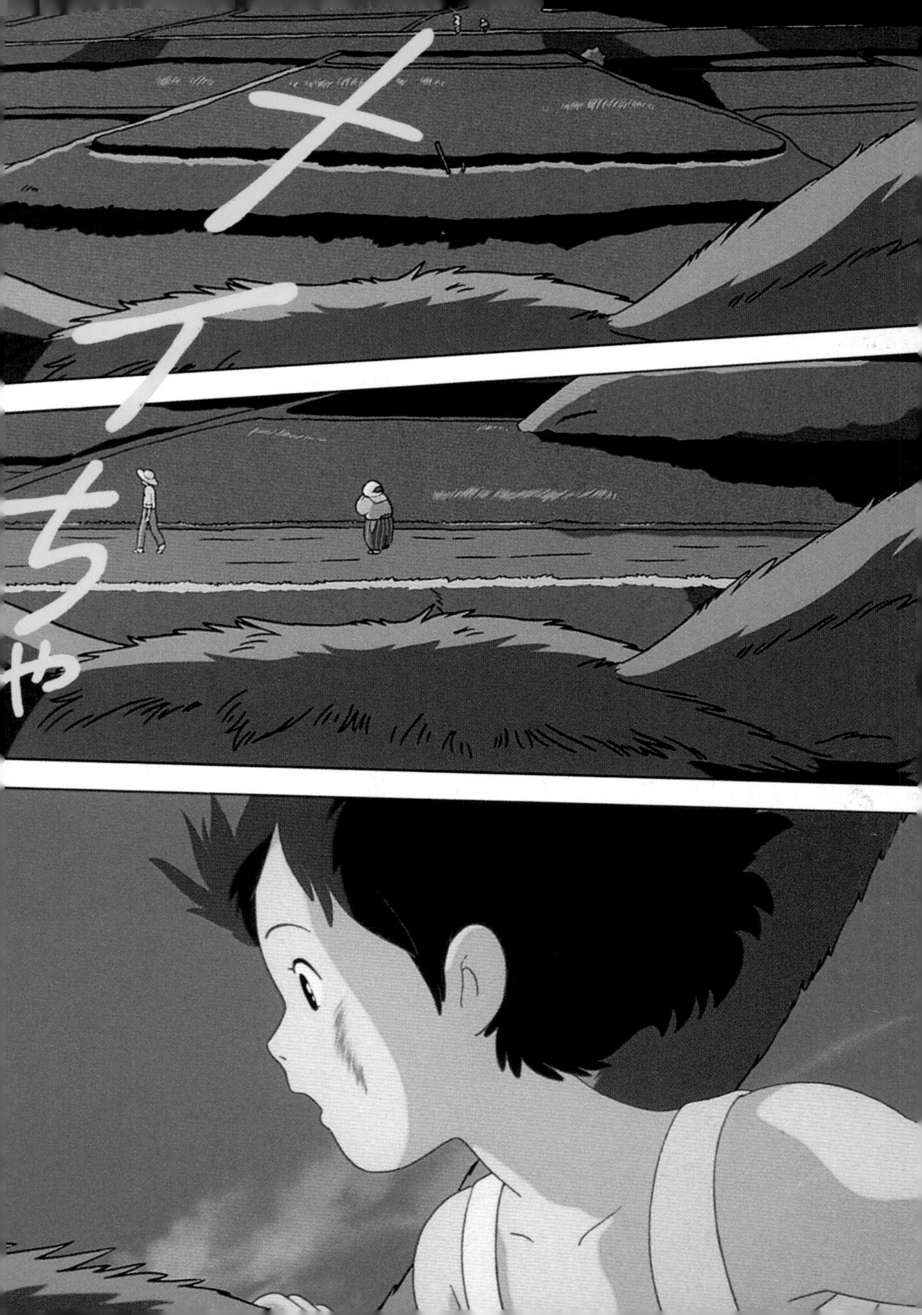
ナイちゃ

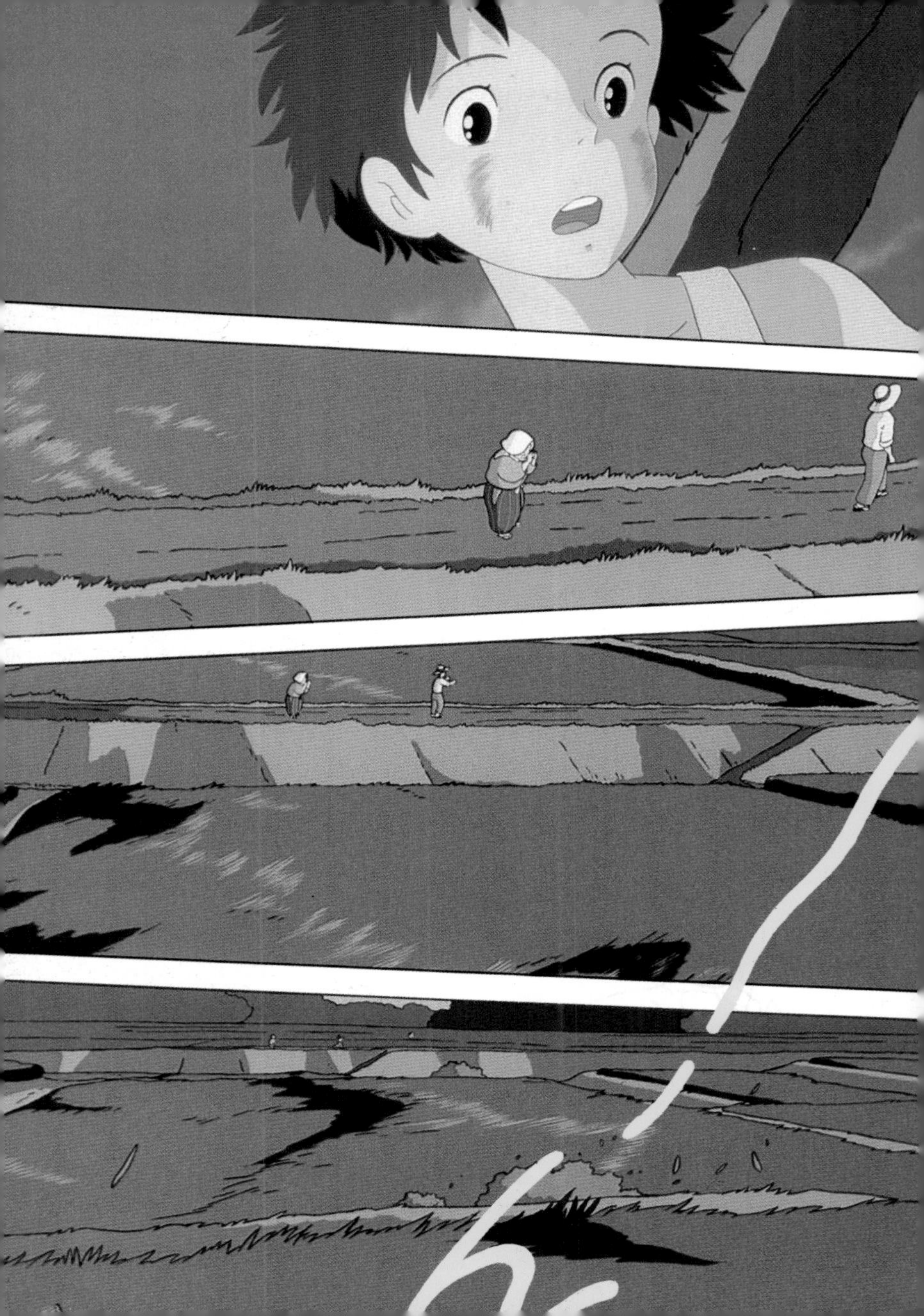

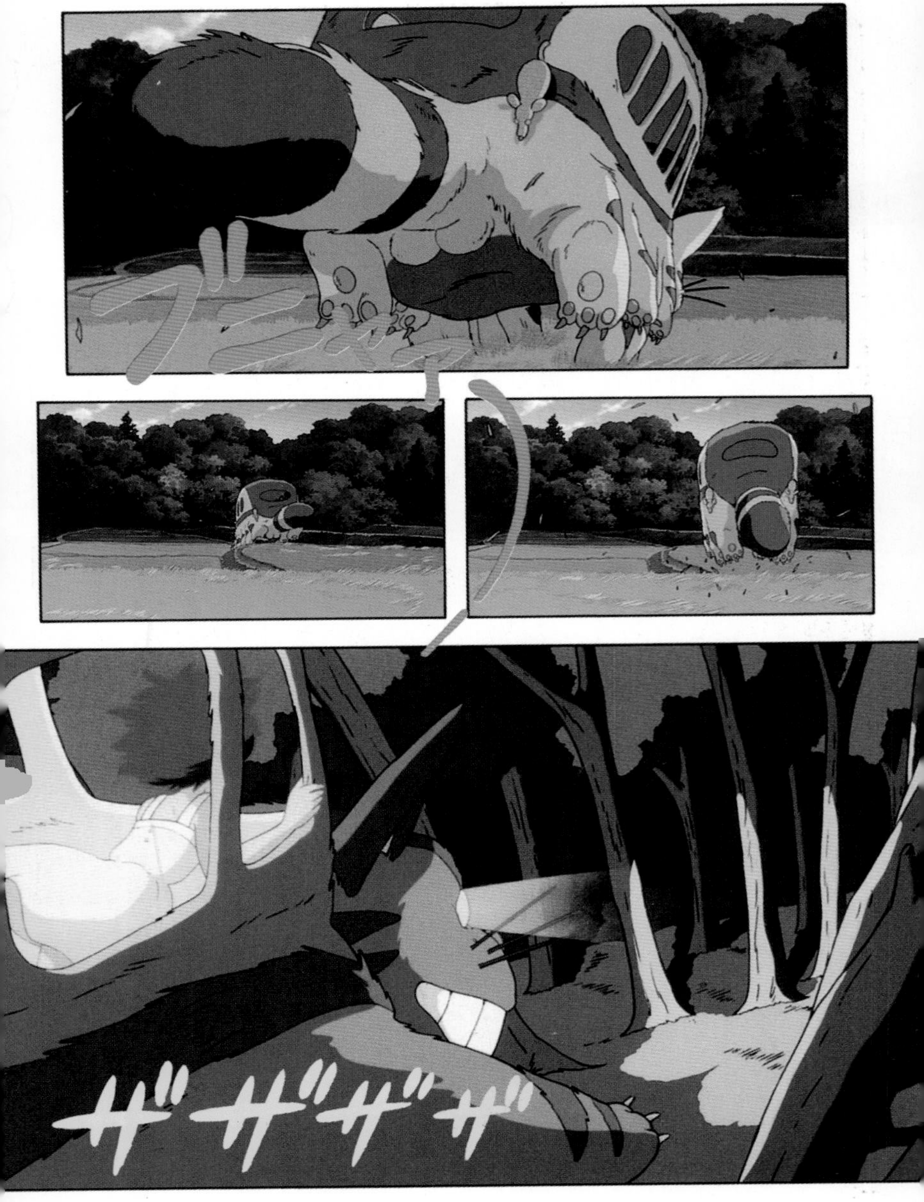
ブニャァー
ザザザザ

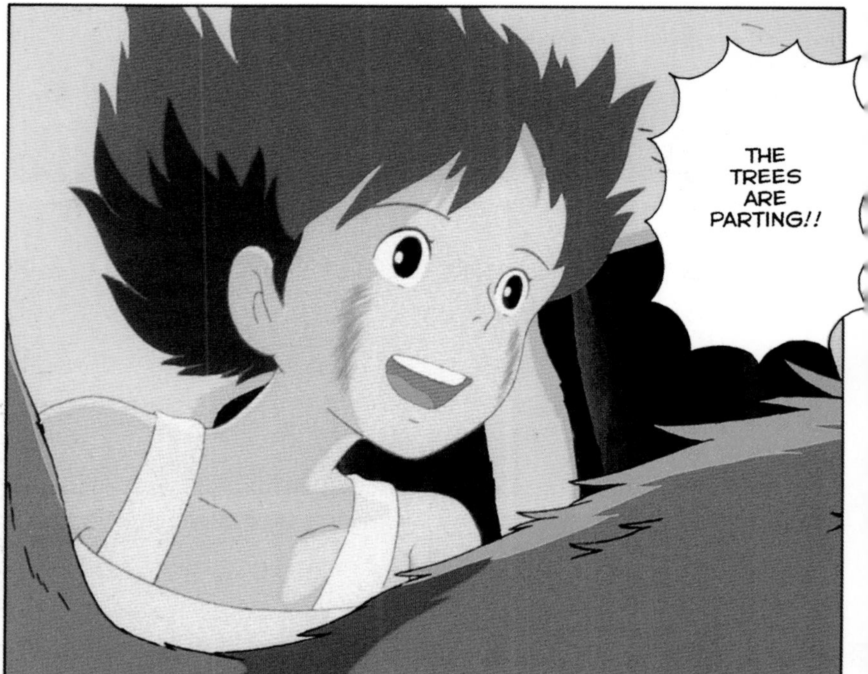
THE TREES ARE PARTING!!

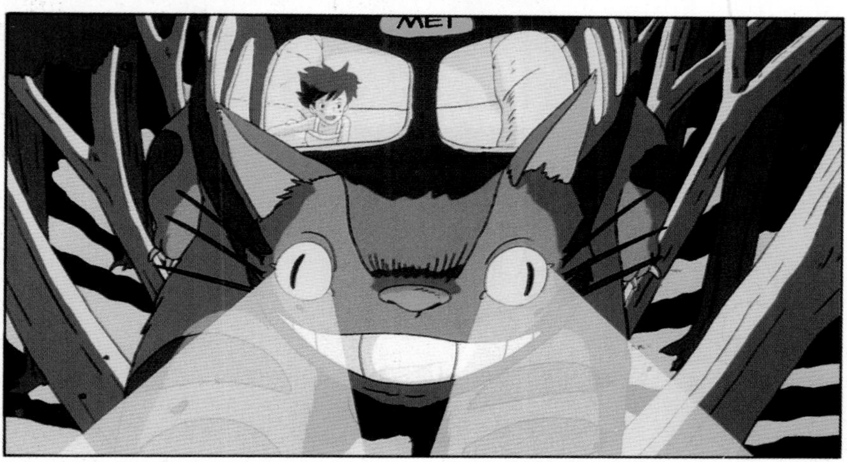

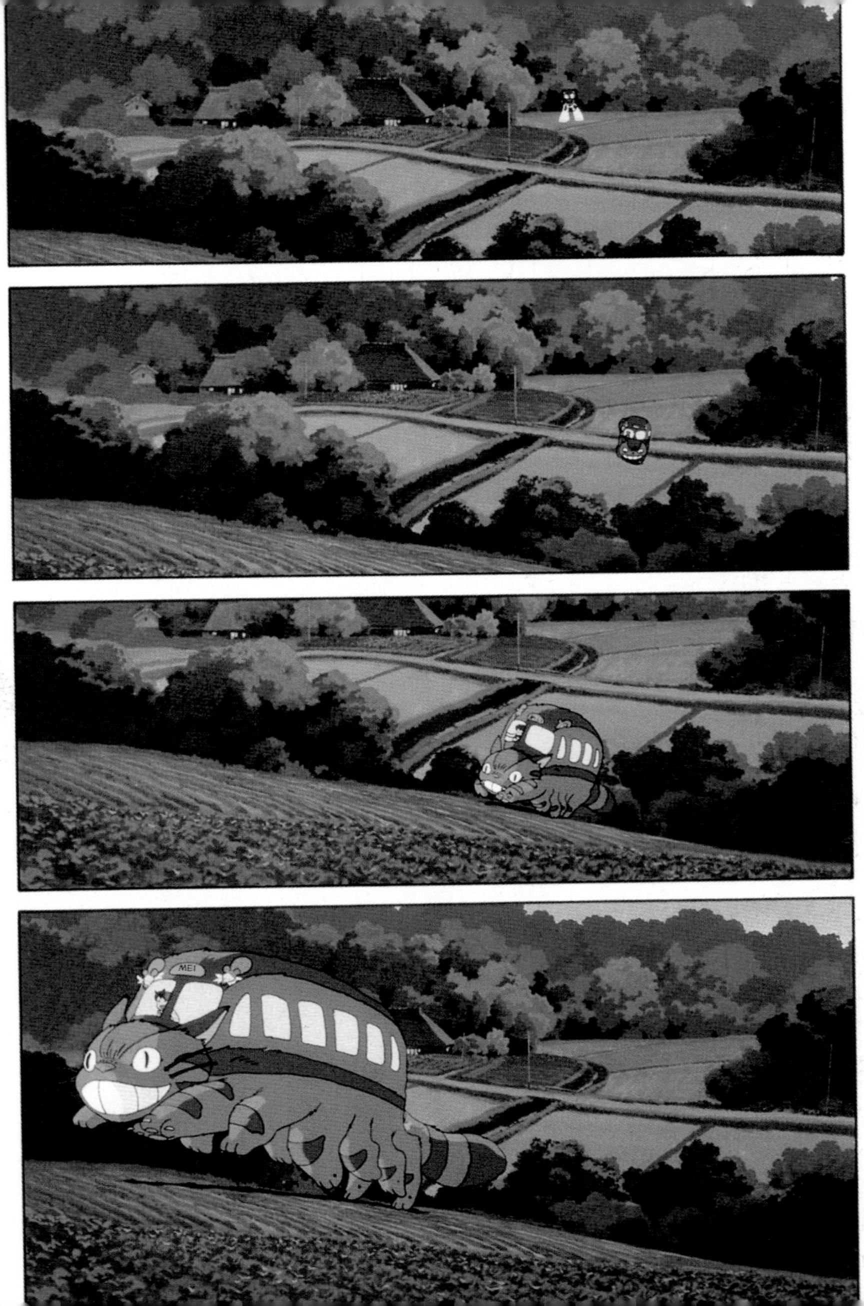
MEI

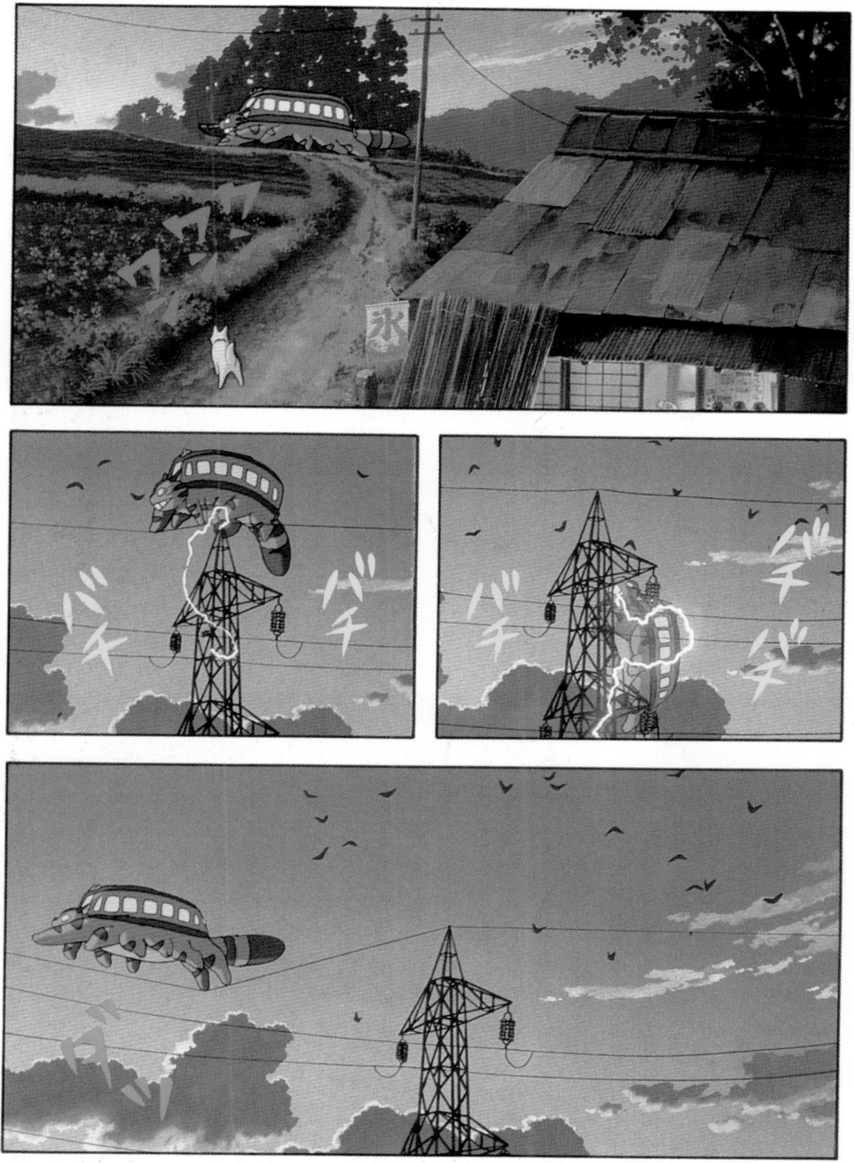
バチ
バチ
バチ
バチ
バチ

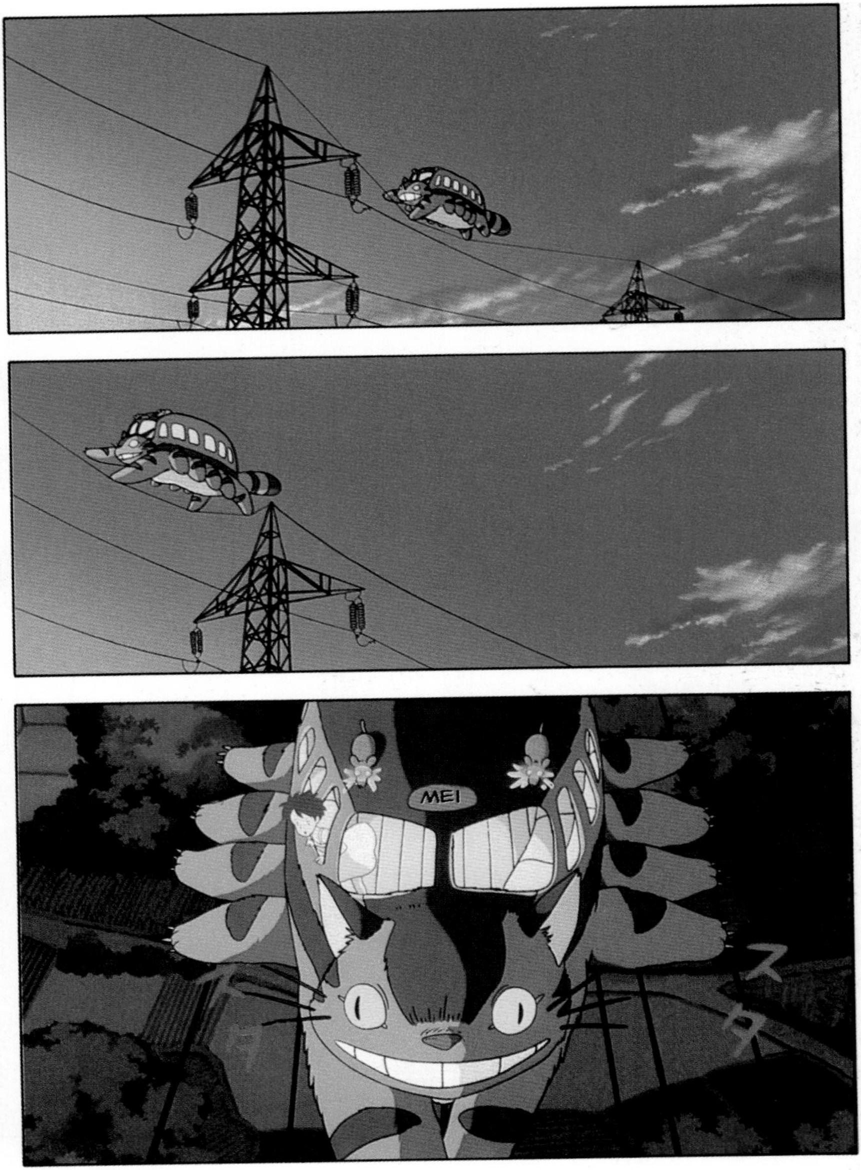
MEI
スタ

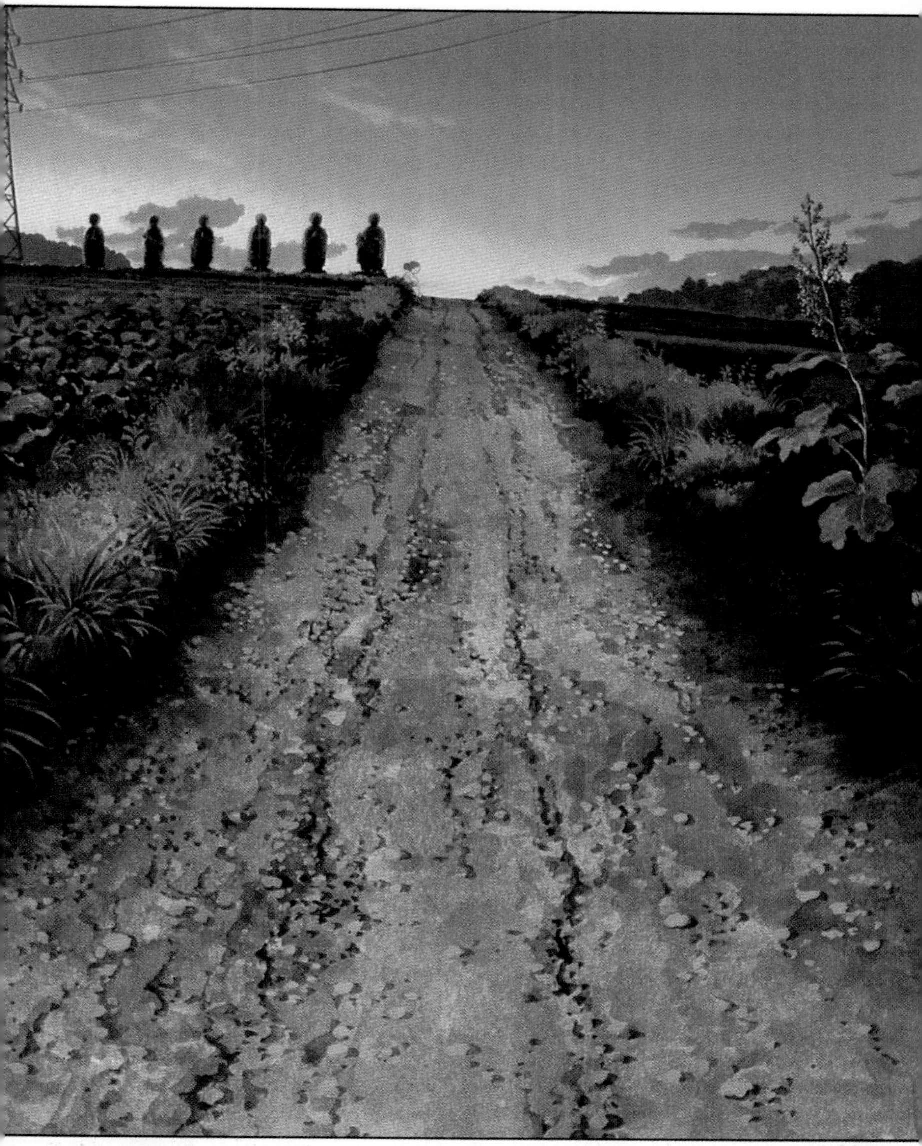

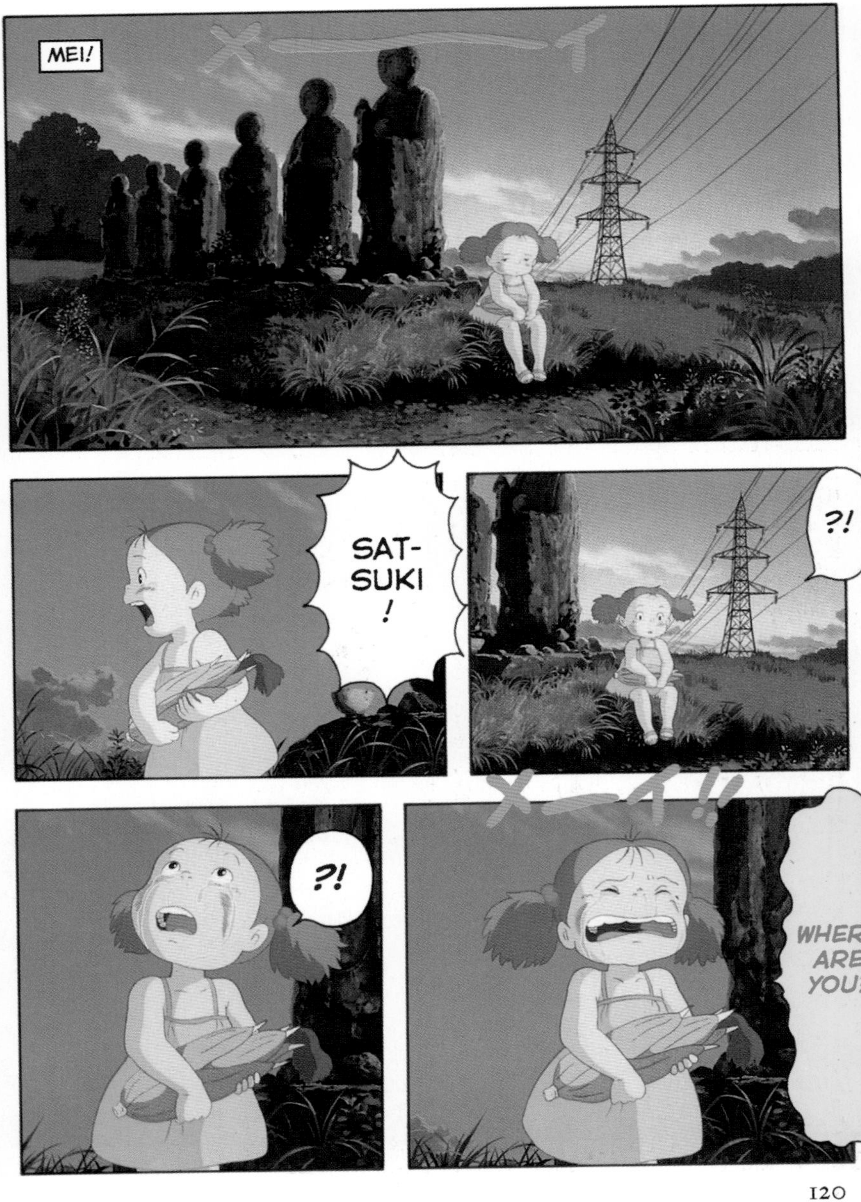
MEI!
?!
SAT-SUKI!
メーイ!!
WHERE ARE YOU?
?!

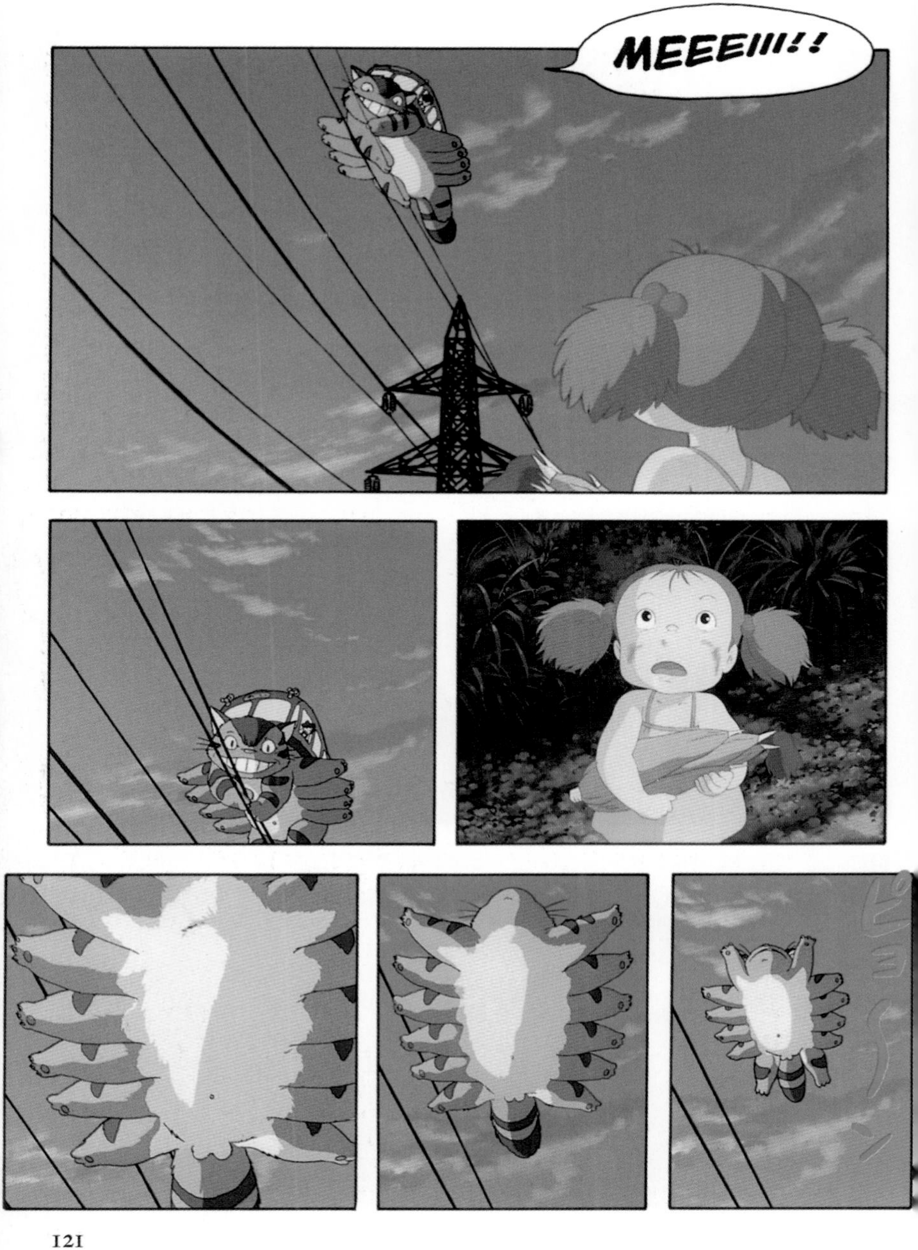
MEEEIII!!

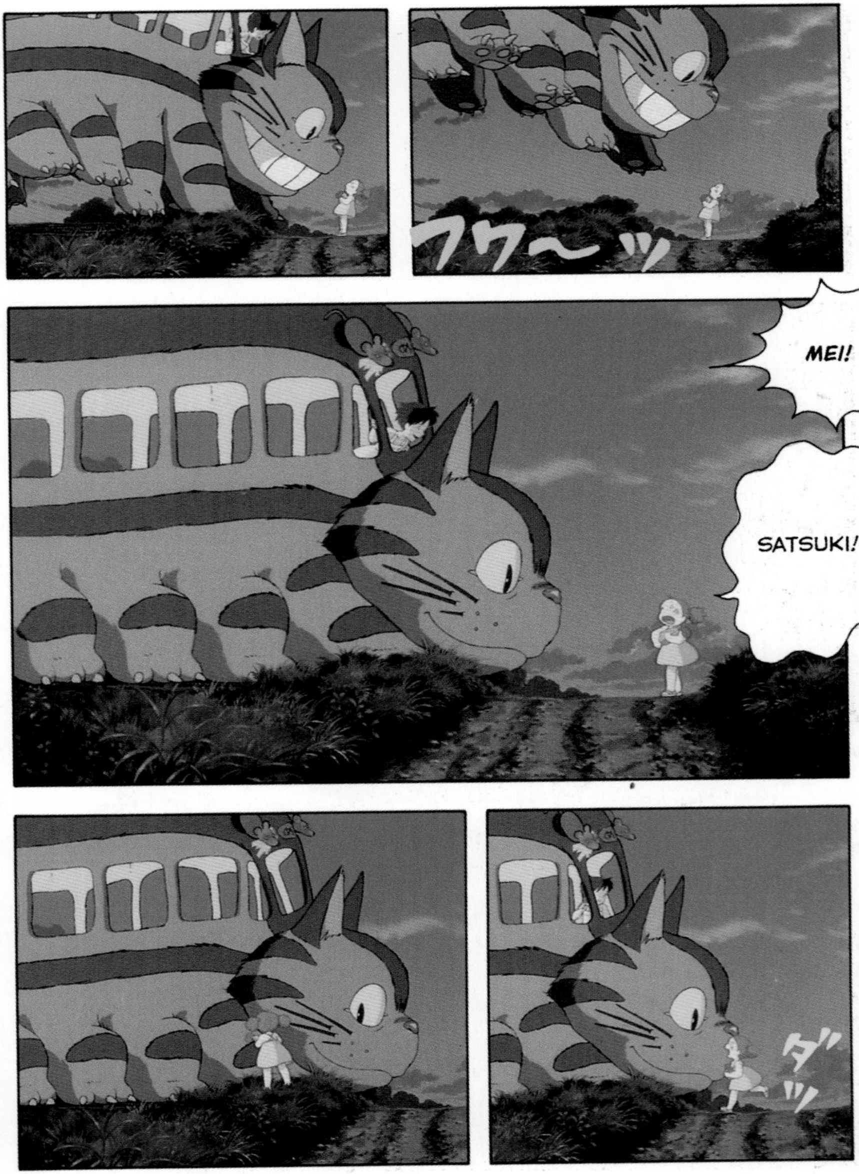
フワ〜ッ
MEI!
SATSUKI!
ダッ

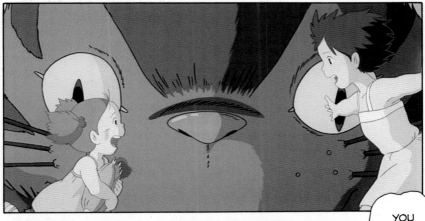

YOU DUMMY.

I'M SORRY.

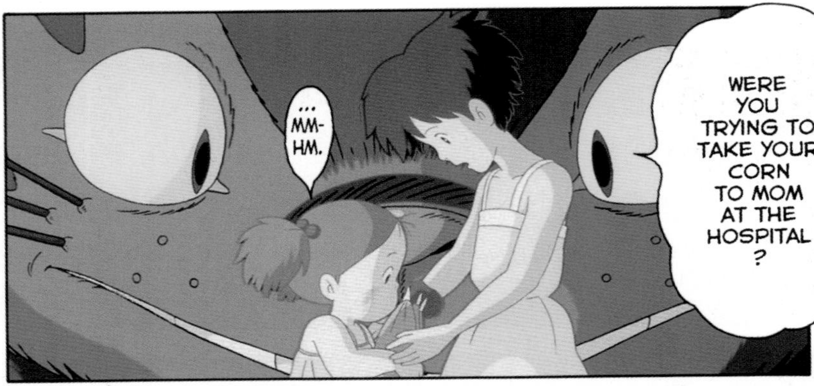
WERE YOU TRYING TO TAKE YOUR CORN TO MOM AT THE HOSPITAL?
...MM-HM.
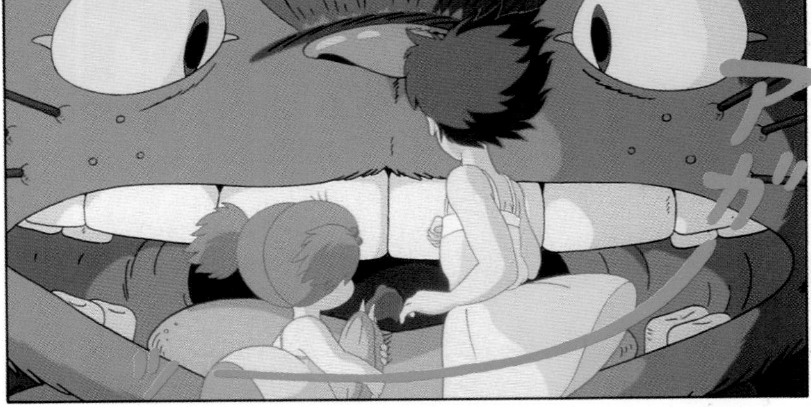
アガ
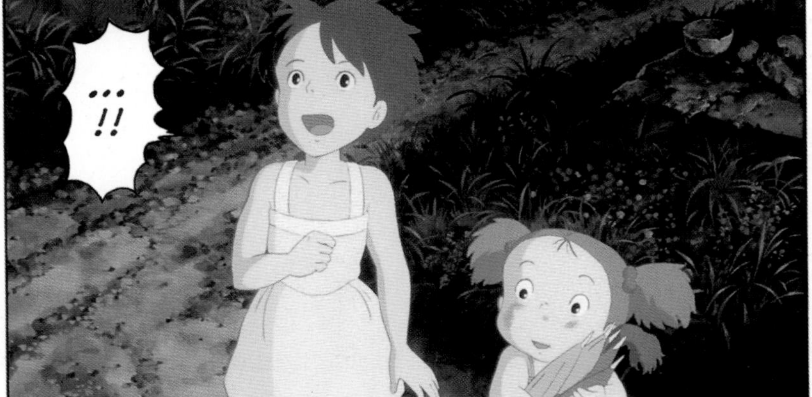
...!!

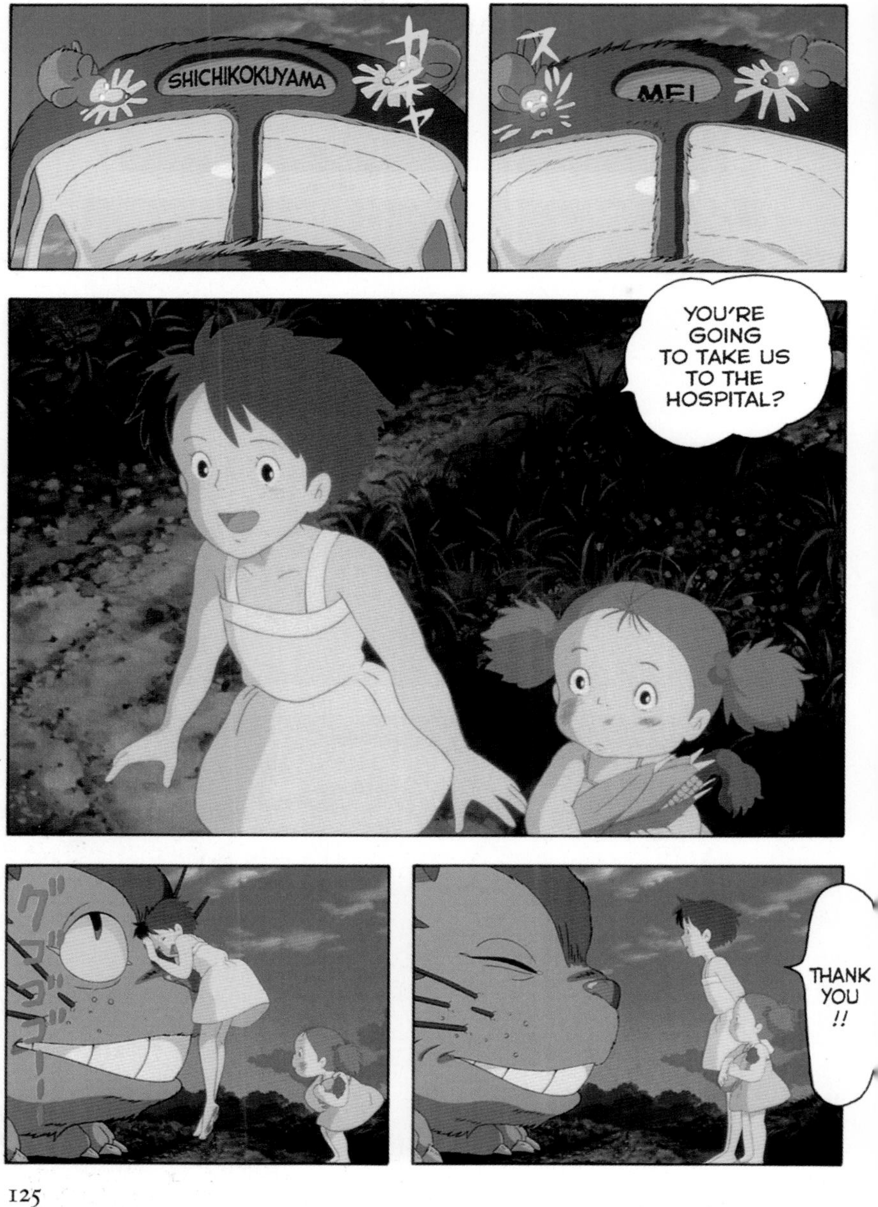
MEI
SHICHIKOKUYAMA
カチャ
YOU'RE GOING TO TAKE US TO THE HOSPITAL?
THANK YOU !!

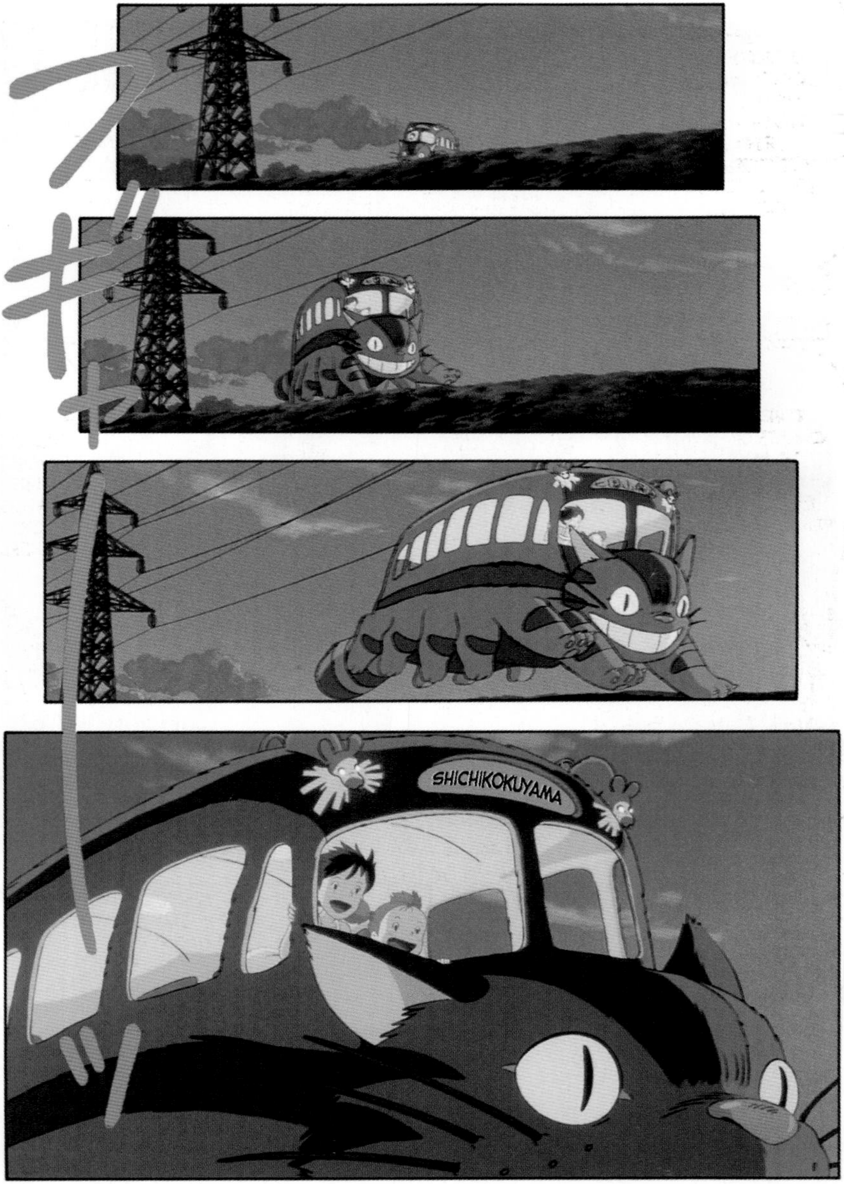
ブギャーッ
SHICHIKOKUYAMA

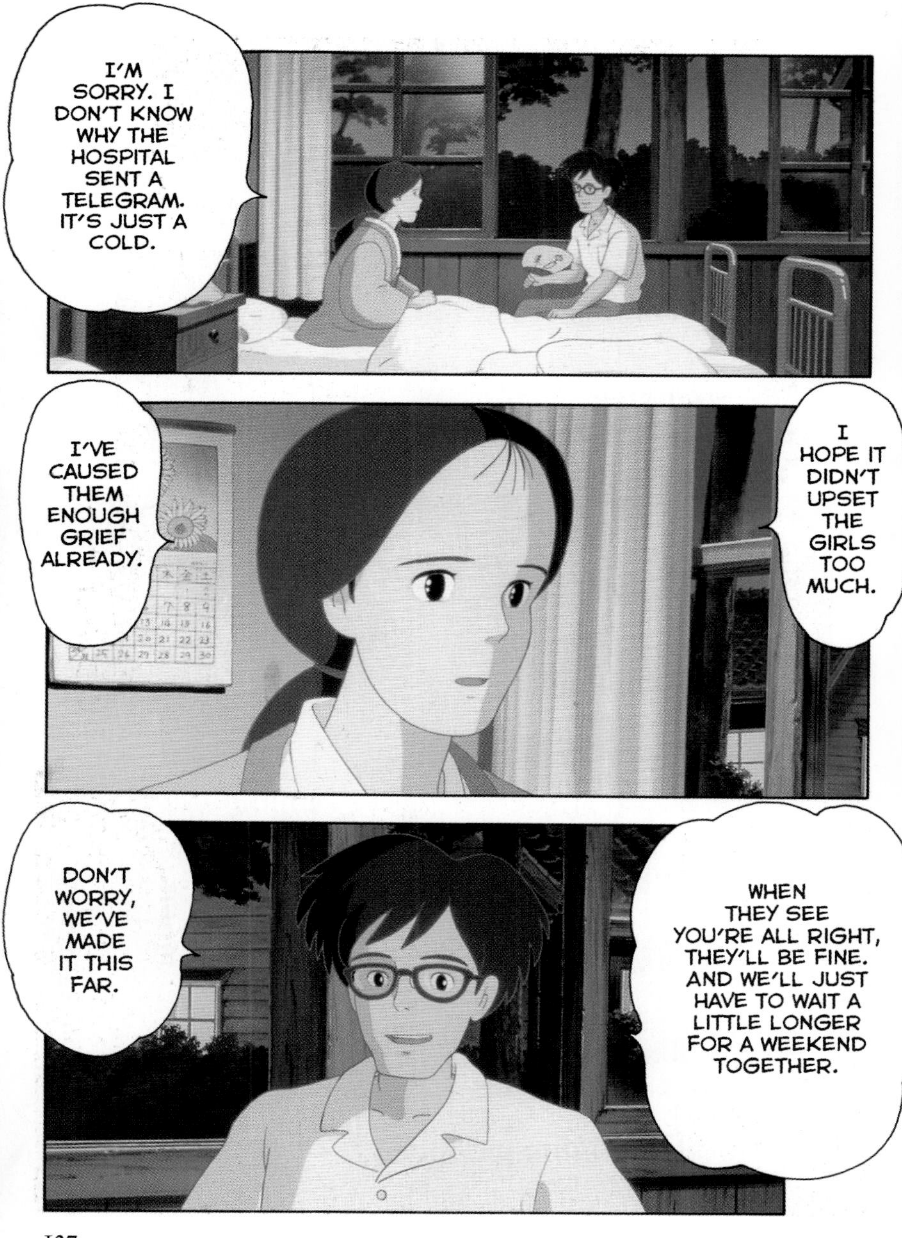
I'M SORRY. I DON'T KNOW WHY THE HOSPITAL SENT A TELEGRAM. IT'S JUST A COLD.
I HOPE IT DIDN'T UPSET THE GIRLS TOO MUCH.
I'VE CAUSED THEM ENOUGH GRIEF ALREADY.
WHEN THEY SEE YOU'RE ALL RIGHT, THEY'LL BE FINE. AND WE'LL JUST HAVE TO WAIT A LITTLE LONGER FOR A WEEKEND TOGETHER.
DON'T WORRY, WE'VE MADE IT THIS FAR.

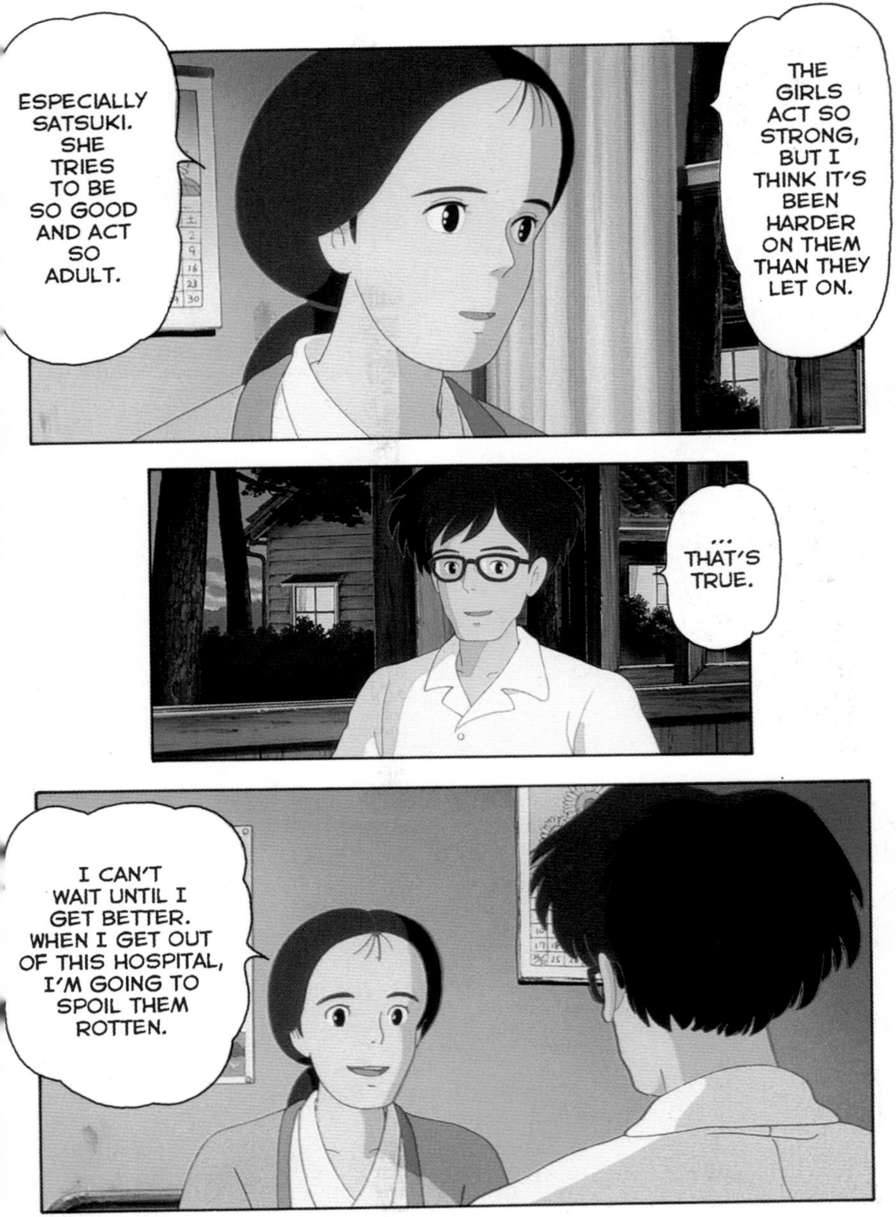
THE GIRLS ACT SO STRONG, BUT I THINK IT'S BEEN HARDER ON THEM THAN THEY LET ON.
ESPECIALLY SATSUKI. SHE TRIES TO BE SO GOOD AND ACT SO ADULT.
... THAT'S TRUE.
I CAN'T WAIT UNTIL I GET BETTER. WHEN I GET OUT OF THIS HOSPITAL, I'M GOING TO SPOIL THEM ROTTEN.

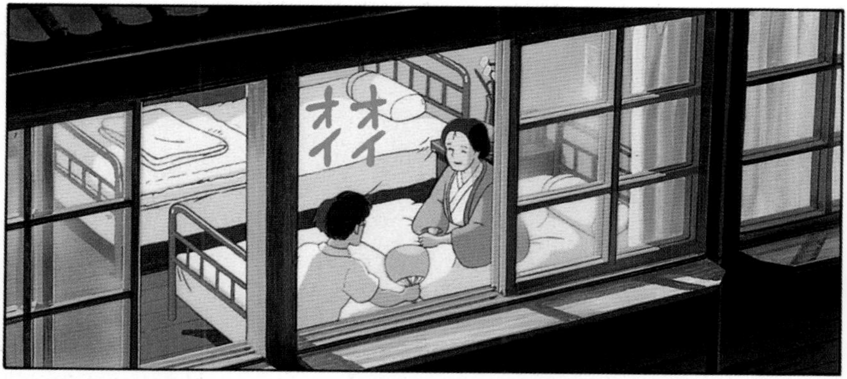
オイオイ

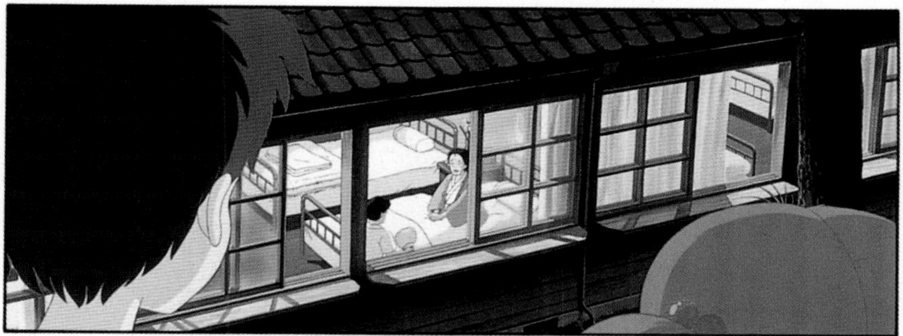

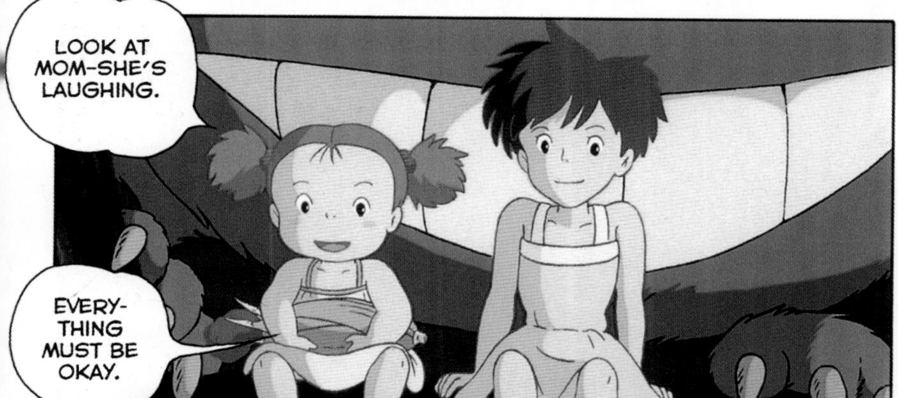
LOOK AT MOM–SHE'S LAUGHING.
EVERY-THING MUST BE OKAY.

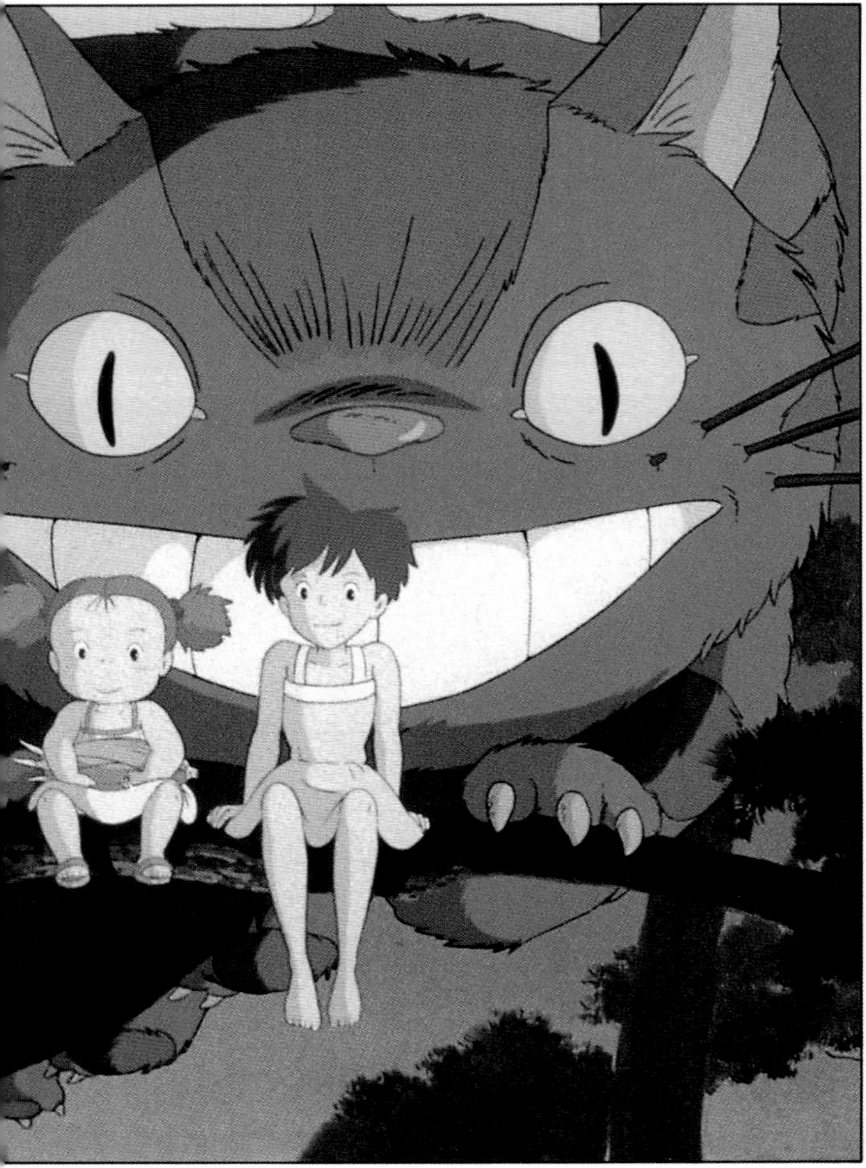

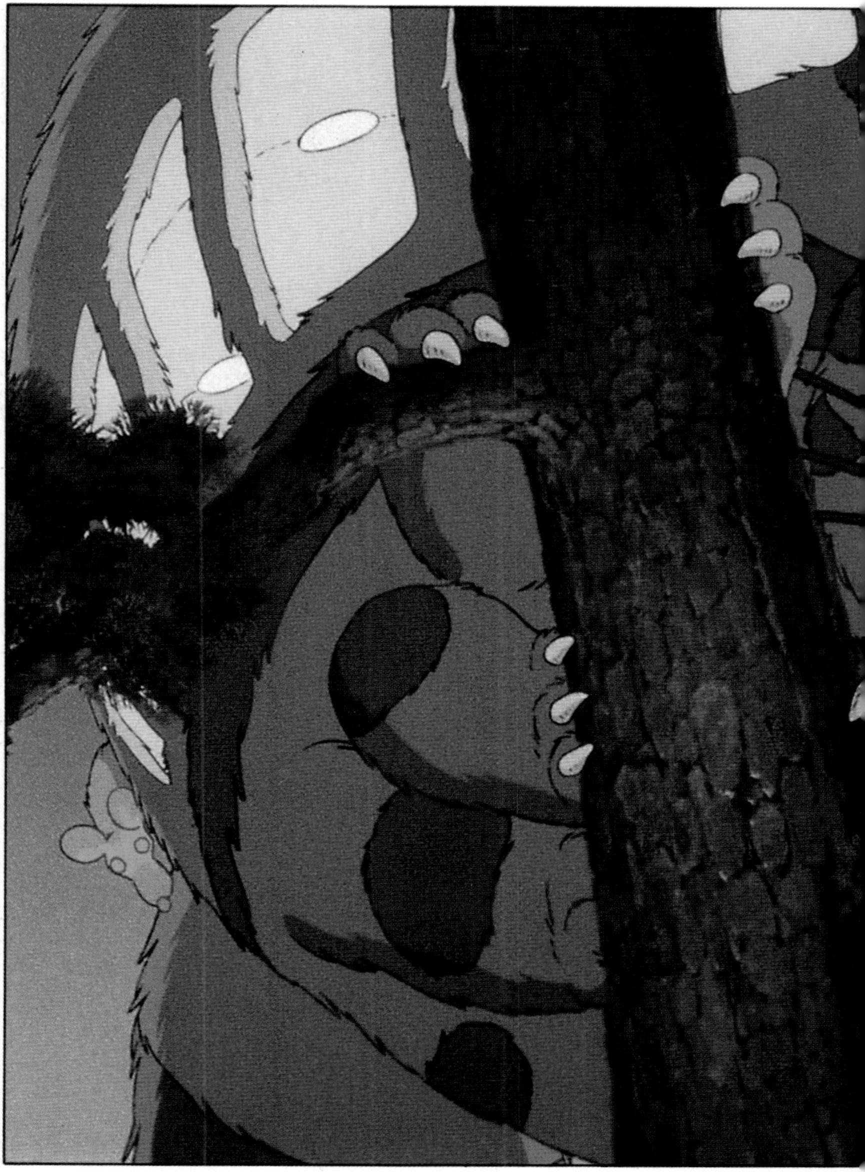

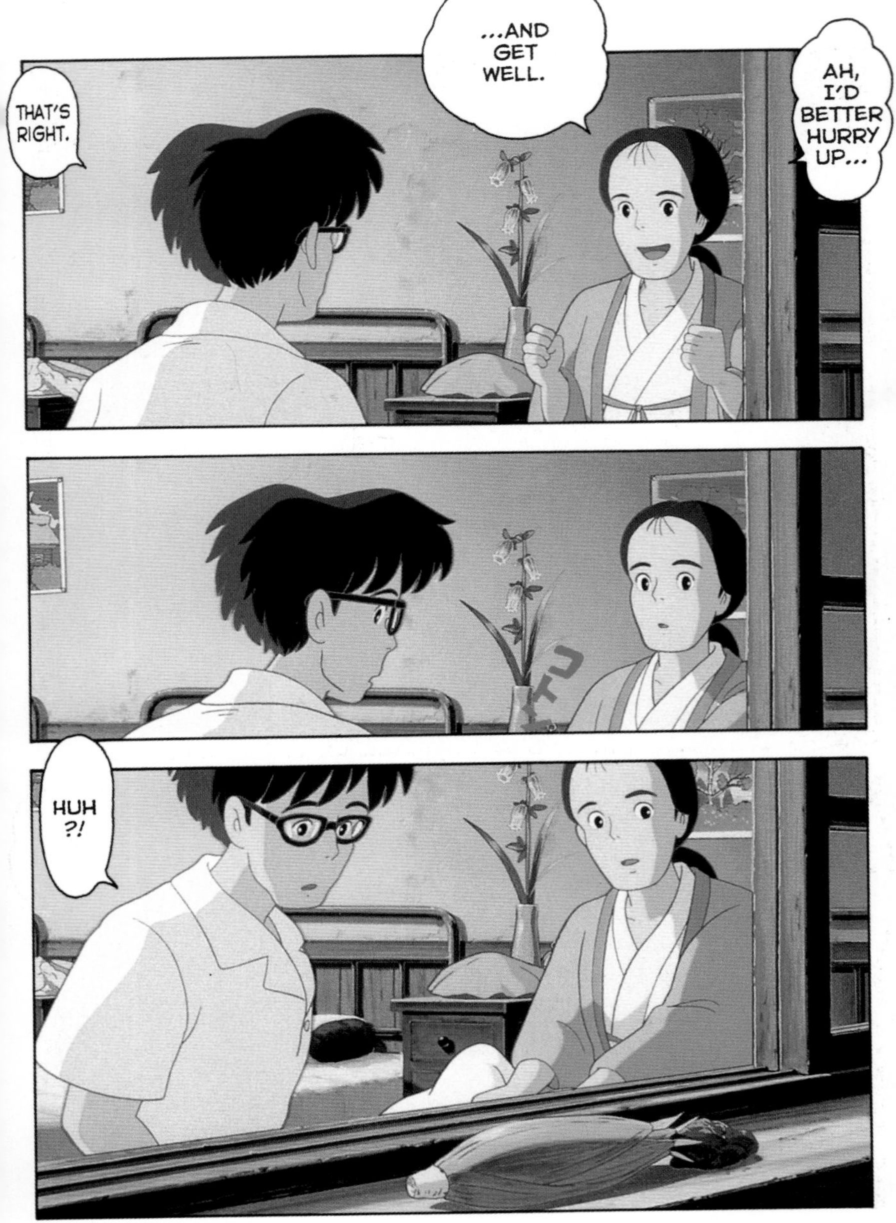
AH, I'D BETTER HURRY UP...
...AND GET WELL.
THAT'S RIGHT.
コト
HUH ?!

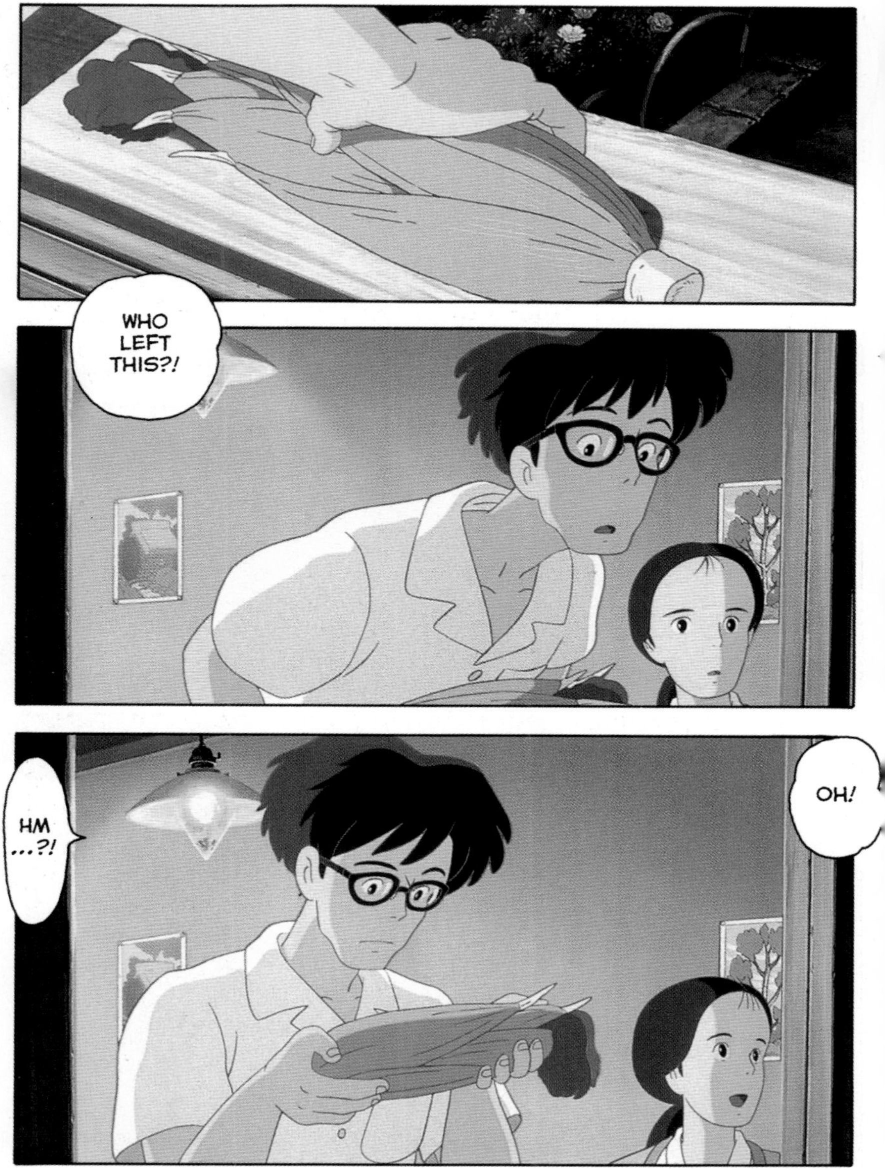
WHO LEFT THIS?!
OH!
HM ...?!

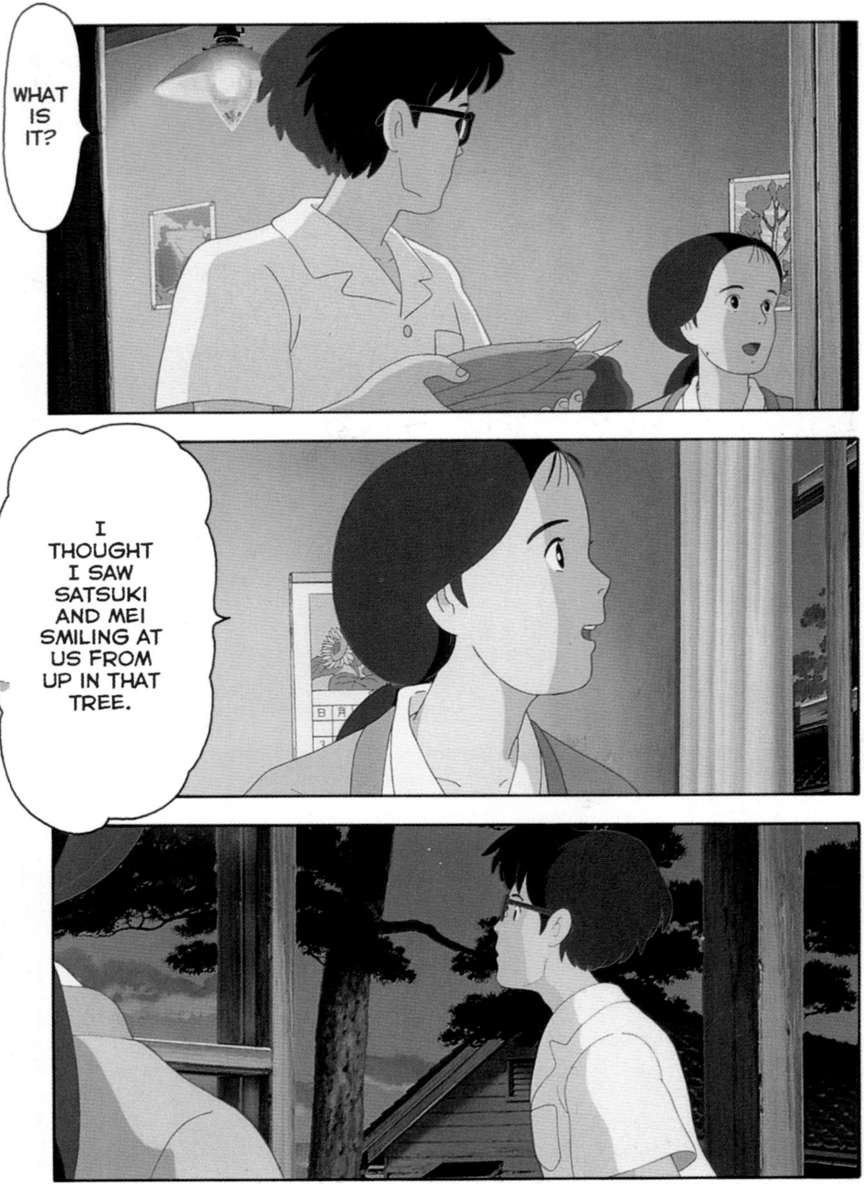
WHAT IS IT?
I THOUGHT I SAW SATSUKI AND MEI SMILING AT US FROM UP IN THAT TREE.

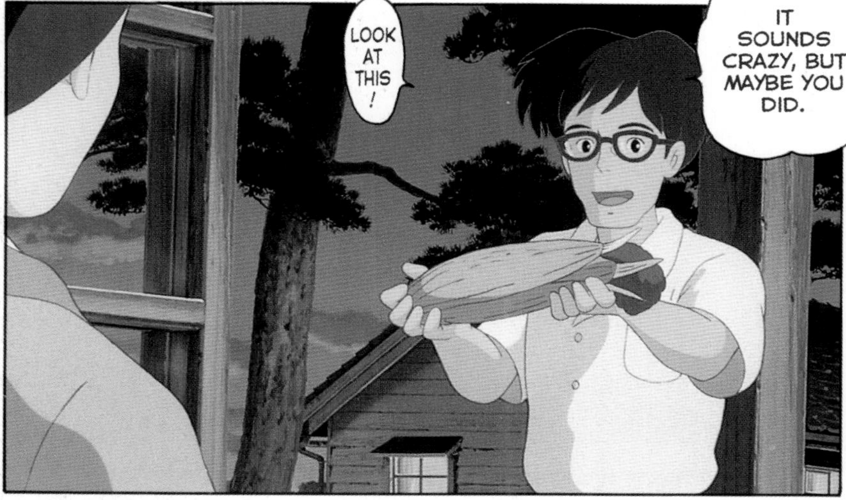
IT SOUNDS CRAZY, BUT MAYBE YOU DID.
LOOK AT THIS!

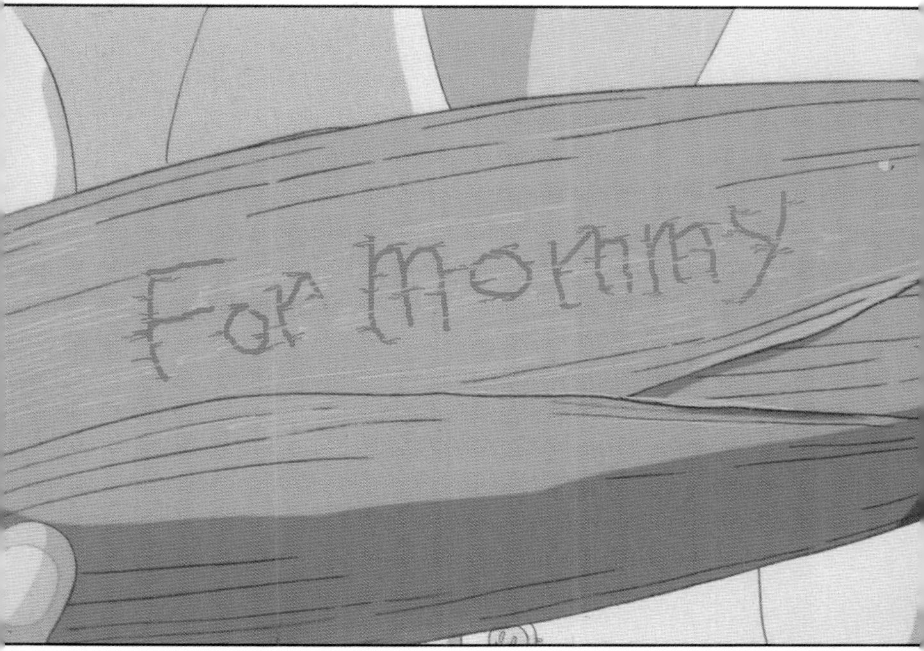
For mommy

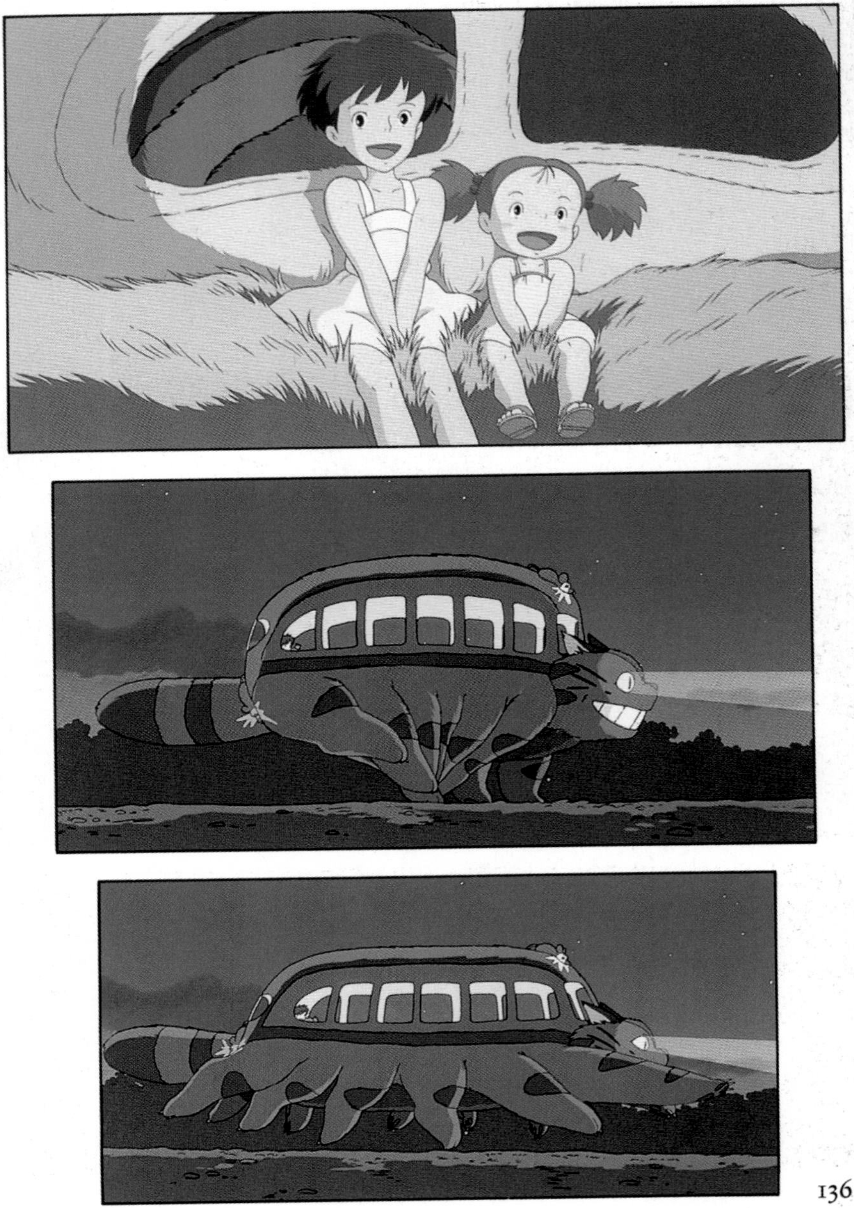

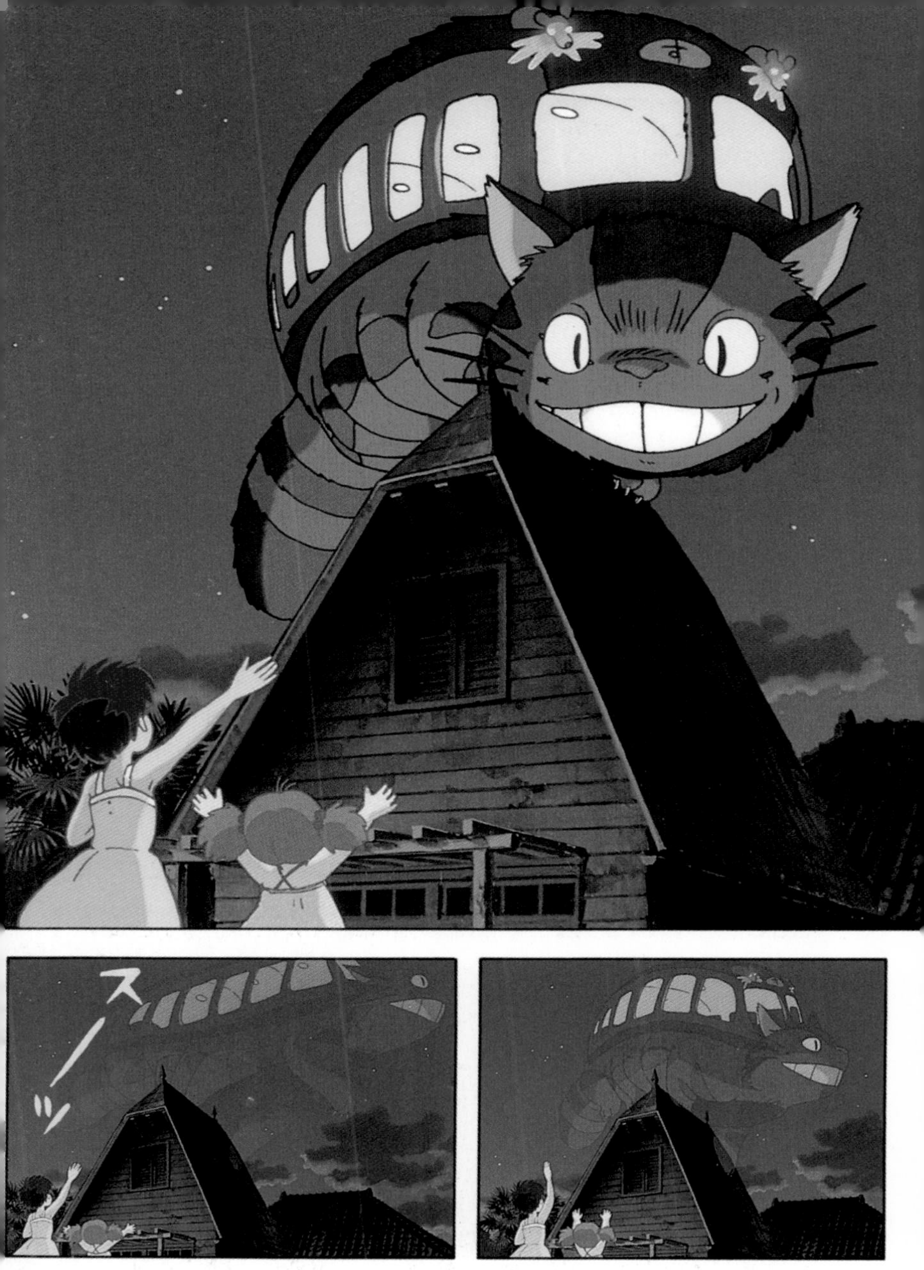
す
スーッ

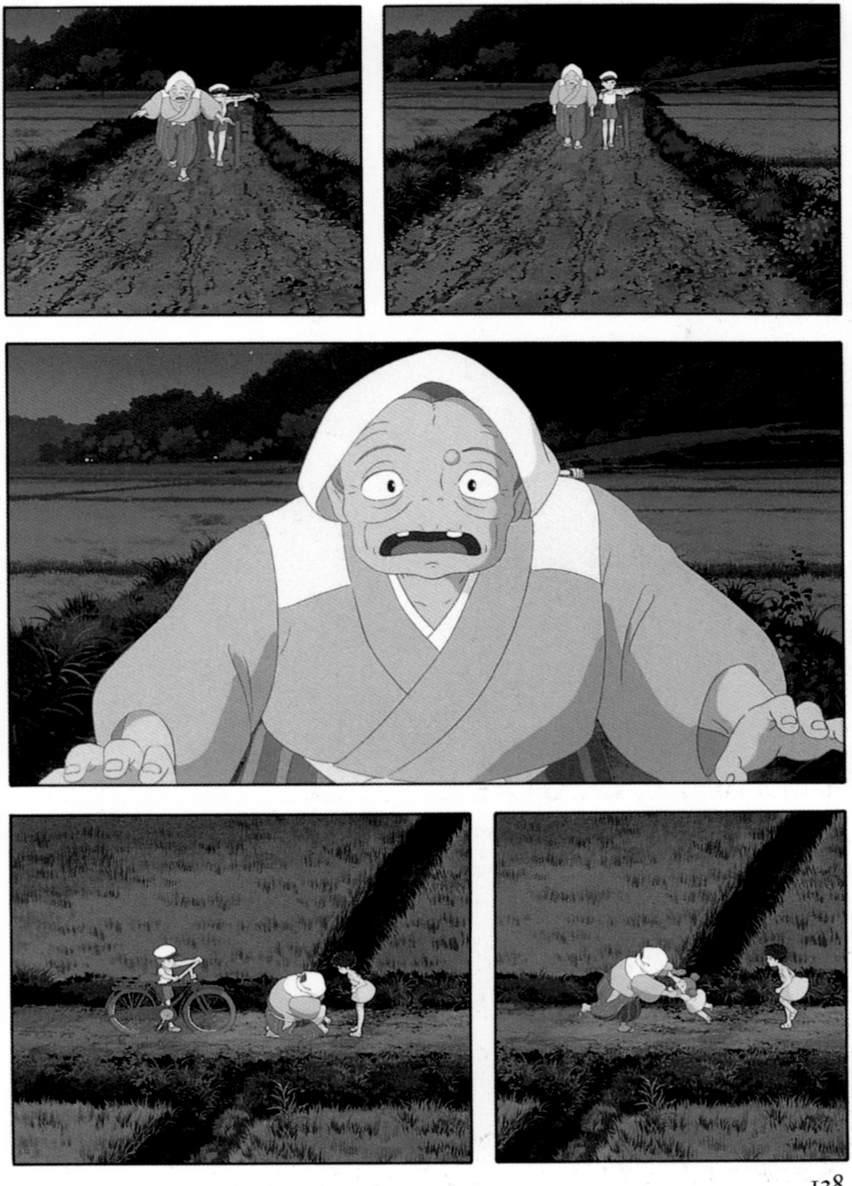

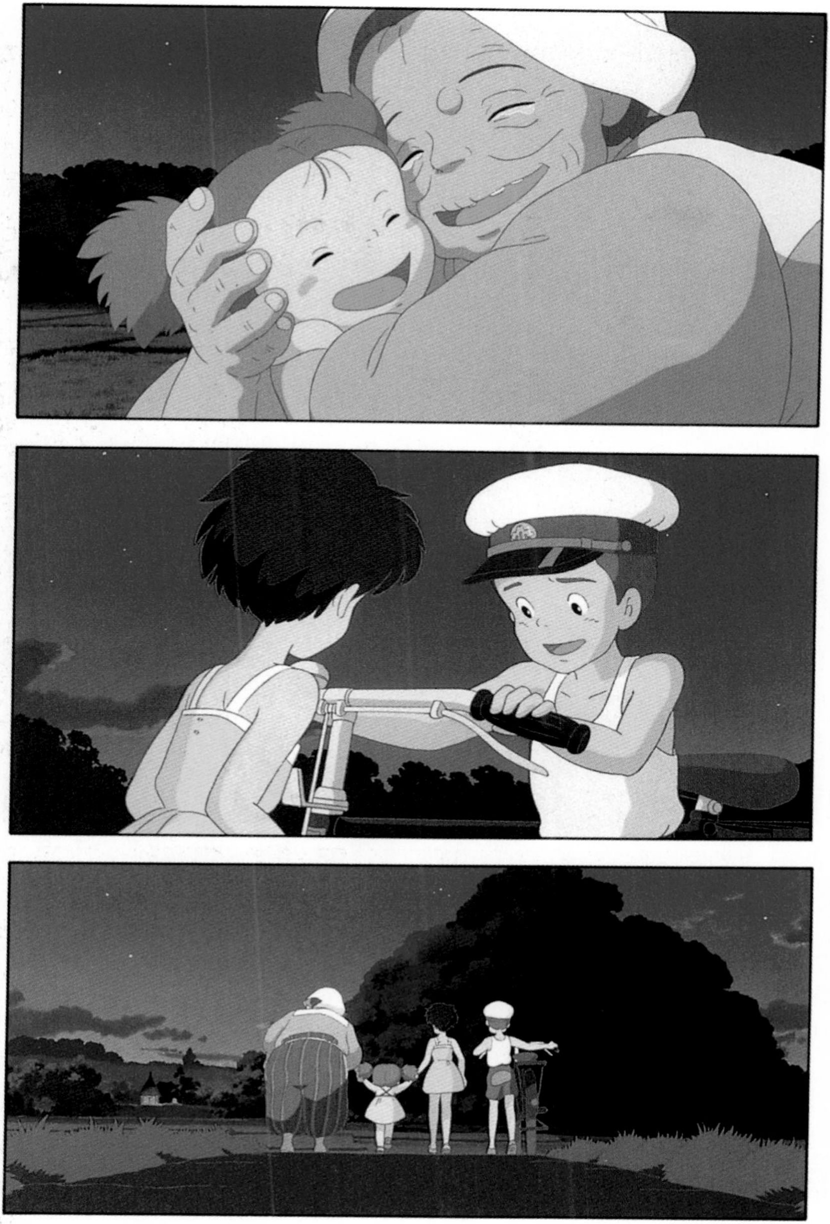

ホ

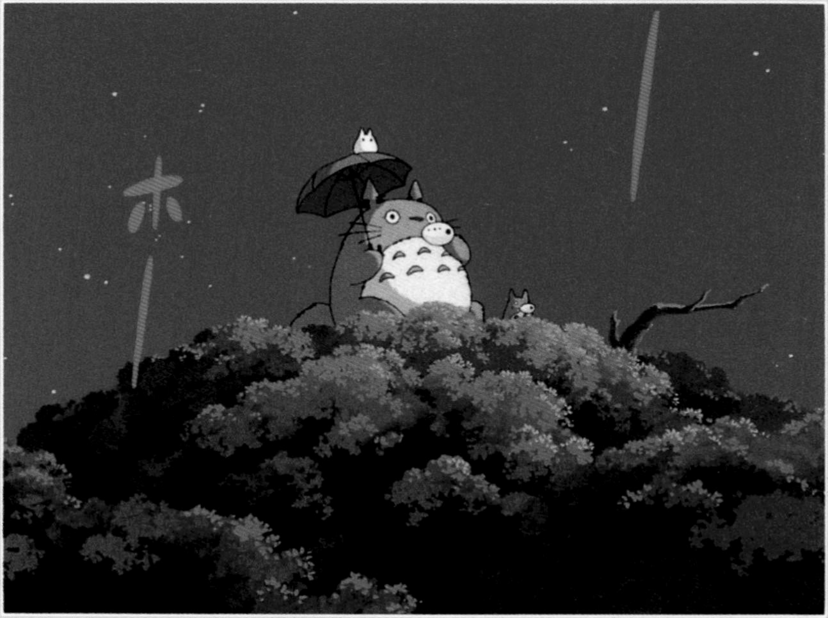
ホ

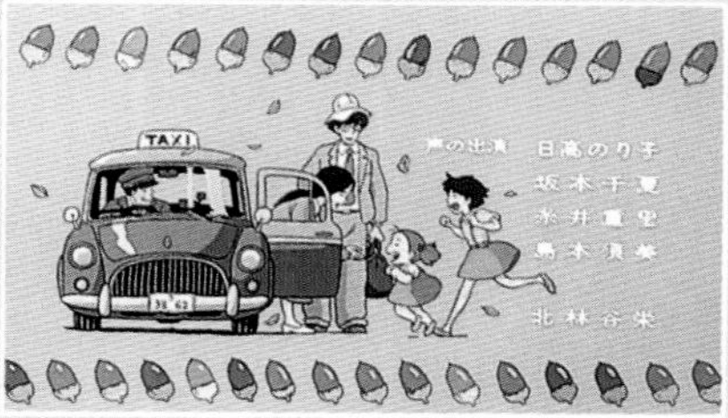
TAXI
声の出演
日高のり子
坂本千夏
糸井重里
島本須美
北林谷栄

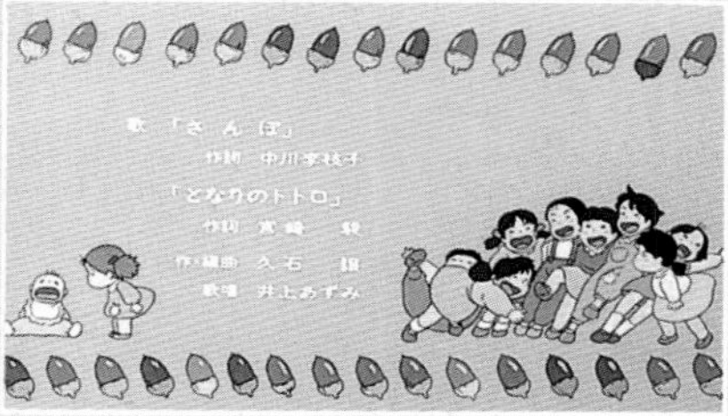
歌「さんぽ」
作詞 中川李枝子
「となりのトトロ」
作詞 宮崎 駿
作・編曲 久石 譲
歌唱 井上あずみ

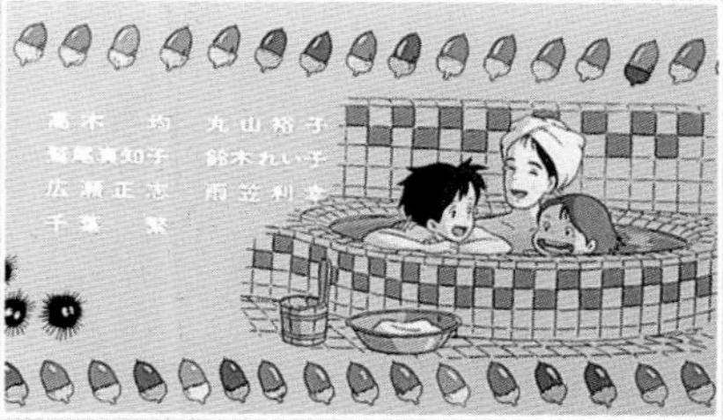
高木 均
丸山裕子
鈴木れい子
広瀬正志
雨笠利幸
千葉 繁

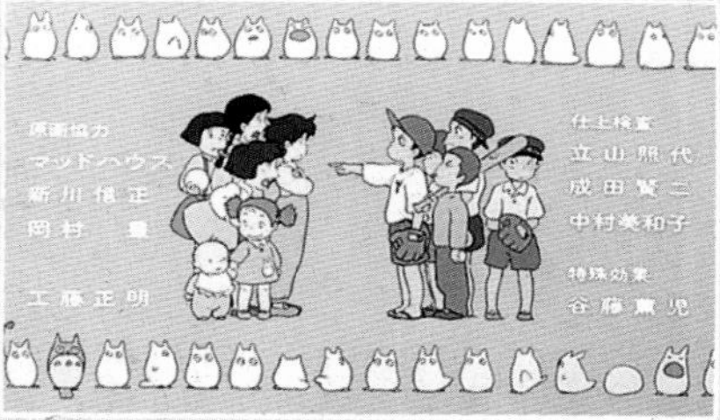
原画協力
マッドハウス
新川信正
岡村 豊
工藤正明
仕上検査
立山照代
成田賢二
中村美和子
特殊効果
谷藤薫児

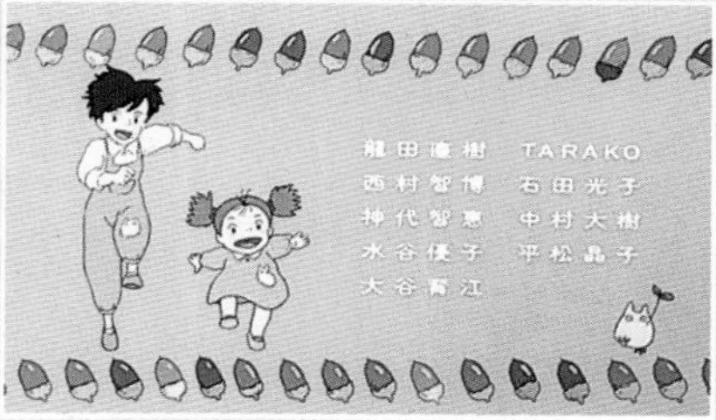
龍田直樹
TARAKO
西村智博
石田光子
神代智恵
中村大樹
水谷優子
平松晶子
大谷育江

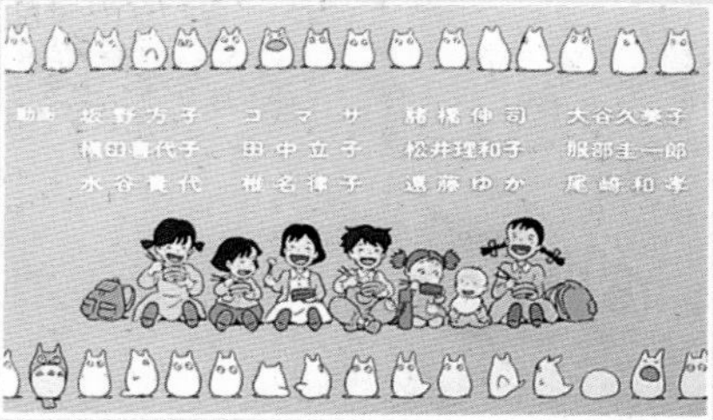
動画
坂野方子
コ マ サ
大谷久美子
田中立子
松井理和子
服部圭一郎
水谷貴代
椎名律子
遠藤ゆか
尾崎和孝

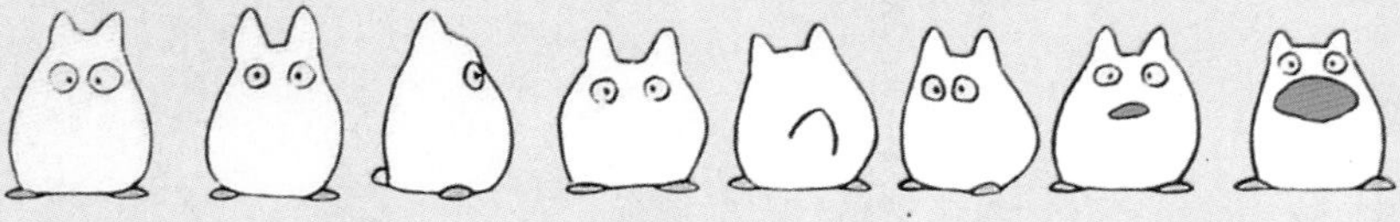

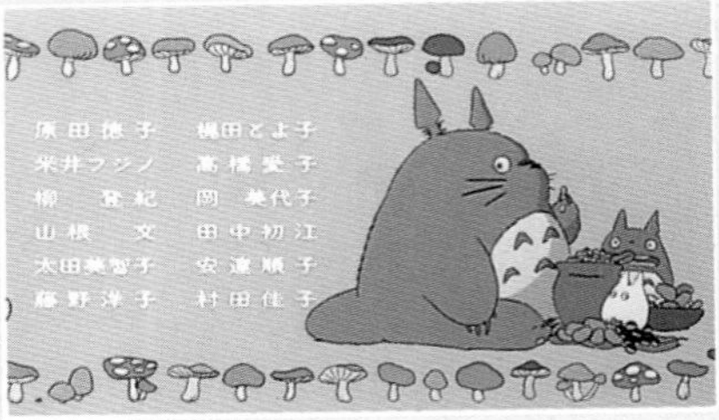
原田徳子　槻田とよ子
米井フジノ　高橋愛子
柳　登紀　岡　美代子
山根　文　田中初江
太田美智子　安達順子
藤野洋子　村田佳子

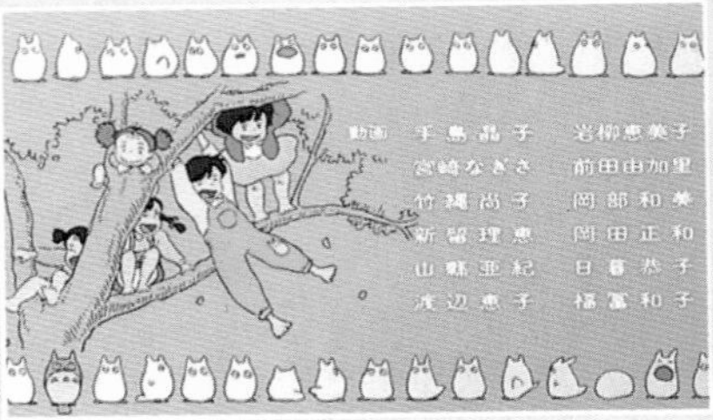
動画　手島晶子　岩柳恵美子
宮崎なぎさ　前田由加里
竹縄尚子　岡部和美
新留理恵　岡田正和
山縣亜紀　日暮恭子
渡辺恵子　榎冨和子

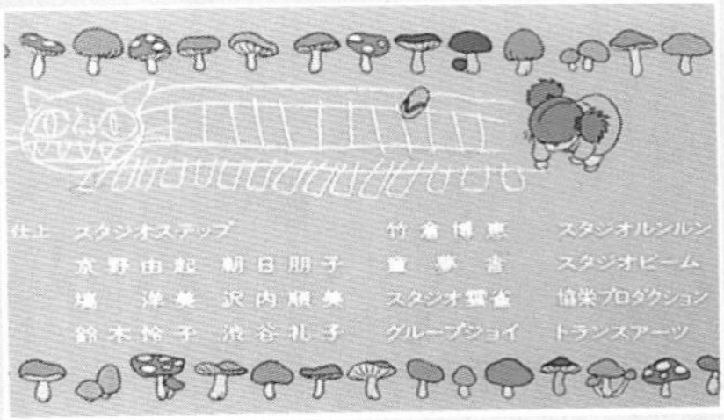
仕上　スタジオステップ
京野由起　朝日朋子
塙　洋美　沢内順美
鈴木怜子　渋谷礼子
竹倉博恵
童夢舎
スタジオ雲雀
グループジョイ
スタジオルンルン
スタジオビーム
協栄プロダクション
トランスアーツ

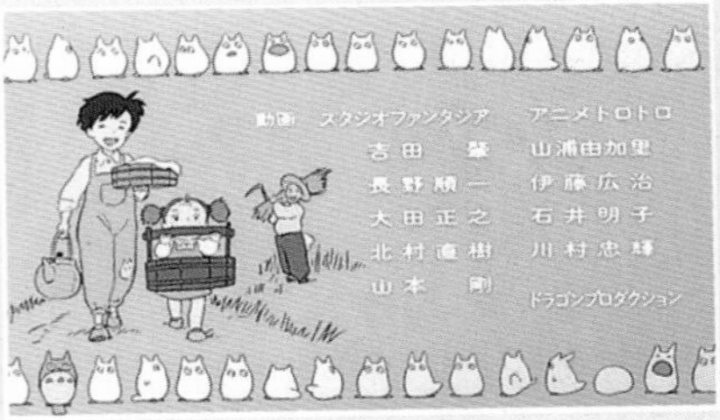
動画　スタジオファンタジア
吉田　肇
長野順一
大田正之
北村直樹
山本　剛
アニメトロトロ
山浦由加里
伊藤広治
石井明子
川村忠輝
ドラゴンプロダクション

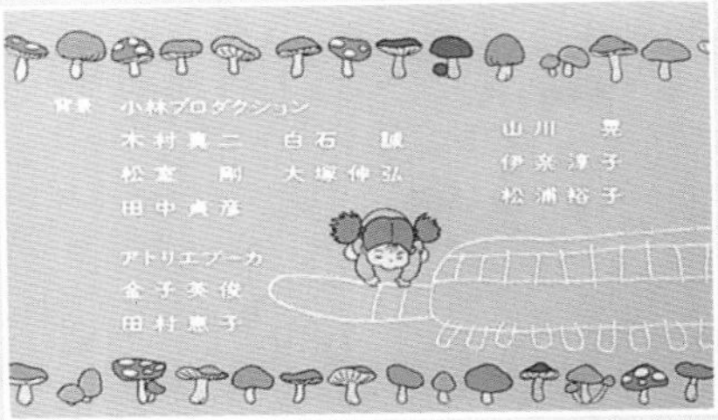
背景　小林プロダクション
木村真二　白石　誠
松室　剛　大塚伸弘
田中直彦
アトリエブーカ
金子英俊
田村恵子
山川　晃
伊奈淳子
松浦裕子

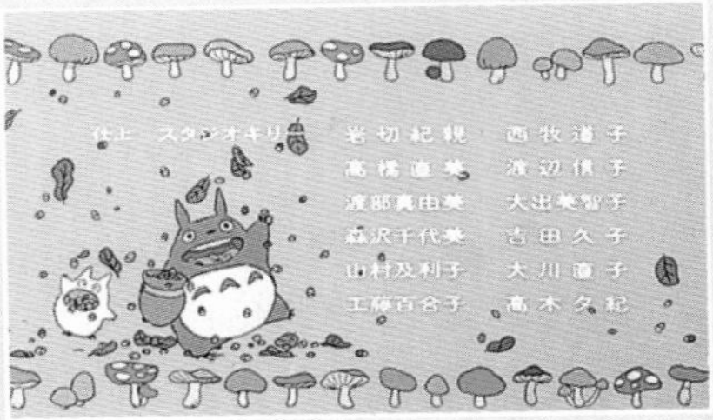
仕上　スタジオキリー
岩切紀親　西牧道子
高橋直美　渡辺信子
渡部真由美　大出美智子
森沢千代美　吉田久子
山村及利子　大川直子
工藤百合子　高木久紀

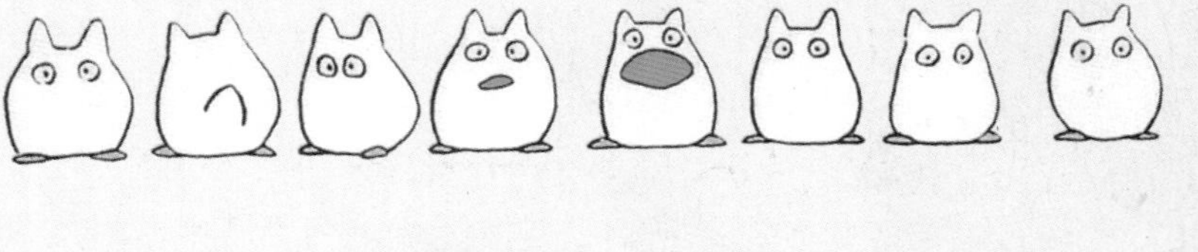

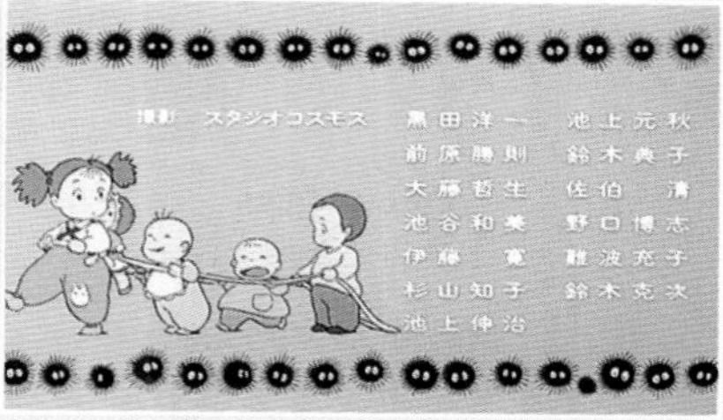
撮影　スタジオコスモス
黒田洋一　池上元秋
前原勝則　鈴木典子
大藤哲生　佐伯　清
池谷和美　野口博志
伊藤　寛　難波充子
杉山知子　鈴木克次
池上伸治

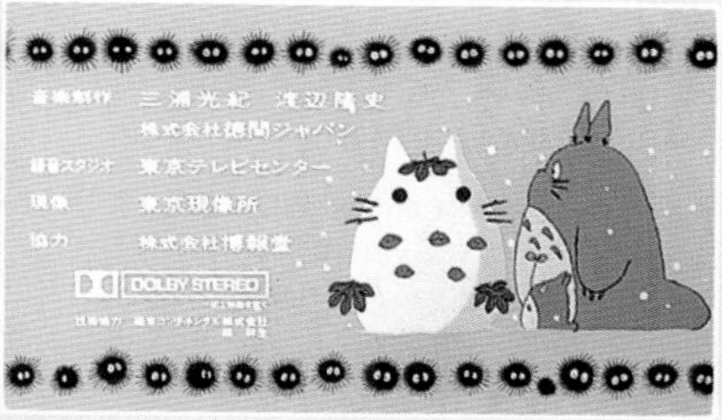
音楽制作　三浦光紀　渡辺隆史
株式会社徳間ジャパン
録音スタジオ　東京テレビセンター
現像　東京現像所
協力　株式会社博報堂
DOLBY STEREO

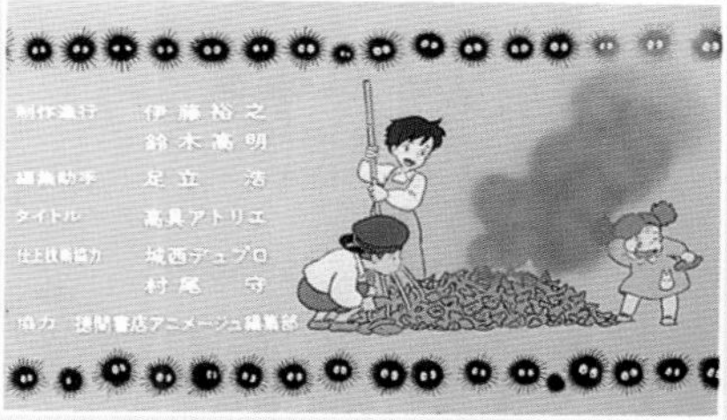
制作進行　伊藤裕之
鈴木高明
編集助手　足立　浩
タイトル　高具アトリエ
仕上技術協力　城西デュプロ
村尾　守
協力　徳間書店アニメージュ編集部

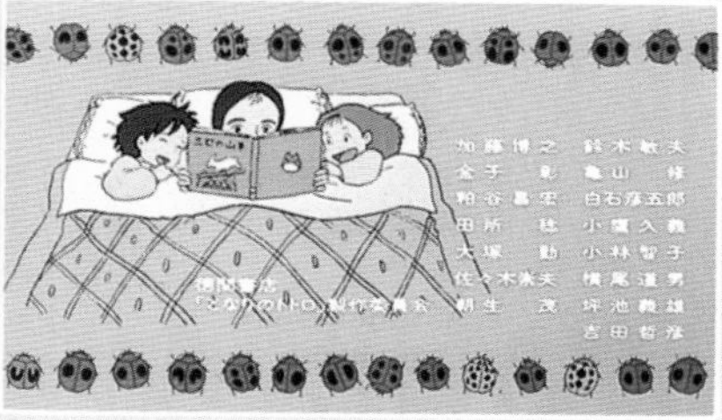
加藤博之　鈴木敏夫
金子　彰　亀山　修
籾谷昌宏　白石彦五郎
田所　稔　小湊入義
大塚　勤　小林智子
佐々木米夫　横尾道男
朝生　茂　坪池義雄
吉田哲彦
徳間書店
「となりのトトロ」製作委員会

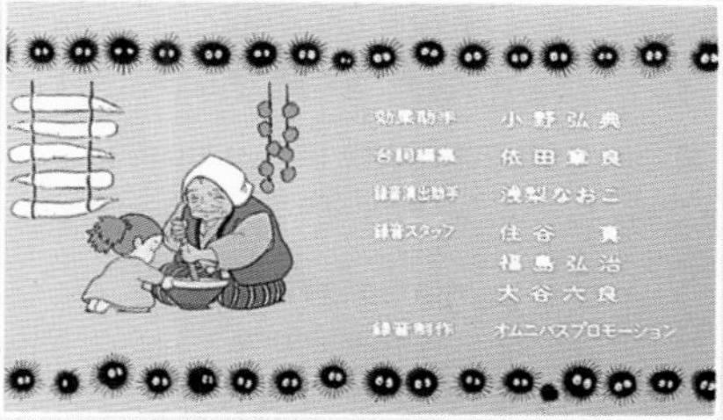
効果助手　小野弘典
台詞編集　依田章良
録音演出助手　浅梨なおこ
録音スタッフ　住谷　真
福島弘治
大谷六良
録音制作　オムニバスプロモーション

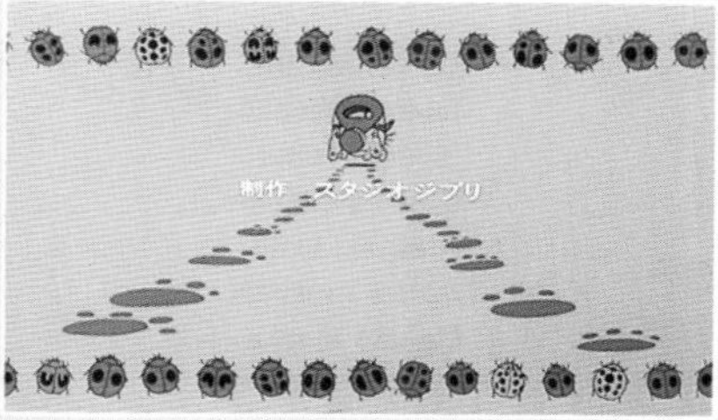
制作　スタジオジブリ

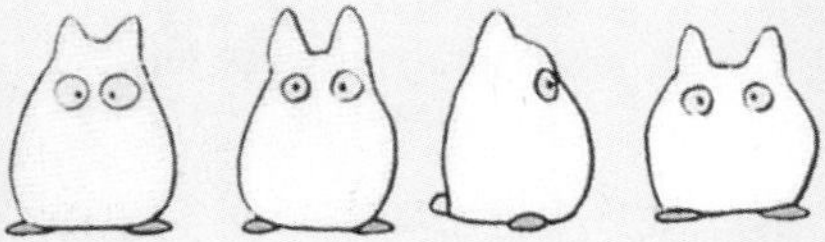

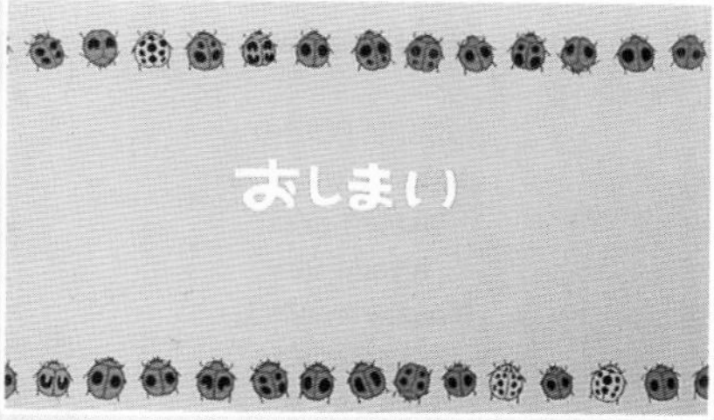
おしまい

COLOR DESIGN
Michiyo Yasuda

CAMERA SUPERVISOR
Hisao Shirai

EDITING
Takeshi Seyama

ANIMATION CHECK
Yasuko Tachiki
Hitomi Tateno

COLOR DESIGN ASSISTANTS
Nobuko Mizuta

INK AND PAINT CHECK
Masae Motohashi

AUDIO DIRECTOR
Shigeharu Shiba

RECORDING AND SOUND MIXING
Shuji Inoue

SOUND EFFECTS
Kazutoshi Sato

PRODUCTION MANAGER
Eiko Tanaka

PRODUCTION DESK
Hirokatsu Kihara
Toshiyuki Kawabata

ASSISTANT TO THE DIRECTOR
Tetsuya Endo

PRODUCER
Toru Hara

Tokuma Shoten PRESENTS
1988
Tonari no Totoro (My Neighbor Totoro)

EXECUTIVE PRODUCER
Yasuyoshi Tokuma

ASSOCIATE EXECUTIVE PRODUCERS
Tatsumi Yamashita
Hideo Ogata

SUPERVISING ANIMATOR
Yoshiharu Sato

ART DIRECTION
Kazuo Oga

MUSIC
Joe Hisaishi

KEY ANIMATION
Tsukasa Tannai
Shinji Otsuka
Masako Shinohara
Masaaki Endo
Toshio Kawaguchi
Makoto Tanaka
Yoshinori Kanada
Katsuya Kondo
Makiko Futaki
Hiroomi Yamakawa
Hideko Tagawa

BACKGROUND
Hajime Matsuoka
Toshio Nozaki
Kiyomi Ota
Masaki Yoshizaki
Yoji Takeshige
Kiyoko Sugawara

INK AND PAINT CHECK
Teruyo Tateyama
Kenji Narita
Miwako Nakamura

SPECIAL EFFECTS
Kaoru Tanifuji

INBETWEEN / CLEAN-UP ANIMATION
Masako Sakano
Komasa
Shinji Morohashi
Kumiko Otani
Kiyoko Makita
Ritsuko Tanaka
Riwako Matsui
Keiichiro Hattori
Kiyo Mizutani
Ritsuko Shiina
Yuka Endo
Kazutaka Ozaki

INBETWEEN / CLEAN-UP ANIMATION
Akiko Teshima
Emiko Iwayanagi
Nagisa Miyazaki
Yukari Maeda
Naoko Takenawa
Kazumi Okabe
Rie Niidome
Masakazu Okada
Aki Yamagata
Kyoko Higurashi
Keiko Watanabe
Kazuko Fukutomi

INBETWEEN / CLEAN-UP ANIMATION
Studio Fantasia
Hajime Yoshida
Junichi Nagano
Masayuki Ota
Naoki Kitamura
Tsuyoshi Yamamoto

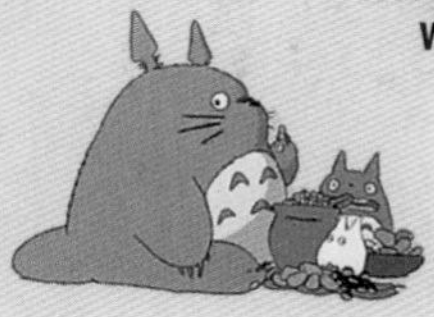

ORIGINAL STORY, SCREENPLAY
WRITTEN AND DIRECTED by
Hayao Miyazaki

VOICES
Noriko Hidaka
Chika Sakamoto
Shigesato Itoi
Sumi Shimamoto
Tanie Kitabayashi

Hitoshi Takagi
Hiroko Maruyama
Machiko Washio
Reiko Suzuki
Tadashi Hirose
Toshiyuki Amagasa
Shigeru Chiba

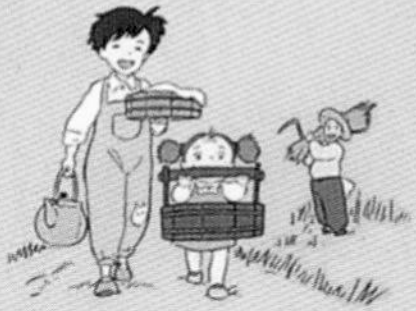

Naoki Tatsuta
Tarako
Tomohiro Nishimura
Mitsuko Ishida
Chie Kojiro
Taiju Nakamura
Yuko Mizutani
Akiko Hiramatsu
Ikue Otani

SONGS
"Sampo"
LYRICS by Rieko Nakagawa

"Tonari no Totoro"
LYRICS by Hayao Miyazaki
MUSIC COMPOSITION AND ARRANGEMENT
by Joe Hisaishi
PERFORMANCE
Azumi Inoue

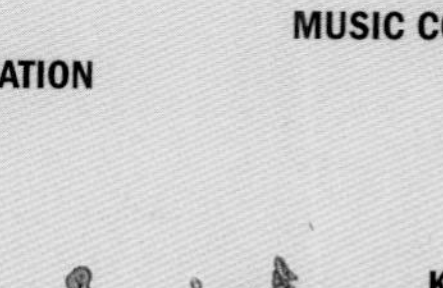

KEY ANIMATION SUPPORT
Mad House
Nobumasa Shinkawa
Yutaka Okamura
Masaaki Kudo

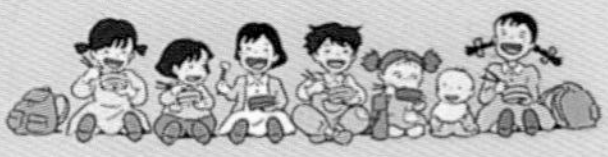

Hiroe Takekura
Studio Runrun
Domusha
Studio Beam
Studio Hibari
Kyoei Production
Group Joy
Trans Arts

BACKGROUND
Kobayashi Production
Shinji Kimura
Makoto Shiraishi
Tsuyoshi Matsumuro
Nobuhiro Otsuka
Sadahiko Tanaka

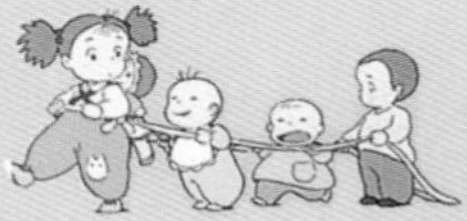

Atelier Bwca
Hidetoshi Kaneko
Keiko Tamura

Akira Yamakawa
Junko Ina
Yuko Matsuura

CAMERA
Studio Cosmos
Yoichi Kuroda
Motoaki Ikegami
Katsunori Maehara
Noriko Suzuki
Tetsuo Ofuji
Kiyoshi Saeki
Kazumi Iketani
Hiroshi Noguchi
Hiroshi Ito
Mitsuko Nanba
Tomoko Sugiyama
Katsuji Suzuki
Shinji Ikegami

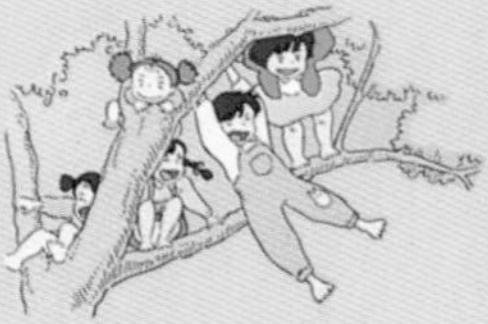

PRODUCTION ASSISTANTS
Hiroyuki Ito
Takaaki Suzuki

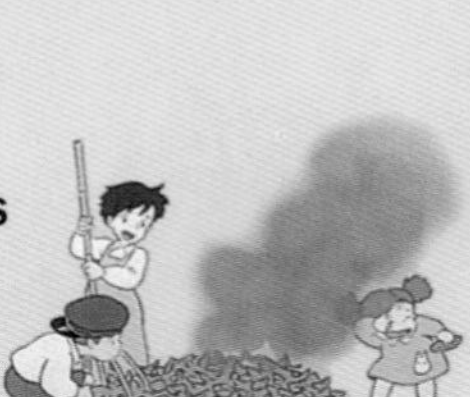

Anime Torotoro
Yukari Yamaura
Koji Ito
Akiko Ishii
Tadateru Kawamura

Dragon Production

INK AND PAINT
Studio Killy
Toshichika Iwakiri
Michiko Nishimaki
Naomi Takahashi
Nobuko Watanabe
Mayumi Watabe
Michiko Ode
Chiyomi Morisawa
Hisako Yoshida
Noriko Yamamura
Naoko Okawa
Yuriko Kudo
Yuki Takagi
Tokuko Harada
Toyoko Kajita
Fujino Komei
Aiko Takahashi
Toki Yanagi
Miyoko Oka
Fumi Yamane
Hatsue Tanaka
Michiko Ota
Junko Adachi
Yoko Fujino
Yoshiko Murata

INK AND PAINT
Studio Step
Yuki Kyono
Tomoko Asahi
Hiromi Hanawa
Yorimi Sawauchi
Reiko Suzuki
Reiko Shibuya

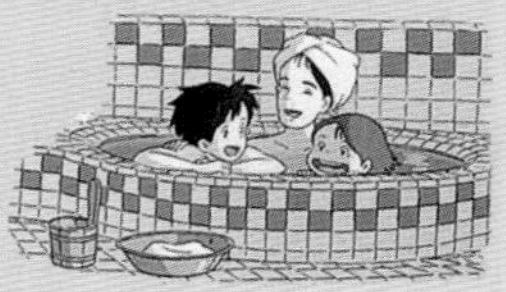

FILM DEVELOPING
Tokyo Laboratory

PUBLICITY SUPPORT
Hakuhodo Inc.

TECHNICAL COOPERATION
Continental Far East Inc.
Mikio Mori

Tokuma Shoten "My Neighbor Totoro"
PRODUCTION COMMITTEE
Hiroyuki Kato
Toshio Suzuki
Akira Kaneko
Osamu Kameyama
Masahiro Kasuya
Hikogoro Shiraishi
Minoru Tadokoro
Hisayoshi Odaka
Tsutomu Otsuka
Tomoko Kobayashi
Takao Sasaki
Michio Yokoo
Shigeru Aso
Yoshio Tsuboike
Tetsuhiko Yoshida

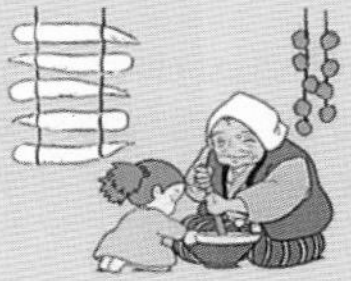

PRODUCTION
Studio Ghibli

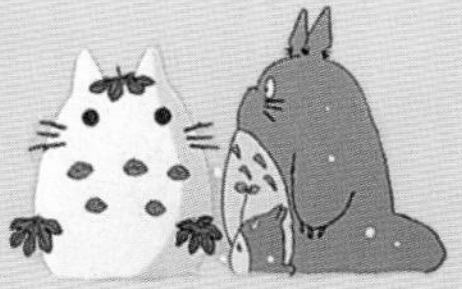

Oshimai (The End)

EDITING ASSISTANT
Hiroshi Adachi

TITLES
Takagu Atelier

INK AND PAINT TECHNICAL COOPERATION
Josai Duplo
Mamoru Murao

MEDIA SUPPORT
Tokuma Shoten "Animage" Editorial
Department

SOUND EFFECTS ASSISTANT
Hironori Ono

DIALOGUE EDITING
Akira Ida

ASSISTANT AUDIO DIRECTOR
Naoko Asari

RECORDING STAFF
Makoto Sumiya
Koji Fukushima
Mutsuyoshi Otani

AUDIO RECORDING
Omnibus Promotion

MUSIC PRODUCTION
Mitsunori Miura
Takashi Watanabe
Tokuma Japan Co.

RECORDING STUDIO
Tokyo T.V. Center

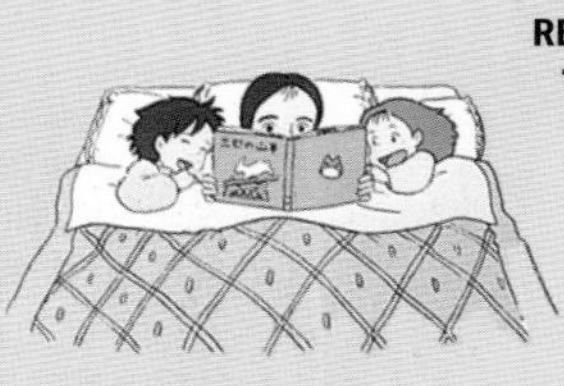

Your Guide to MY NEIGHBOR TOTORO Sound Effects!

To increase your enjoyment of the distinctive Japanese visual style of MY NEIGHBOR TOTORO we've included a listing of and guide to the sound effects used in this comic adaptation of the movie. In the comic, these sound effects are written in the Japanese phonetic characters called katakana.

In the sound effects glossary for MY NEIGHBOR TOTORO, sound effects are listed by page and panel number, for example, 5.1 means page 5, panel 1 – if there is more than one sound effect in a panel, the sound effects are listed by order (so, 9.3.1 means page 9, panel 3, first sound effect). Remember that all numbers are given in the original Japanese reading order: right-to-left.

After the page and panel numbers, you'll see the literally translated sound spelled out by the katakana, followed by how this sound effect might have been spelled out, or what it stands for, in English. It is interesting to see the different ways Japanese people describe the sounds of things!

You'll sometime see a long dash at the end of a sound effects listing. This is just a way of showing that the sound is the kind that lasts for a while; similarly, sounds that fade-out are indicated by three dots. When a sound effect goes through more than one panel, a hyphen and number indicate the panels affected.

Now you are ready to use the MY NEIGHBOR TOTORO Sound Effects Guide!

15.1	FX: UNGU UNGU [krrr]	5.1	FX: MIIN MIIN [tweet tweet]
15.2	FX: BAKI [krak]	5.2	FX: MIIN [tweet]
15.3	FX: HAAA [hooof]		
		6.1	FX: MIIN MIIN [tweet tweet]
18.3	FX: PAKU [mnch]		
		7.2	FX: CHIRIIN [ting]
19.2	FX: TA TA TA TA [tp tp tp tp]		
		9.3.1	FX: GYU [tugg]
24.1	FX: DA [tmp]	9.3.2	FX: UN UUN [hm hmm]
24.4	FX: DA [tmp]		
		10.1	FX: GUI [tugg]
25.1	FX: TA TA TA... [tp tp tp...]	10.2	FX: BOKI [krik]
25.2	FX: DA DA [tmp tmp]	10.4	FX: NIKKO!! ["sound" of smile]
25.3	FX: TA TA TA TA [tp tp tp tp]		
		11.3	FX: BOKI [krik]
26.1	FX: DA DA DA [tmp tmp tmp]		
26.4	FX: TA TA TA [tp tp tp]	13.2	FX: ZASA [fssh]
27.3	FX: DOTE [wump]	14.2	FX: KAPU [mnch]
27.4	FX: KORO KORO [plok plok...]	14.3	FX: PU [hak]
		14.4	FX: GABU [chomp]
28.1	FX: MUKU [fwup]	14.5	FX: MOGU MOGU [mnch mnch]
28.2	FX: SHIKKARI ["sound" of clutching]		

59.1	FX: ZA ZA [fich fich]
59.2	FX: KYORO [fwim]
59.3	FX: DA [tmp]
60.2	FX: DA [tmp]
60.3	FX: TA TA TA [tp tp tp]
61.5	FX: TA TA TA [tp tp tp]
61.6	FX: ZA [fich]
62.3	FX: KANA KANA KANA- [chirrup chirrup chirrup]
63.4	FX: ZA ZA ZA... [fich fich fich...]
64.3	FX: DA [tmp]
64.4	FX: HAA HAA [huff huff]
65.2	FX: HAA HAA HAA [huff huff huff]
65.3	FX: KYORO KYORO [fwim fwim]
65.4	FX: DA [tmp]
66.1	FX: TOTA TOTA TO... [putt putt putt...]
66.3-5	FX: KIKIII [kreeech]
69.1	FX: TOTA TATA... [putt putt...]
69.2	FX: DA [tmp]
69.3	FX: GIIKO GIIKO [twook twook]
73.3	FX: DA [tmp]
75.1	FX: HAA HAA HAA [huff huff huff]
75.4	FX: HAA HAA [huff huff]
76.1	FX: HAA HAA HAA [huff huff huff]
77.1	FX: HAA HAA HAA [huff huff huff]
77.2-3	FX: DA DA DA DA DA- [tmp tmp tmp tmp tmp-]
79.1	FX: NAMU AMIDA BUTSU, NAMU AMIDA BUTSU [Buddhist prayer]
80.4	FX: NAMU AMIDA BUTSU [Buddhist prayer]
83.3	FX: GOKU [gulp]
84.2	FX: HAA HAA HAA [huff huff huff]

28.3	FX: DA [tmp]
28.5	FX: KYORO KYORO [fwim fwim]
29.2	FX: TA TA TA [tp tp tp]
29.4	FX: TA TA TA TA [tp tp tp tp]
30.3	FX: TA TA TA [tp tp tp]
30.4.1	FX: KURU [fwip]
30.4.2	FX: TA TA TA... [tp tp tp...]
31.3	FX: GACHA!! [chak!!]
32.1	FX: JIRIRIIN [brrring]
35.1	FX: GACHA [chak]
36.1	FX: NMEEH [BAAA]
37.1	FX: NMEEH [BAAA]
37.3	FX: NMEEH [BAAA]
37.5	FX: DA DA [tmp tmp]
38.1	FX: TA TA TA... [tp tp tp...]
38.2	FX: KUI [fwip]
38.3	FX: TA TA... [tp tp...]
38.4	FX: DA [tmp]
44.1	FX: JIII... JIII... [bzzz... bzzz...]
49.4	FX: EHHN [aieee]
51.5	FX: SA [fsh]
52.2	FX: TA TA [tup tup]
52.3	FX: TA TA [tp tp...]
52.4	FX: TA TA [tp tp tp...]
55.1	FX: KANA KANA KANA KANA- [chirrup chirrup chirrup chirrup]
55.2.1	FX: GASA GASA [fich fich]
55.2.2	FX: KANA KANA KANA KANA [chirrup chirrup chirrup chirrup]
56.1	FX: KANA KANA KANA KANA KA... [chirrup chirrup chirrup chirrup chirr...]

104.1-3 FX: FUNYAA [zwoosh]
104.4 FX: NIKA ["sound" of smile]

105.1 FX: SA [fsh]
105.2 FX: FUWA [fwom]
105.3 FX: SUU [zoosh]
105.5 FX: FUWAA [fooomsh]
105.6 FX: FUNYUU [fween[

106.2 FX: KASHA KASHA KASHA [klak klak klak]
106.3 FX: KASHA [klak]
103.4-6 FX: FUNYAAAAA [Maaaeioow]

107.1 FX: FUUU [hmmm]
107.2 FX: FUNYAAAAA [Maaaeioow]

108.3-109.3 FX: HYUUUN!! [fwooosh!!]

112.1-113.1 FX: "Meeeiii!"

114.1-3 FX: FUNYAAAAA [Maaaeioow]
114.4 FX: ZA ZA ZA ZA [fich fich fich fich]

117.1 FX: WAN WAN WAN! ["Arf Arf Arf!"]
117.2 FX: BACHI BACHI [krakkl krakkl]
117.3 FX: BACHI BACHI [krakkl krakkl]
117.4 FX: DA [tmp]

118.3 FX: SUTA SUTA [fump fump]

121.4 FX: PIYOOHN [pwiing]

122.1 FX: FUWAA— [fwomm]
122.4 FX: DA [tmp]

125.1 FX: SU [fsh]
125.2 FX: KACHA [klak]
125.5 FX: GU GO GO GO... [vrrrrrr...]

126.1-4 FX: FUNYAAAAA [Maaaeioow]

129.1 FX: OY OY ["There, there"

132.2 FX: KOTON [klik]

137.3 FX: SUUU [fwooosh]

140.1 FX: HOOH— HOOH— [whoo whoo]

86.5 FX: DA [tmp]

87.5 FX: GASA GASA [fwich fwich]

88.6 FX: DA [tmp]

89.1 FX: TA TA TA... [tp tp tp...]
89.3 FX: KA SA SA... [fp fp fp...]
89.5 FX: KA SA SA [fp fp fp]

90.1-2 FX: DAA- [fwoom]
90.3 FX: DA [tmp]
90.4 FX: GA [tugg]

91.2 FX: DOHN!! [whump!!]
91.3 FX: FUWAHN [fwom]
91.4 FX: DOSA [whud]

94.4 FX: NIKAA ["sound" of smile]
94.5 FX: MUKU [fup]

95.1 FX: BYUU [fweee]
95.3-4 FX: GWEEN [vween]

96.1 FX: BYOHHN [vwomm]
96.3-5 FX: FUWAAA [fwoooom]

97.1 FX: SUPO [foop]
97.2 FX: TO TO [tp tp]
97.3 FX: TO TO TO TO TO TO... [tp tp tp tp tp...]
97.4 FX: SUBO [pwok]

98.1 FX: SUU [hmmm]

99.5 FX: DO DO DO DO!! [whud whud whud whud!!]

100.2 FX: DOOHHH [zwoosh]
100.3 FX: GOHHH [rrrrr]

101.2 FX: TA TA TA [tmp tmp tmp]
101.3 FX: TA TA... [tmp tmp...]
101.4 FX: BA!! [fwoosh!!]

102.1 FX: FWAAA [fwoom]

103.1 FX: PYON [pwing]
103.2 FX: ZUZA [fwich]